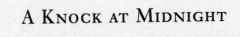

A KNOCK AT MIDNIGHT

A KNOCK AT MIDNIGHT

A Story of Hope, Justice, and Freedom

BRITTANY K. BARNETT

 CROWN
NEW YORK

Published in the United States by Crown, an imprint of Random House,
a division of Penguin Random House LLC, New York.

CROWN and the Crown colophon are registered trademarks of
Penguin Random House LLC.

LIBRARY OF CONGRESS CATALOGING-IN-PUBLICATION DATA
Names: Barnett, Brittany K., author.
Title: A knock at midnight / Brittany K. Barnett.
Description: First edition. | New York : Crown, 2020.
Identifiers: LCCN 2020007214 (print) | LCCN 2020007215 (ebook) |
ISBN 9781984825780 (hardcover) | ISBN 9781984825797 (ebook)
Subjects: LCSH: Barnett, Brittany K. | Criminal defense lawyers—
Texas—Biography. | Prisoners—Legal status, laws, etc.—
United States. | Judicial error—United States. |
Clemency—United States. | Jones, Sharanda—Trials, litigation, etc.
Classification: LCC KF373 . B37 2020 (print) |
LCC KF373 (ebook) | DDC 340.092 [B]—dc23
LC record available at https://lccn.loc.gov/2020007214
LC ebook record available at https://lccn.loc.gov/2020007215

Printed in the United States of America on acid-free paper

randomhousebooks.com

1 2 3 4 5 6 7 8 9

First Edition

Book design by Edwin Vazquez

In memory of my grandmother Lena Reed Barnett,

the purest love I have ever known

Contents

A KNOCK AT MIDNIGHT

On the last day of her trial, Sharanda found a parking spot with a two-hour limit across from the courthouse. Early, she sat for a few minutes, admiring the blackbirds lining the branches of a small elm on the corner, both birds and tree silhouetted against the crisp Dallas sky. People complained about the birds, said they were too noisy, but Sharanda admired their tenacity. And they looked pretty, fanned out on the tree branches like that. It was late summer but the air was still cool from the air-conditioning in her car, and she shivered a little in her light blazer. As on every week-day morning, she'd been up since four to prep-cook at her soul food restaurant, Cooking on Lamar, and she relished a few quiet minutes in the car. She had no way of knowing that these private moments of peace would be her last for a long, long time.

Cooking on Lamar was her pride and joy, and though the hours were long, Sharanda enjoyed every minute of it. While her eight-year-old daughter, Clenesha, snored lightly in a blue vinyl booth, Sharanda would chop vegetables for the salad bar, set tomorrow's brisket in marinade, smother ribs in dry-rub. At eight thirty this morning, she'd taken her break, dropped Clenesha off at McKenzie Elementary, and headed back downtown to the courthouse.

Now that her trial was finally ending, Sharanda felt relieved. It had been an ordeal, but at least it was over. Based on the obvious lies from the witnesses and the sympathetic glances the jurors shot her throughout the long week, she was sure she would be acquitted. Her attorney agreed. "The only challenge is the conspiracy charge," he said. "Kind of hard to counter hearsay. And that's basically all they need." He shrugged. "I wouldn't worry about it too much. Based on this evidence? You're looking at probation. Worst case, five years." Five years? Sharanda's eyes had filled with tears. In five years, her baby would be a teenager—no way she could do five years in federal prison.

The lawyer patted her on the shoulder reassuringly. "Don't worry," he said. "Pretty sure you're looking at a full acquittal."

She'd prayed, stayed positive. All the signs in her life were good. The restaurant was finally taking off, her house ready to flip. And Clenesha was an angel. Being a mom was the greatest joy of her life. Sharanda smiled a little, thinking of her daughter's thrilled face the night before when she'd tried on the bright red leotard she'd wear to her gymnastics practice and the imitation beam routine she'd done on the way up the school steps this morning.

Reminding herself to check Clenesha's practice time, Sharanda slipped on her heels and fed the meter. At the last minute, she tossed her purse into the backseat of the car. No reason to drag it around the courthouse. She figured she'd be right back.

During closing arguments that morning, Sharanda tried to follow what was going on but gave up after a while. The prosecutor kept saying the same things he'd said throughout the trial. Her attorney didn't say much. Just as she started to worry about the parking meter, the judge came back to the bench to announce the verdict.

Sharanda's attorney gripped her arm. "The marshals just came in through the back," he whispered urgently. "No matter what happens, stay calm."

"What?" Sharanda looked at him, not understanding. Then her stomach dropped.

She never saw her purse, her car, or her restaurant again. By the time Sharanda was able to set eyes on her daughter as a free woman again, Clenesha was twenty-four years old and a mother herself.

I FIRST SAW Sharanda Jones in a YouTube video. Hair half up, neatly pressed. Dimples like dimes. Her boxy tan top could pass for a Dickies work shirt, in that early-nineties style, and at first glance she looked like any beautiful young woman on her way to class, to work, to see a movie with her girls. But the beige brick wall behind her had no windows, and there was a number printed on a white sticker above her left chest pocket. Sharanda wasn't on her way anywhere. She was a woman in federal prison, serving the harshest sentence possible in America short of execution: life without the possibility of parole.

How could such a beautiful, vibrant woman be spending the rest of her natural life in prison? In the video, the narrator decried a wrongful sentence for a drug offense, but surely there had to be something more to the story—some history of violence, a lengthy criminal record. I adjusted my headphones and leaned closer to my laptop screen. It was late in the evening at the Southern Methodist University Underwood Law Library, and only one other student sat with me at the mahogany table, a preppy-looking white guy who'd been staring blankly at the same torts textbook for over an hour. I was twenty-five and had just transferred here after my first year at the University of Houston Law Center.

Off camera, the interviewer asked Sharanda a question about her daughter, Clenesha. Pain flickered over Sharanda's otherwise calm features before she answered with a small smile.

"My sister brings her to visit. Every time she comes it's hard. She's grown up from an itty-bitty girl to almost a grown-up woman. I only get to see her once a month."

She paused to compose herself and continued, her voice full of pride and conviction.

"My dream is just to show up at her school. I know they gave me life, but—I just can't imagine not being at her graduation. Her high school graduation. I just can't imagine me not being there."

Onscreen, the camera zoomed for a close-up of the number on Sharanda's tan prison uniform before panning back up to her face. My breath caught in my chest.

I flipped my laptop shut and sat frozen in my seat. The torts student looked at me curiously as I fought back tears. I understood all too well the emotions I saw flickering across Sharanda's face as she spoke longingly of her daughter. I stared straight ahead, breathing deeply, and tried to shake the seven-digit number burning in my brain: 1374671. It wasn't Sharanda's number that haunted me.

Prisoner number 1374671 was my mother.

Part One

TRAVELING

Black love is black wealth and they'll
probably talk about my hard childhood
and never understand that
all the while I was quite happy.
— NIKKI GIOVANNI

Chapter 1

DEAR MAMA

Mama was always heavy-handed, and I was tender-headed. I'd sit between her legs on the worn rust-brown shag carpet separating my bare legs from the cool cement floor of our old wooden house in Fulbright, Texas, trying to hold in my protest as she dipped the brush in water to pull through my thick hair. Mama's hands, cool on the side of my head and ear, smelled of Blue Magic hair grease, and I relished the touch of her palm even as I squirmed from the comb. "Hand me that barrette, Britt," Mama would say, and I'd reach into our pink hair box for the red one I knew she meant. Jazmine—or Jazz, as we called my little sister—would be dancing her carefree self around the TV, pantomiming the Tom and Jerry carnage playing out on the screen, her hair already combed in perfect pink barrettes that matched her short set, red with pink flowers, lace on the straps. It might have been the last time in her life she'd look so girly without a fight, but at four, she wore it well. As soon as Mama finished torturing my head we'd be free to go sit outside on the faded porch swing and eat sweet plums from Aunt Opal's tree across the road, the best spot in the whole town of Fulbright to catch a breeze in that sweltering Texas midsummer heat.

My mom was a tall, long-waisted, young Black woman with the deep-set paisley eyes and the high, full cheekbones of her Filipina and half-Cherokee grandmothers. Her skin shone like a burnished penny, and her glossy black hair framed her face in a perfect curly halo. Physically, she was striking—an exotic beauty of Hunt County. Even when she was a small girl, her biting wit and sharp-tongued fury could not be contained. Before adolescence, other kids mocked her "Chinese" eyes and bony frame; when she grew into herself, the attention from men of all ages was both blessing and curse. She cultivated a tough exterior. In photos, she's always giving the camera side-eye, jaw set, lips a flat line. Even then she's gorgeous. Too much for her small town, for her small world, a world made smaller by my arrival when she was only eighteen, and Jazz's a year later.

Mama had grown up with her mother in Greenville, notorious even in the South for the sign that stretched across its main street for decades: WELCOME TO GREENVILLE: THE BLACKEST LAND AND THE WHITEST PEOPLE. Though some would claim that "the whitest people" referred to the moral purity of Greenville's citizens, Black folks from inside and outside the town knew the truth. Mama's mama, who I called Granny, was named after Ida B. Wells, and she was as fierce and loving as her namesake. A prayer warrior, she was a straight shooter who would tell you exactly what was on her mind, regardless of whether you were ready to hear it. My mother took after her in temperament. Always willful, Mama took pride in controlling her own destiny—nobody could tell Evelyn Fulbright what to do. Greenville schools didn't reward precocious intelligence in young Black girls, and Mama played the rebel more than the achiever. Still, at seventeen she scored extra high on the entrance exam for a basic training and airborne program at Fort Jackson in South Carolina, which would have led to a year in Germany and the nursing training she desired. Then I came along.

I was born in 1984 when both my parents were still living with their own parents. Mama was seventeen when she got pregnant with me, and Daddy just sixteen, a sophomore in high school. Mama says that Daddy was "mesmerized" when they met in the Greenville park where she held court with her friends, seniors to my daddy's crew of gangly sophomore boys. She had a barely healed divot under her eye from her latest fight and shorts that showed every inch of her long brown legs. Daddy was indeed struck dumb, by the force of her character as much as her uncommon beauty. "All I wanted was to see her smile," he would say. "Prettiest woman you ever saw, but boy did she act mean!"

Mama joked that when she saw that handsome young Barnett boy drive through the park in Greenville she'd have been a fool not to fall for him. Leland Barnett drove a brand-new Z28 with the T-top, flashing his gap-toothed smile from beneath his Michael Jackson curl, a perfect single twist on his forehead just like on the *Thriller* cover. Everyone knew my daddy's family, the only Black family in all of Campbell, a small town about fifteen minutes' drive from Greenville, with six handsome brothers and a real pretty piece of land. My daddy's daddy had picked cotton and had only a third-grade education, but he managed to build one of the most successful cement contracting businesses in the area. He also owned Sudie's, a thriving after-supper club in nearby Commerce. And here came my daddy, fine as could be, earnest and smart and with the exact opposite personality as Mama. He met her hot temper and sharp tongue with a sweet smile and calm demeanor, her extroverted sass with shy introversion, her decisive action with his languid dreams. They fell for each other hard, in that first flush, can't-tell-nobody-nothing kind of love.

That's the kind of love that burns out fast, especially under the pressure of two newborns. Mama entered the deferred enrollment program for Fort Jackson, but she was reluctant to be away from me, her first baby. Granny told her, "That little black-eyed pea don't want to go to no Germany!" So Mama relented.

Jazz was born a year after me, and by the time she was a year old my mom and dad's relationship was all but over. For the next year we bounced around within a ten-mile radius in Hunt County, Texas, between Granny's house in Greenville and my dad's family home in Campbell, under the loving care of our dad's mom, Mama Lena. Mama appreciated the help, but she wanted out from under all of it—away from her mama's house, away from Hunt County, and especially away from my dad's new girlfriend. So when Mama's daddy, Pa-Pa, offered to fix up the old house he'd grown up in for us, it was a big deal for her—a chance, finally, for my headstrong, independent mother to be on her own with her girls.

Pa-Pa's own daddy had built that house with his two hands, and by the time we moved in, it had seen better days. Still, it was ours. Pine trees grew out back, and the sky was sharp with electricity during tornado season. Fireflies delighted us on summer nights, and torrential downpours turned the red earth redder, releasing everywhere the sweet smell of new growth so potent it permeated our clothes drying on the line. Despite the cement floors and bare bulbs, the thick plastic nailed over windows for insulation in the winters and the pipes that froze all winter long, we had joy in that house, and so much love.

Pa-Pa's family constituted more than a quarter of Fulbright's one hundred fifty residents, and most of us lived on that same two-mile stretch of Fulbright Road—not quite dirt but not quite paved either, the old blacktop crumbling back into the rich soil. We were the first house you'd come to if you turned up that road, a little ways after the old church where we'd go some Sundays, gospel hymns shaking the wooden floorboards. My cousin Charla lived across from us with my great-aunt Mary Ann, and a few paces down the road my great-aunt Opal made my favorite plum jelly from the massive trees in her front yard. Just around the bend my great-grandmother, Mama Toni, tended her flowers and cooked up sweet rice with carnation milk and sugar from her family's recipe in the Philippines. Across the road from her was Pa-Pa's house, my grandfather Edward, who worked in the coal mine. Pa-Pa's cattle and horses grazed in the fields around the house, and in the summer he and Uncle Willie would be in the field all day with their rumbling tractor, pitching hay that fell loose from the fresh rolled bales. There we all were—descendants of Fulbrights, living on Fulbright land in a town that bore our mama's name. There was rich history in that small East Texas town. We knew we could knock on any of those family doors on Fulbright Road if we needed to. And we knew we had a proud, hardworking mother, who dressed every weekend in the white nurse's uniform she'd bought secondhand at a store in neighboring Lamar County and starched and ironed until it looked almost new.

The year was 1988 and my mother was only twenty-three, with two toddlers underfoot. Though she'd given up her dreams of the military, she was determined to make something of herself. She attended nursing school all day in Paris, Texas, through the week and worked the evening shift Thursday through Sunday as an aide in a nursing home. Mama would carry us to the car, asleep, and when she knelt by the backseat to wake us and usher us into daycare, it would still be pitch black, no other children there but us.

When Mama's financial aid package got cut as part of President Reagan's austerity program that closed several hospitals in the area and cut drug treatment programs, childcare initiatives, and education, daycare was no longer an option. Without daycare, Mama's future was in jeopardy. Mama Lena offered to take us, but Evelyn wasn't having it. "They're my girls, Lena," she said. "I'll figure out a way." And with grit and determination, she did.

The whole family pitched in. Pa-Pa left his truck at the end of our driveway when he came home from the coal mine at night and walked the rest of the way home so Mama would have a vehicle to drive to the nursing home to work second shift. And every weekend, without fail, Mama Lena came to collect us and spoil us rotten at her home in Campbell while Mama was at work. Everyone pitched in to make sure we didn't want for anything. At least, if we did, we didn't know it. In our family, as in much of the South, Black love was Black wealth.

JAZZ AND I were sitting on the edge of the front porch, our skinny arms circling the peeling slats, when a huge blue and silver Silverado truck, set way up high, rolled up the driveway of our little house in Fulbright. We looked on with interest as a brown-eyed, handsome man with a box haircut slid out from behind the wheel of the truck. He was shorter than our daddy but sturdily built, with a round face and wad of snuff tucked in his lower lip. He wore a thick TXU work jacket and a wide, kind smile that put us immediately at ease, and at the bottom of the porch steps he stopped to pay his respects to us as if we were grown-ups. "What you know good?" Billy said, and we appraised him for only a moment before Jazz clambered off the porch, walked straight up to him, and said, "Do that truck fly?"

That's how Mama's new boyfriend, Billy, always seemed to us—a superhero. And we, his apprentices, to whom he worked to impart all of his steadfast values from the day we met him, just as though we were his own blood. That day, he laughed his quiet laugh and took Jazz to sit in the shiny cab, showed her how the controls worked, didn't even complain when she got Teddy Graham crumbs on his seats. Just like that, Billy became a part of our family. We loved to see him coming and ran outside whenever we heard his truck rumbling down the road. We joke now that he rescued us from that old drafty Fulbright house, and he did.

When I started kindergarten, Jazz was left by herself, gathering the last of the sweet plums, feeding stray pups, sneaking out to ride bikes with our cousin Chauncy while Mama slept off the night shift. Each day she waited loyally for the mailman at the big tin mailbox in front of our house so she could proudly carry in the letters.

One afternoon Jazz was standing outside waiting for me to get off the bus after school—I could see her standing there on one leg like a stork, using the other to worry a scab on her calf, her hair a wild mess because Mama hadn't had time to put the comb through it.

"Brittany," Jazz announced as soon as I was in earshot, her eyes wide with wonder at the day and the pleasure of the telling. "Yo mama gone crazy today!"

"What happened?" I said.

"Yo mama's so happy she's gone crazy!" Jazz said. "Jumping around, hugging me—she spun me around and around! Yo mama got her driver's license!"

"Mama already has a driver's license," I said, in the bossy old wise woman tone I used whenever I explained anything to Jazz in those days. "What are you talking about? How you think we drive everywhere?" But sure enough, Mama—never one to show much affection—met me on the porch, her smile wide as I'd ever seen it, and swung me around, too.

"We did it, Britt! We did it! Your mama is a *nurse!*"

That night Billy took us all to the Tip-Top in Bogata to celebrate. We toasted Mama's success over the Tip-Top's should've-been-world-famous burgers and thick homemade milkshakes. We were so proud of her, and she was so happy. "I am a *nurse!*" she kept saying. "All those long nights, all those days of dragging you poor girls to the daycare at the crack of dawn! *I am a nurse!*"

She was our hero.

MAMA WORKED HARD to enrich our lives. When she was home, despite what must have been her extreme exhaustion, she read storybooks, made French toast, and played Candyland and Uno. When she could she took us to the movies, to the circus, to county fairs. And she did whatever teachers asked of her. One time she stayed up after working a full shift to help me make a poster for class, a public service announcement to keep folks from messing with the power lines. That poster took us hours: MC Hammer's face realistically rendered, his trademark glasses mirrored with carefully applied glitter, 3-D speakers in the corners blasting "Don't Touch This!" with power lines in the background.

In 1991, Mama married a smitten Billy in Mama Toni's front yard, wearing Granny's old wedding dress. Jazz, six by then, was the flower girl—happily tossing the flowers to guests on only one side of the aisle—and I carried Mama's train. A year later, they decided it was time to get out of the rickety old house in Fulbright for good. With Mama a full-fledged nurse and Billy's coveted benefits job at the coal mine, they bought a house in the town of Bogata—pronounced entirely Texan, with an "uh" sound for the *o* and a long *o* for the first *a*—about seven minutes up the road from Fulbright.

Bogata was another small Red River County town, but with a population of twelve hundred, a thousand more people than Fulbright, it dwarfed our old neighborhood, let alone that road with our family in every house. While our road in Fulbright had been peopled with our grandparents, cousins, great-aunts and -uncles, Bogata was almost all white. My cousin Charla and I were the only Black students in my class, and there were only a handful of other Black families living in the town. Even today, if you pull into the road leading to our old house, you'll see the bright blue letters announcing DIXIE KITCHEN against a Confederate flag backdrop. But sheltered by my family's love, I was shielded from racism growing up. The Bogata of my childhood was an idyllic country town, and my memories of those first few years there bring me nothing but pleasure.

Mama worked in the nursing home, and Billy worked in the coal mines in week-long shifts, seven days on, seven days off. We spent those off weeks as the tightest-knit family you can imagine. Biking down Main Street to the snow-cone stand, making signs to root for our football team while Billy drenched ribs in his secret-recipe barbecue sauce. Jazz playing out back with the horses while I sat inside on the couch, inhaling another book from the *Babysitter's Club* series. My mom perched on a lawn chair, shaving her long legs in the water hose as Billy fixed the fence and teased her about her feet, Jazz hollering at me to get my nose out of the book and come play catch. Me and Billy shooting hoops in the front yard around our Little Dribblers trophy while my mom and Jazz put extra glitter on their Dallas Cowboys poster. Always the sound of laughter. I had a happy country childhood in our small rural town. But those times didn't last.

I didn't know then about the system of law and order closing like a vise around my community, my family. I wouldn't really know until years later. I was a kid, enjoying my kid life in my doors-unlocked-and-windows-wide-open piece of rural East Texas. But when the drug war came for us, it came with a vengeance. When the drug war came for us, it came straight for my mom.

Chapter 2

HERO ON GROUND ZERO

"Come *on*, Jazz! What are you doing in there? I gotta pee!" I banged on the bathroom door. I'd already been standing there for what seemed like a whole episode of *The Fresh Prince of Bel-Air*. I could hear Jazz being her little Jazz self in there—humming, singing, probably making a mess with the toothpaste. *"Jazz!"* Lord knows I loved her, but my little sister was a handful.

Just when I'd about given up, the bathroom door opened. Jazz stood in the doorway, in no hurry at all, clearly unconcerned about my bladder. She held a pair of Mama's cut-off jean shorts in one hand—the ones Mama always kept near her makeup bag on the bathroom counter these days—and a tubelike object in the other.

"Hey Brittany," she said, as if surprised to see me there. "Brittany, what's this?"

She held out the tampon-shaped object and, exasperated, I peered at it. It wasn't a tampon. When I realized what it was, the air rushed out of me, and with it all my thoughts about peeing and the *Fresh Prince* rerun I was missing. All I could see was what my little sister held in the palm of her hand: a crack pipe, from the pocket of Mama's summer shorts.

Jazz had no idea what she was holding, and all I knew was that I didn't want her to know. "Dang, Jazz! I've been out here forever! Why you touching Mama's stuff?" I grabbed the pipe and shorts, pushed past her, and slammed the door behind me. I stuffed the glass cylinder back in Mama's pocket and laid the shorts where I thought I'd seen them last, trying to do it so no one could see they had been disturbed. Then I sat on the edge of the bathtub and just stared at the wall.

I was only ten, still tender. But this was the early nineties. Drugs were everywhere in popular culture, from movies like *New Jack City* to "Just Say No" campaigns and "This Is Your Brain on Drugs" commercials. I knew what that pipe was, and I knew what it meant.

Suddenly so many things made sense. Jazz had spent weeks selling Girl Scout cookies for her troop, but when it came time to turn in the money she'd kept so carefully in a box on our bedroom shelf, it was gone. A set of Billy's brand-new tools went missing, and a prized bow and arrow he used for hunting. One day when I got home from school, the TV was gone from my room. Our Nintendo games disappeared the same way. Each time something went missing, Mama would pull one of her all-nighters. Her mood would swing wildly. Sometimes she'd sleep a lot.

Over the past few months, my mother had been going through a slow transformation, and with her our world. The changes had crept up on us. Mama still went to work, and we still had our fun days as a family. But many nights now, Mama paced manically through the house late into the night, banging around, in and out of the bathroom. Night after night, gentle Billy, who never yelled at anyone, raised his voice at her, pleading late into the night— "Dammit, Evelyn! You got to stop this!" Lying next to Jazz in the queen bed we shared, I'd listen as their voices grew softer and then crescendoed again. More than once I heard feet pounding in the hall and the bathroom door slamming, the toilet flushing as Billy tried to get rid of the drugs. Then Mama would lose it, screaming outside the door, rattling the handle, banging on the wood, cussing at Billy for all she was worth.

Mama was what used to be called a functioning addict, which in some ways made the growing problem even harder to confront. She made it to work, never missed a school event, presented herself to the outside world as if nothing had changed. But her addiction kept getting worse.

The summer I was to enter the fifth grade, Billy finally convinced our mom that things had gone far enough. She entered a residential rehab. Billy still worked long, hard hours at the coal mine and couldn't be home to watch us all the time. So Jazz and I moved to Campbell, to live with our dad and his parents for the school year, until our mom came home, until she was better.

Our extended family was strong and had always been a part of our lives. The move seemed almost natural to us, a long weekend at Mama Lena's that stretched into the next, and then the next. It wasn't until the first day of that year's Little Dribblers basketball season, when I walked onto the court, filled with nervous adrenaline as I always was at the beginning of the season, that I realized how much had really changed. It was like everything hit me at once. For the first time since I started playing basketball in the first grade, Billy would not be my coach. And this wasn't my Little Dribblers team from Bogata, but a whole new group of girls. Everything was different now. No Billy to coach me after school and on weekends. No riding my bike with my friend Krisha to the Scholastic book fair. No seeing the same teachers I'd had all my life—a few of whom had been Billy's teachers, too. And the worst part: Our mama was sick. Very sick. So sick we didn't even live with her anymore.

I don't know how I got through the rest of that practice. It was like every time the whistle blew it was a reminder of who wasn't blowing it. I missed Billy. I missed home even though I knew that Mama Lena's house in Campbell was home, too. It always had been. But that night, not for the last time, I couldn't sleep for the nightmares.

Mama's addiction had brought with it a confusion that my ten-year-old mind couldn't fully comprehend. I was too young to process the urgent sense of responsibility and anxious worry that arises when a child is watching disaster unfold an arm's reach away. I wanted to save her and protect her from drugs, to rescue her from this demon that had crept into our lives, that wouldn't leave us alone. It didn't occur to me that I was the child and she was the mother, that the weight of her addiction was not mine to bear. Or that I couldn't save her. When Mama went to rehab it gave me hope and lifted some of that burden. I trusted that she was going to get better.

That year, Mama Lena dropped us off at school and picked us up again in the afternoons. She taught me to bake and spoiled me with every kind of cake decorating tool you can imagine: piping bags and tips, fondant knives, sugar flowers—you name it, we had it in our Campbell kitchen, in a special case with my name on it. Jazz and I each had our own room and got to choose how to decorate it ourselves, new paint colors and everything. When our dad got home from his job at the Dow Chemical plant, he helped us with our homework. While I read my books, he sat next to me and drew or wrote poetry in quiet companionship; Mama Lena sat in her plush blue recliner in her pretty blouse and matching slacks, pantyhosed feet tucked under her, glasses settled on the end of her nose, writing her sweet potato pie recipe in a small notebook. After school I'd walk down to the pond in front of the house with my grandpa, who we called Daddy Sudie, and watch him fish while he told me stories that shaped my view of myself and the world. In Campbell, we had sit-down dinners together every night. After dinner, my daddy took us outside to peer through his telescope, showing us the constellations in the vast night sky.

Still, Jazz and I missed our Bogata house and friends. We missed Billy, and we missed our mama. Especially, we missed who our mama had been before the addiction took hold.

———

WHEN MAMA CAME out of rehab, Jazz and I came back to Bogata. I was going into the sixth grade and Jazz the fifth. As ever, Billy held us together, adding to the lifelong lessons imparted to us in Campbell in his steady, no-frills way. After a two-hour basketball practice, he'd have me back out in the driveway to "practice what we practiced." He drilled me to hit fifty baskets, but they had to be done the right way, with perfect form.

"Nope," he'd say after I swished one through, nothing but net. "Didn't count."

"What do you mean, it didn't count?" I'd gasp, my arms starting to throb. "That's thirty-six shots!"

"Nope, you didn't hit the backboard, Britt," he'd say, in his even-tempered way. Rolling my eyes, I'd bounce the ball twice, laser-focused on the red square, and make a perfect shot off the backboard. "*That's* thirty-six," he'd say, reaching in his pocket for his tin of chewing tobacco. "Only fourteen more to go."

To Billy, winning wasn't about the moments of glory, the swish of a nothing-but-net shot, the roar from the stands. It was about the journey: staying focused, putting in the time, hitting your benchmark goals even if your arms were tired, even if you wanted to quit. Hard work was paramount. For him, victory was all about showing up to do the work. About staying even-keeled, even when times were rough. That was how he loved, too.

His teaching and strong example couldn't have come at a better time. Rehab hadn't made Mama better. If anything, she was worse. Our house seemed ruled by the highs and lows of Mama's chemical cravings. In between highs, when she was drug free, we'd cling to the Mama we knew best, to signs of normalcy, to hope. Some mornings she'd get up and make French toast, just like the old days, the banter between her and Billy keeping us all laughing.

But when I'd get home from practice in the evening, that Mama would be gone, and I'd end the day seething in resentment. There was a catastrophe unfolding within our mother, one we tried not to acknowledge with words. The dope sickness took us all on the roller coaster of her mood swings. She still went to work, keeping up a functional facade. Physically, she was there. But she operated on the fringes of our family life. Sometimes, in the room we shared, Jazz and I would talk about it without talking about it. We knew when her paydays were, and we knew that the money made it worse. I wondered if Mama knew how much we worried about her, if she knew the higher she got, the lower Jazz and I sank.

But we didn't talk to her about it, ever. She'd always been feisty, and, like most people who struggle with addiction, she had fine-tuned patterns of self-defense, turning her guilt and anger on you in a second. We gave her a wide berth.

Still, I tried to fix it, to fix her. I would ask her to come to basketball games, school events, to walk down the road with Jazz and me for shakes and burgers. She wouldn't. When he wasn't working, Billy came instead. He took us out for Friday night dinners at the Sirloin Steak House in Paris. More often than not, Mama didn't come. Billy's way of coping was to ignore her absence, to carry on as usual, to make sure Jazz and I were good. We didn't talk about any of it. We just carried on, as if the center of our lives hadn't spun out of control.

Every other Friday of each month, Mama would bring me her paycheck. I'd be lying on my bed doing homework, listening to Aaliyah or Tupac playing in the background. Music was my escape now as much as reading, the rhythms washing over me and taking me away from scenes like this.

"Hold this, Britt," Mama would say, handing me several hundred-dollar bills tucked neatly in a white envelope. "Keep it safe." Safe from her, she meant. I'd look up at her and hold out my hand for the envelope, wordlessly put it in my top drawer under my stereo. Little by little, though, she'd come for it.

"Britt, let me get a hundred," she'd say, almost like she was asking. "I'm just gonna get a hundred."

I'd sit still on the bed, watching in silence as she opened the drawer, took the bill out of the envelope, and hurried out of the room. By the end of the weekend the money would be all gone, its only trace a fog of putrid-smelling smoke clouding the bathroom. I was twelve.

I understood even then that my mother wasn't well. People in their right minds don't put that kind of responsibility on a child. She needed help, treatment. But it was 1996, and America's War on Drugs was in full throttle. Resources for drug treatment were scant, while money was being poured into law enforcement and prisons. People with addiction like Mama didn't stand a chance. And neither did their kids, caught up on the front lines.

I was still at the top of my class, still competed in statewide academic competitions, still starred on my basketball team, and still spent endless afternoons shooting hoops in our driveway under Billy's watchful eye. But I was well aware of my mother's addiction by now and of the ways my life differed from those of the Bogata friends of my childhood, for whom drugs were foreign. Slowly we drifted apart. I had more in common now with a different set of girls, like my new friend Jonandrea. She lived with her grandparents just as I had the year before, and just as I still did most weekends. Both of Jonandrea's parents struggled with addiction. Later, her dad would die of an overdose, and her mom would go to prison. Jonandrea, a skinny, dark-haired white girl with a dimple in her chin and bottle-green eyes, didn't require any explanation from me about the weird things going on in my house. She knew. We never talked about any of it, but we drifted together, united by shared experience.

I thought more, too, about the Threadgills, one of the only other Black families in town, about the ways their story diverged sharply from my family's and yet still seemed more familiar than that of the kids with whom I used to spend my time. Demitrice Threadgill was a grade above me, and we'd never been tight. But like me, Demitrice's mom was addicted to drugs. By the seventh grade we shared an awareness of one another that none of us could put into words. We didn't hang out together, weren't close friends, but a bond hung in the air between us whenever we were around each other, a kind of unspoken kinship.

I remember sitting next to Demitrice on a school field trip to Dallas. Her grandmother, called Blue Eyes for the striking contrast between her rich, dark brown skin and marble blue eyes, had just been killed in a car accident. I knew somehow that Blue Eyes had been more of a mother to Demitrice in the past several years than her own had been. We didn't say much during the bus ride, but I could tell by the way her body relaxed when I sat down, her nod of recognition, the way she leaned into my shoulder sometimes when the bus turned a corner, that my presence was welcome. At some point during a long stretch of highway, a white egret rose from fields on our side of the bus and flew beside us for a time, its long black-tipped wings working in perfect, elegant unison, its blue eye parallel with our own.

"Maybe that's your grandma," I said, and Demitrice looked out at the bird and nodded. We sat in companionable silence the rest of the way, quiet in the knowledge of what we shared, and what we knew. Far too much for our age.

DRIFTING ON A memory, Ain't no place I'd rather be, than with you-ou-ou-ou. . . .

It's two o'clock in the morning on a school night and the silky tones of the Isley Brothers waft through the house. Jazz sleeps deeply beside me, her arm warm against mine, her steady breathing uninterrupted by the jarring sounds of the last three hours— the heavy slap of Mama's footsteps on the floor as she paces the house, the repeated slam of the bathroom door, the stereo being turned up or down depending on which Isley Brothers song is playing. Billy's working the night shift at the mine. I have a history test tomorrow and Mama has work. But it's two A.M. and both me and Mama are wide awake.

I can't stop the thoughts running through my head. *Why is she still up? Don't she know we have school tomorrow? Don't she gotta be at work in the morning? How can Jazz be so clueless?* I have to pee, but I'll hold it until I can't hold it anymore. I don't want to walk into the acrid smell of crack smoke piercing the heavy cloud of air freshener Mama uses to try to cover it up. My body is tense with a whole range of emotions: anger, sorrow, resentment, worry, fear. Every time I close my eyes I may as well be in the living room with her. By this time, I know that scene all too well.

There's our beautiful mama. She sits in the corner of our blue sofa close to the stereo, her feet curled up under her. She's got a half-burnt cigarette in her left hand, the curling smoke backlit by the blue light of the TV, muted hours ago. The light flickers on her face, highlighting eyes that have lost their way. Sometimes she leans forward, slow as molasses, and tips a tube of gray ash into the growing pile of half-smoked Benson & Hedges, a few still smoldering in the glass ashtray on the table. If her cigarette ash tumbles to the floor before she remembers, she'll curse.

For the love of you . . . She tries to sing along, but she's moving in slow motion, the sides of her mouth gummy with spit, the words coming out garbled, as though her jaws are glued together. There are three empty Michelob bottles on the coffee table next to the ashtray, and one that's almost empty, but she doesn't reach for it anymore. Her beautiful high cheekbones have gone slack with the weight of the chemicals coursing through her body. Her agitated temper of the last few days is nowhere to be found. It's like someone doused the very flame inside her with that chalk-white milk coating the corners of her mouth.

That's my mama out there on that couch. My *mama.* In a state where I can't even recognize her, but that I know by now like the back of my hand.

Those were bad dream nights, except that I was awake. Alone in our room, sleepless, I'd try to wrap myself in the smooth sounds of Ronald Isley's soothing voice, drift with him and his brothers on their dream that Mama had somehow managed to rewind and play again.

Sad to see . . . A new horizon slowly comin' into view, yeah I wanna be livin'. For the love of you, oh, yes, I am. All that I'm givin' . . . is for the love of you, all right now, oh . . .

Wrapped in the music, I'd try to get my mind to catch onto something else. Anything but what had taken hold of our mother. I never could manage it.

MY MOM HAD become an unstable, unpredictable individual I hardly knew, and I wanted none of it. Every weekend, I called Mama Lena. And every weekend, she drove the hour to and from Bogata to take me and Jazz home with her to Campbell. She'd sing Al Green the whole way home, smoking her Salem 100s and sipping out of the Pepsi she kept in the drink holder—it was a soothing ritual to take sips out of Mama Lena's cup of ice-cold Pepsi. She never asked questions, and to this day I don't think she knew how bad things had gotten with my mom. If she did, she kept it to herself, her full-body hugs telling me everything that I needed to know—that I was surrounded by love.

On these weekends, I would go to church with Daddy Sudie, who, in the few hours of the day he wasn't fishing, loved to sit at his black desk and highlight verses in his Bible. And I needed it. To have your family crumble before your eyes under the weight of addiction—it can shake a person, especially a teenager. Granny went to the same church, and it felt good to stand shoulder to shoulder and pray with both sides of my family. Being in church, surrounded by the swaying and singing choir, listening to the sonorous voice of the preacher rise and fall from the pulpit, feeling those wooden floors shake with the gospel under my feet—even now the memories bring me a sense of healing and solace.

On Sunday afternoons, Mama Lena and Daddy Sudie's house filled with all five of my dad's brothers and his sister, countless cousins, and their kids. One by one family members would pull up the quarter-mile concrete driveway Daddy Sudie had laid himself, pile out of the cars, and make their way through the kitchen to admire the cornucopia of dishes that would soon grace the Sunday dinner table, a tradition so strong it was almost a religion unto itself. By two o'clock, the lowing of the dairy cows on the property beyond Mama Lena's back fence would be drowned out by the laughter of at least twenty-five people, all family.

Mama Lena's soul food was healing and made with love. She'd call everyone on Saturday night to make sure they all had a dish coming that they wanted to eat. Meatloaf, mac and cheese, cabbage, candied yams, jugs of sweet tea—the house would be full of the aroma of soulful cooking and the resounding laughter of my dad's brothers. My great-grandmother, still vivacious at eighty-four, would be holding court from her seat on the end of the couch, catching up one family member after another on the latest family drama. Uncle Gerald would have his clippers out, cutting a couple of my boy cousins' hair just outside the bathroom. Aunt Felicia was the only girl and like a big sister to me—I hung on her every word. By early evening, we'd be spent with laughter, our paper plates scattered around the living room, bellies full and minds brimming with old family stories and new family secrets.

One Saturday evening I followed my grandpa to the pond, jabbering away. I was his namesake—our shared middle name is just the initial "K," signifying our bond to each other—and in early photos I'm constantly by his side, grinning proudly as he holds up his latest prize catch.

"Daddy Sudie," I said as we picked our way down the path, my grandpa carrying both our poles and the bait I refused to touch, "I made straight A's on my report card *and* on two tests last week. My teacher said my book report was the best she'd read in a while. So I was thinking, maybe you could give me some kind of special award. I mean, my friend Kelly gets five dollars for every A. And I got all A's! What are you gonna give me?"

Daddy Sudie listened patiently. While I passionately justified my case, he baited my hook for me as he always did, so I wouldn't have to get my hands dirty. When I'd run out of arguments for my cause, he handed me the pole and looked me dead in the eye.

"I'm not giving you anything," he said.

I kept my eyes on the worm dangling from the hook, a sight I usually carefully avoided. My grandparents hardly ever told me no, and my feelings were crushed though I tried not to show it. When Daddy Sudie spoke again his tone was firm, but kind.

"I'm not going to reward you for doing what you are supposed to do, Big Girl. You are smart. Straight A's—that's what you're supposed to do." That was a lesson in responsibility I would carry for years to come.

During these weekends in Campbell, I got to spend a lot more time with my dad, since he still lived at home with his parents, which was wonderful. In his late twenties by now, my dad was as central a figure as ever to us. His Michael Jackson curl had given way to a neat fade, but he was still baby-faced and always poised to envelop his daughters in a proud hug that could cure any blues. In every way, he groomed me for success: counting my "ums" during practice presentations until they were vanquished from my vocabulary, urging me to smile during phone calls to project confidence over the line, practicing firm handshakes with eye contact. He fawned over all of my accomplishments while, in his calm, quiet way, insisting on more and better.

But my father also suffered from addiction. Once, when we still lived in Fulbright—I must have been about eight—I remember standing in the doorway of his darkened room in Campbell while Mama Lena called to him. "I'm taking the girls back to their mama," she said. "Get up, now. Say goodbye." But my dad didn't even stir. "High as hell," Mama Lena muttered, and went to shake him, push at his arm, tried everything to rouse her son from his bed. It was the middle of the afternoon, but she couldn't get him to budge, not even when she raised her voice. Finally, she rolled him over and took a wad of cash out of his pocket. "Here, Brittany," she said. "Take this. He'd have given it to you if he wasn't knocked out."

Like Bogata, Campbell was a white town, but much smaller, with only about five hundred people. Most of my dad's friends were white, and they partied hard—LSD, alcohol, and powder co-caine. They weren't the addicts who graced the covers of *Time* and *Newsweek*—all Black, all from the so-called inner city—but even in the eighties, country white kids were rampant drug abusers. And though, predictably, none of my dad's white friends ended up in jail for drugs, they paid the price of addiction in other ways. Around the time Mama went to rehab, one of my dad's best friends went fishing and drowned in a stoned, drunken stupor. A few weeks later, another overdosed on cocaine. Another had a bad trip that led to a psychotic break. Still another committed suicide.

I didn't know it then, but my father, so young and surrounded by death and destruction, believed he was next. He wrote poems furiously into the night and illustrated them with pencil sketches, the best of which he did with his eyes closed, completely by inter-nal vision. I'd wake in the mornings in Campbell to find pages taped to my bathroom mirror, filled with poems dedicated to me, the messages he wanted me to carry if he himself didn't make it out of the struggle.

I was fourteen by then and full of myself—I wanted to apply lip gloss in the mirror, not read my father's soul on the page—and I sometimes found the poems annoying, as all things parental can seem at that age. But somehow I had the wherewithal to hold on to them, and they remain among my most cherished possessions. They were full of gems, I recall to this day: "Brittany, remember your happiness and well-being are not open for debate," and "Sweetheart, whatever you want in life, put and keep God first and go and get it," and

> May God enhance all positive abilities in my lovely daughter
> may she not forget the lessons her daddy taught her
> Let her know her daddy will always love her and care
> Her daddy will always be there
> if not in the flesh
> eternally in spirit.

When I got older, I could read his own internal struggles be-tween the lines. But at the time, all I saw was my dad's unwavering support and encouragement. From the beginning, he drilled into me that I could do anything in this world I set my mind to, and reminded me constantly that I held all that I needed to succeed within myself—that my future was whatever I imagined it to be.

When finally Daddy decided enough was enough—that he wished to live, and to live he had to leave the drugs—he got him-self sober. While he waited to shake the chemicals' hold on his body, he studied my grandfather's contracting blueprints and began to envision a new life for himself as a cement contractor as successful as his own father had been. "If you can build a sidewalk, you can build a stadium," my grandfather told his son. With the evidence of his own father's achievements in front of him, my daddy knew that despite being at the lowest point of his life, his success as an entrepreneur depended only upon his own dedica-tion and belief. He studied the Bible, he studied his blueprints, and he began rebuilding his life.

While my daddy taught himself about cement, sitting in his armchair color-coding blueprints, I sat beside him with my own pen, and my own dreams. "What college do you want to get into, BK?" he'd ask. At thirty, he had abandoned his Michael Jackson jackets for a collection of suave leather vests and trousers that he wore with turtlenecks of the same color. He peered at me seri-ously from behind his round glasses.

"I don't know, maybe University of Texas," I said. He found me a picture of their logo in a magazine and had me cut it out and hang it on my bedroom wall.

"How are you gonna make that happen?" Daddy would ask. "You gotta set your intentions, BK. You got to know what you want and believe in it. Speak it into being."

Way before tech-age gurus were making millions for TED talks speaking the same truth, my father taught me the power of inten-tion: You can't be it unless you can believe it.

Chapter 3

THE HOLE

My sister, Jazz, is the opposite of me and always has been. Carefree, laughing, entirely free with herself, her words, her emotions. She lives her life fully, without layers—always bringing all parts of herself to the table, regardless of the table—and I envy her that poise and conviction. In our relationship I've always been the guardian, but even when I give her a hard time for her free-spirited ways, I've always admired her ability to be one hundred percent herself at all times. I look up to her for this quality, and always have. With Jazz I can be totally free—free to be silly, to cuss, to act ratchet Brittany, to live life without any masks. I'm so grateful for that—and I don't know where I'd be without having Jazz to laugh and feel whole with.

Which makes it harder, I guess, when I think of how I abandoned her to move to Campbell.

I was only in the ninth grade. Objectively, I know it wasn't my responsibility to stay in Bogata and take care of Jazz, take care of my mom. But I also know that Jazz saw a lot of things I never had to. And if I had stayed, she and Mama wouldn't have ultimately followed me to Commerce, where drugs were plentiful and Mama got worse. But at the time, I wasn't thinking about all that. All I wanted was to get away.

Life with my mother had become intolerable. Her functional time between binges was shortening by the week. We couldn't pretend we were normal anymore, not by a long shot. I was fourteen years old and full of anxious worry and confusion, which sometimes gave way to resentment and anger at what my mother was doing to us, to Billy, to our life as a family. I had no real understanding or empathy for what the disease of drug addiction was doing to her, the ravaging. I coped by doing what I did best— taking responsibility. I made sure we stayed out of her way, made sure we ate when Billy was on his shift and Mama had disappeared for a couple of days.

At first I thought that if I did these things, made it easier at home, I could help cure what ailed her, could bring her back to us. But by 1998, I'd lost faith in that. At school, the DARE program brought friendly police officers into our classrooms to convince us that drug abuse was everywhere, a mortal threat, and that only the weakest, most morally bankrupt individuals would succumb to it—the losers, those who didn't love themselves enough or weren't strong enough. I loved Mama through and through, but it was hard not to internalize that message, not to view Mama's habit as the worst kind of moral failure. My experience with my mom collided with the conflicting realities of what people said about people on drugs and the people I knew who were on drugs to create a painful double consciousness. I was sad, deeply disappointed, and wounded, but in a teenager this all comes out most easily as hostility. Mine was the blind, vindictive rage of an adolescent girl who was growing up too soon and savvy enough to know the cause— or to think I knew, at least. It was as if the drug controlled all of us, and I didn't want to be controlled.

And so I left. I left the Bogata of my childhood, those innocent days walking down Main Street to the Kwik Korner for a burger, the hours in my bedroom reading any book I could get my hands on. I left Billy. I left Mama, and I left Jazz. I left Jazz with Mama at her most ill and unstable.

But I was a teenager, and I couldn't wait to get to what I saw as the faster-paced excitement of Commerce, a town of nearly eight thousand people five minutes from Mama Lena's house in Campbell. As much as I was running away from my mama's transformation, I was also running *to* something. The love and stability of my grandparents. The big high school in Commerce. And the first Black community besides my own family that I ever really felt a part of.

Commerce was where the action was: step shows at the Texas A&M–Commerce campus, where the Q-Dogs stomped in their purple bomber jackets and the pretty-boy Kappas shimmied and twirled their red-and-white canes. On weekends during the run-up to the high school basketball championships, all the top schools from the surrounding area would converge on Commerce for the weekend. It was like the Black population in town tripled overnight, with a true *Friday Night Lights* kind of energy, but with flavor. Master P's "Make 'Em Say Uhh" blared from the speakers at halftime, and the stands would be packed with cute boys. My friends and I would put on our Tommy Hilfiger gear and shake the stands with DMX's "Stop . . . drop . . . shut 'em down, open up shop" whenever our team took the court. I had my hair cut in an asymmetric blond bob like T-Boz from TLC, faded in the back courtesy of Dino's Barber Shop, a painted belly button like Aaliyah, and way too many pairs of Air Max to match my clothes. All that Southern Blackness was medicine to my wounds.

At Commerce High I continued to excel academically, whipping through my classes despite sketchy attendance caused by a series of debilitating migraines, which I later realized were probably stress related.

My grandparents' house in Campbell, my sole and soul refuge during my adolescence, was home to me now. But like most teenagers, I no longer spent my free time at home. I had my own life, and I threw myself into it. I spent most of my time in Commerce, with a whole new set of friends, with whom I felt, maybe for the first time in my life, entirely myself.

As in many larger rural towns in the South, the railroad tracks in Commerce marked the dividing line between Black and white. On one side of the tracks was the commercial center: the college, city hall, businesses, white residential neighborhoods—carefully kept that way, first by deliberate redlining and later by Jim Crow. On the other was the lower back end of Commerce, neglected by the city, with very few businesses and many signs of disrepair and government neglect. Through the sixties, the city of Commerce was known as a "sundown town"—any Black person found on the streets after dark was in danger of being lynched. The only place where Black citizens were safe from the threat of white violence was also the only place Black people were legally allowed to reside: Norris Community, known fondly by younger generations as "the Hole."

The Hole was the Commerce hood. It was set in a valley and locked in by the tracks on two sides and a large field with no road at the far end. When you drove down into it from the high school—which we did almost every afternoon—you really drove down. The Sunrise Housing Projects in the Hole resembled most projects in the rural South, with small yards in front of single-story pink brick units, surrounded by a couple of feet of grass and a chain-link fence. From the outside, they couldn't look more different from the high-rise stacked apartment complexes that stretch city blocks in big urban hoods. But in many ways, the conditions that led to them and shaped the lives of their residents were entirely similar. Beyond the innocuous-looking front yards and country porches of Commerce, most people struggled to survive.

But the Hole was ours, and I loved it. It was *our* hood, buzzing with the energy of Black people living their daily lives: *our* music blasting from houses and cars, *our* laughter from porches and corners. People gathered on their front steps to catch up after a day's work. Kids rode their bikes in packs, swooping in and out of driveways from the sidewalk to the street. Mothers and grandmothers yelled for those same kids to come and eat. Teenagers drove slowly down the block, showing off shiny new rims. Other than our family road in Fulbright, I'd never been in a place where there was nothing but Black people. I felt more comfortable and at home than I ever had in my life. The energy of the Hole spoke powerfully to me. I felt a gravitational pull to culture, a pull as strong as an ocean tide.

Late afternoons, after school was out, we crossed the tracks to hang out in the Hole at the home of my new best friend, Ashley, who we called Sissy. Sissy recognized my soul and understood me. She was short and thick, with beautiful dark-chocolate skin, a pixie cut, and perfect teeth from her years in braces. She lived with her grandmother in a white clapboard corner house, next door to her aunt Cookie. The houses had twin dirt yards in the front and a big old oak tree on Aunt Cookie's side that supplied shade in the blazing late-afternoon sun for all but a few short winter months. We'd sit in the shade in folding chairs in Sissy's front yard with her grandma. Aunt Cookie came in and out of the conversation through the screen door from her front kitchen, where she was busy preparing potato salad for her weekly card game. I practically lived at that house in my high school years.

From Sissy's place, we'd stroll down to visit Ms. Reynolds, the neighborhood Candy Lady, for watermelon Now-and-Laters and Frooties, sometimes a Kool-Aid pickle. Sissy was a sunflower seed queen, able to deshell multiple seeds with precision in her mouth and neatly deliver the seeds back to her bag. Almost every day, we'd sit in Sissy's yard eating seeds, sipping our freeze cups, and gossip about everybody who drove past.

From that corner yard, Sissy's grandmother and Aunt Cookie had the best view in town. On Fridays, when everyone got their checks, the drug corner ran nonstop. The yard had a clear view of the intersection that ran down to the busiest block in the Hole— the block where guys hung all day and night, slanging dope.

"There goes Rita's boy," Aunt Cookie would say a few moments after he passed, shaking her head. "Damn shame. Got a good job at Sherwood but won't keep it long. This is the third time this week I seen his car."

The older women would talk about every car that drove up to the dope block, and sometimes those that didn't, too. They knew everybody and everybody's business. But when a silver two-door Pontiac Grand Am came through from up the street, Sissy's grandma would get up from her chair.

"Who wants some sweet tea?" she'd say. "I got some cake in there, too. Sissy, come on and help me get some more ice. Brittany, you come, too."

The gossip would stop for a few minutes, the yard quiet, a gentle pause in the laughter and cutting up.

It was my mama in that car, and everybody knew it.

Like Sissy and her family, my friends in Commerce did the best they could to shield me from feeling the shame of Mama's addiction, even if, living in the supply zone as they did, they were eyewitnesses to it. Mama and Jazz moved to Commerce soon after I did, the middle of my ninth-grade year, and I wasn't pleased about it. I wanted space from that life, space from my mother's struggles, from the pain of witnessing her decline. Mama had unraveled by this point and was no longer containing her addiction to the privacy of the home. My friends in the Hole knew when she came through in the middle of the night to buy. Many of them had seen her at her worst, but they said nothing to me. They let me go on being the good girl who lived with her grandparents on the other side of the tracks. For those of us born and raised during the height of the War on Drugs—and on our communities—having a loved one who sold crack or was addicted to crack was a shared reality, a shared experience. It didn't mean we weren't cruel to one another about it, that we didn't break each other down over it. We did. But the truth is, for me, for my friends in Commerce, my friends from Bogata like Jonandrea and Demitrice, having lost a loved one to drugs was the norm. In the Hole, I was protected.

———

TWO WHITE SHERIFFS in cowboy hats and big metal belt buckles looked me and my Granny up and down as we walked through the parking lot and up the steps of the old Clarksville courthouse. I felt Granny stiffen beside me. I'd already suffered the embarrassment of having to stand in the office of the principal, Ms. King, to explain that I'd be missing school that day, even though I'd accumulated the maximum absences for the semester.

"What's the reason for your absence, Ms. Barnett?" she asked. Her stern expression softened when I answered: "My mom's in jail. I gotta go to her court hearing."

Clarksville is the county seat of Red River County, located about fifteen minutes from Bogata. Tourist blogs and websites describe it as a quaint town with an authentic Old South feel, and that's about right. Of course, for Black people, the Old South is nowhere you want to visit. A statue of a lone Confederate general towers over the Clarksville town center. To hear my grandpa tell it, the general was built looking sternly over at the Black side of town as a warning regarding where the town's heart lies. As if there were any question.

Clarksville had a majority Black population and almost entirely white law enforcement. In the courthouse, a historic building that still houses the original bills of sale for many of the region's first Black residents, rural injustice along color lines runs rampant. "Instead of hanging Blacks from trees, nowadays they do it in the courtrooms," says Fred Stovall, a Black pastor from the next town over. At the Clarksville courthouse in the late nineties, a dime bag of weed could get you twenty years or more—if you were Black. No one really disputes that racial inequity haunts law enforcement here—the numbers make it foolish to do so. ACLU Texas director Tom Baker bluntly stated, "Marijuana enforcement is just a tool of law enforcement to target communities of color" in the region. In a neighboring county, Blacks were charged for marijuana possession at a rate thirty-four times that of whites, despite equal usage. Red River County numbers weren't much better.

With their own windfall from the War on Drugs, which gave

financial incentives for drug arrests regardless of convictions, Clarksville renovated their jailhouse in the late eighties, even while other businesses shuttered around it. But the old courthouse was left exactly as it had always been, right down to the basement file cabinets and the records of slaves bought and sold.

I sat next to Granny on the straight-backed dark wooden benches of the old courthouse, our eyes on the door where they would bring Mama in from the jail. When the door opened, I heard Granny's sharp intake of breath, heard her whisper "Lord have mercy" through clenched teeth. Granny was a fierce woman who didn't stoop for anybody, but even for her, this sight was too much. There, shackled at her feet and wrists, prodded along roughly by a white sheriff in a cowboy hat, was my mama. She wore a soiled uniform with thick black-and-white horizontal stripes more reminiscent of Looney Tunes cartoons than real life. It was like she'd stepped back in time.

When we saw each other, we smiled, or tried to. I still remember the feeling of horror in my throat, in my chest. I had never seen anything as demeaning and archaic as that uniform in my life. The uniform was clown-like: oversized, hanging off her shoulders and long in the arms. Mama had tears in her eyes when she saw us, but beyond that there was a sheepishness, a shame—and my mama didn't show shame, not ever.

It wasn't like our family wasn't acquainted with law enforcement. We were a rural Black family in East Texas, where the arm of the law had quickly replaced the slave owners' shackles as a method of social and economic control of its Black population. I had uncles and cousins who had been to jail. Mama wasn't even the first in my immediate family to go—my father served thirty days when I was a freshman in high school for writing a bad check for construction materials. That was all it took: a bounced check when his previous job failed to pay him in time for it to clear. In he went. I remember his orange jumpsuit, I remember the visits. I knew what he was there for, and I knew when he was getting out. It wasn't that big a deal to me. But this was my mama. There's something about seeing your childhood hero, your guiding star, fallen. It rocks you to your core. Add the striped Looney Tunes suit, the white judge and lawyers, my mom's shamed expression—it's a primal wound, to see your mother like that. I will never forget the pain of seeing her in the run-down, time-warped courthouse in Clarksville, Texas. Whenever I think of Mama in prison, that image of her in humiliating stripes is still the first one I see.

Mama had already been in the Clarksville jail for two months pending court. That day she was given five years' probation and released to Granny. She went back to work, and back to using.

Chapter 4

OTHER SIDE OF THE GAME

In our senior year of high school, Sissy's grandmother passed away, and she moved to Dallas. When I drove up to visit her, my boyfriend, Red, came with me. Red always paid for gas, and always put a couple hundred on top for me, for my time. On the way, I'd stop off in East Dallas at a white clapboard house with pretty daisies and a gentle brindle pit mix in the front yard. Red would go in the house. Ten minutes later, he'd come out with a bundled package wrapped in several layers of plastic that he'd slip under the front seat. I knew what was in it. But we didn't talk about it. At the end of the trip, I took the money he handed me without a thought.

My boyfriend was a drug dealer, and I knew it.

I met Red when I was a freshman in high school and he was a senior. His older brother, Courtney, also known as C-Money, was a beloved figure in the Hole, handsome and popular, with an infectious smile and a mouth full of gold teeth. C-Money and Red's cousin Gerald—we called him Black—organized the block parties and summer Hoodfests, where everybody would come from towns all around, park their cars on a stretch of empty land, set up chairs and tables, play bones and spades all afternoon, and then party into the night. These gatherings were the social events of the summer, almost like huge family reunions. We'd sit on the backs of cars with paper plates on our laps, eating BBQ and drinking E&J Brandy out of Styrofoam cups, the girls' hair stylish with Marcel iron curls and stiff with Pump It Up hair spray. The guys wore denim shorts with a crisp crease, painstakingly ironed with generous use of Sta-Flo starch. As a teenager, it was about seeing and being seen.

Red was easy to talk to, charming, and funny—so funny. He had heavy-lidded, light brown eyes that were always half-closed from smiling, and looked just like Brandy's boyfriend, Q, on *Moesha*. He was slim and muscled with skin the smoothest brown and a pure white smile to contrast with his brother's gold grill. He'd talk to anyone about anything and anybody and could have a room of us rolling with laughter in no time at all. We were friends for a long time before we started dating, but it was still nothing serious until I was a senior. By then, he was two years out of high school and on the grind pretty much full-time. I was taking extra classes before and after school to stay on track to graduate in three years instead of four.

By then the good, or even just steady, jobs that our elders had held—jobs on the Cotton Belt and Southern Pacific, Sherwood Manufacturing, in hospitals and even in retail—had long ago dried up. Under Reagan's economic programs, several hospitals had closed. Small businesses had been wiped out by the arrival of a Walmart, and there were just two grocery stores and a few fast-food restaurants left. These jobs generally went to college students. There weren't a lot of opportunities available for young men and women coming out of generations of poverty in East Texas. But there were drugs. Lots of them. A steady supply to feed an ever-expanding demand. The drug game was a lucrative hustle, and whole families ran businesses out of their homes. The risks were high, but as long as you didn't get caught up, the immediate rewards were great.

There I was, graduating from high school a year early, at the top of my class, about to begin a full-time job at a bank and my first year of college, nothing but a gleaming future ahead. But I was also a young woman immersed in a culture where some level of drug involvement was the norm. I didn't think much of Red's dealing at the time, but when I look back now, the truth hits me hard.

MAMA GOT OUT of Clarksville jail right in time for my graduation and even took me and Jazz on a mini college tour of the University of Texas at Arlington for orientation. We lounged around in the hotel room, laughing and loving just like we used to in the old days in Bogata. I was the first person to go to a university in my family, and even if it was just a few hours away, we were all excited.

I've always been driven. Billy once asked me and Jazz what we wanted to be when we grew up. At five, I knew for sure. "I'm gonna be a lawyer!" I said, chin lifted, that stern expression on my face that everybody said I'd gotten from my mama. I loved *The Cosby Show,* and I might have been Rudy's age, but I idolized Clair Huxtable—an attorney, beautiful, stylish, and always in control.

Up through the sixth or seventh grade I never wavered from wanting to be a lawyer, but as you get older your dreams begin to shrink, narrowed by what's around you—so slowly you don't even realize it. No matter how many times my dad urged me to reach for the stars, my understanding of the universe was still confined by the world's limited notion of what a Black country girl from the South could do or who she could become. By high school the idea of myself as an attorney had receded. I didn't know any lawyers, not a single one, and I had begun to internalize some of the harder messages of my environment. Being a lawyer seemed out of my league.

Around that time, I read Bebe Moore Campbell's novel *Brothers and Sisters,* in which the protagonist is the operations manager for a Los Angeles bank. She enjoyed her career, and her lifestyle seemed glamorous to me. Just reading about a Black career woman gave me something to hold on to. *I could do that,* I thought, and I set my sights on majoring in finance and becoming a bank VP.

My dad urged me to go to the University of Texas in Austin instead of the satellite campus in Arlington—he'd leave different university booklets with his poems, encouraging me to aim high in my applications. I would have gotten into Austin, too; I was in the top ten percent of my class, which means automatic admission to any Texas university. But I didn't listen to him. Even though I had successful businessmen as role models in my own family— my grandfather with his cement company and nightclub, my dad who by this time was growing his contracting business—their success was local, rooted in our corner of East Texas. Austin seemed way too far away for me, too big-time, too other—let alone the out-of-state colleges my dad encouraged.

Besides, I was seventeen and in what I thought was love. Things between me and Red had gotten serious. Tragedy drew us even closer. During my senior year, his brother C-Money had been pulling stunts and wheelies in front of their grandmother's house when his motorcycle spun out of control. He was in a coma for three days before he succumbed to his injuries. The entire neighborhood mourned C-Money the same way the nation mourns the loss of a celebrity. After the funeral, we gathered in the street where the accident had happened wearing T-shirts screen-printed with his beaming face and favorite phrase, "You do the math!" We drank alcohol and smoked blunts in a tragic imitation of the beloved Hoodfests C-Money had so diligently organized, trying to numb our disbelief that he was really gone.

Red told funny stories about his brother so we could mix laughter with our tears, but the angle of his shoulders and the hoarse, desperate sound of his voice told of his pain. He had to put on a hard front. With C-Money gone, he had more responsibility. Both the game and his grief took their toll on him. He didn't laugh as much as he used to, didn't joke. Unbeknownst to me, he'd started to use cocaine. All I knew was that the boy I loved was hurting.

We decided to move to Arlington together. I had already lined up a job for the fall at Chase Bank. For Red, it would be a fresh start, away from the pressures and memories of his family home. He talked about getting out of the game. I believed him.

A week after I graduated from high school in 2001, Red and I were sitting on his couch, sharing the pepperoni pizza I'd just brought over to his apartment, the game on the TV. "You talked to Jay lately?" I asked Red, reaching for the napkin that had fallen off the glass coffee table. "I saw him at the corner store when I got the soda. He's doing real good, just got a new job over at Raytheon. He was telling me about the benefits and everyth—"

Crack!

The blow came so hard and fast it knocked me from the couch to the carpet.

I didn't even know what had happened until I looked up from the floor. I don't even think I made a sound. I was so surprised. Red had never hit me before. Nobody had.

Red stood over me, his face twisted with rage. "Bitch, you talked to *who*? Why the fuck you talking to Jay, Brittany? Huh?"

"Red, what the hell?" I said, starting to sit up, confused.

With his heel, he stomped down hard on my face. I blacked out.

When I came to, the whole side of my face was pounding, my head heavy and hurting like I'd been hit with a brick. My eyesight was blurry, my right eye already swelling shut, though I wouldn't see the extent of the damage until later. I could barely make out Red pacing the apartment. He stalked in and out of the tiny kitchen, paused now and then to curse and hit the wall. "Look what you made me do, Brittany!" he kept saying, angry at first, then despondent. "Just look what you made me do!"

"I'm sorry," I said. "I'm so, so sorry."

I avoided my family the rest of that summer, hiding my swollen face behind oversized sunglasses. I knew if Daddy or my uncles saw my eye, they'd find Red and kill him. And like a lot of young women trapped in a cycle of abuse, I was sure I loved him. He'd never hit me before, and I hoped he wouldn't again. I'd go from work to Red's, avoiding any store where I might see a cousin or anyone who knew my family. I was doing so much hiding that summer—hiding my mom's addiction from my friends and colleagues, my boyfriend's abuse from my family, any sign of weakness or pain from myself.

When I began my job at Chase three months later, my eye was still bruised. I told my co-workers I'd been in a minor car accident.

"Good thing you have that nice boyfriend to take care of you," one of them said kindly.

IT WAS A confusing time in my life. On one hand, I was an ambitious young woman on the rise; on the other, a teenage girl emotionally adrift without her mom, trying to take care of her sister while falling into an increasingly abusive relationship. I did well in college from the beginning, even while holding down a full-time job at the bank. I was good at my job, too. I came to see it's partly how I cope with stress and chaos—I do what I'm supposed to do, like Daddy Sudie taught me, control what I can control, move forward with purpose.

When I started at Chase, I met one of the people who I've been fortunate to encounter all my life, mentors and friends who guide my path, who nudge me in directions that, once I take them, seemed to be there for me all along. I think of them as my angels, and my friend Ken Chuka-Obah is one. There were a lot of college students that worked in my department, and Ken was a few years ahead of me at UTA. When he learned I was majoring in finance, he took me to lunch and, in his lilting Nigerian accent, said, "Brittany, you should switch your major to accounting."

"Why?" I was skeptical. Even when it came from friends as good as Ken, I never did like being told what to do.

"It's not much of a difference, but accounting is three-sixty. You can still do finance with an accounting degree, but you can't do accounting with a finance degree. Way more job options."

That made perfect sense to me. And so I switched. In my sophomore year I'd enter the business school and begin as an accounting major.

But my relationship with Red was going from bad to worse. He hadn't stopped dealing or using, and the abuse wasn't daily, but it was bad. I kept the whole thing under wraps—no one but Sissy knew anything was going on at all.

It took six months for that first black eye to heal. We had moved together to Arlington, over my mother's tearful protests. She had figured out the truth about my bruised eye and was livid. Plus, she knew all too well how Red made his money. She wasn't doing well herself—after getting out of jail in Clarksville her drug use had accelerated, the weight of her addiction stronger than the threat of more jail time for probation violations. But she was still my mom, and she tried hard to persuade me not to go. I was as stubborn as she was, seventeen, and in love. "I will be fine, Mama."

"You're making a huge mistake, Britt," Mama said, her voice quavering with the urgency of getting the message across to me. I didn't listen, but my mama was right.

The next time Red stomped my face, he wore a boot.

SOMETIMES A SERMON comes just in time.

Ms. Eleanore Murrell, a co-worker at Chase, could see straight through me. She was an older Black woman, about my mother's age, short and impeccably stylish, with the sweetest smile and a way of putting her hand on my shoulder and calling me baby that made me feel all was right in the world. Eleanore was a single mom of three kids and brought me into her fold as if I were one of her own. She made me lunches and took me home to have dinner with her and her family. We'd sit and eat her famous lasagna and laugh about the day just like family. In spite of my academic success, my positive persona, my internships, my tall tales of a happy home life, Eleanore could tell I was hurting. And though she never said anything about it, I'm pretty sure she knew that there'd never been any car accident.

Lord knows I needed her kindness. On Sundays, she took me with her and her kids to Morning Star Baptist Church. I loved that church. It was a big church but had real pews and wooden walls, like the country churches of my childhood. Pastor Taylor had a beautiful, honeyed voice, and he sang through much of the service. As soon as the organ swelled and the first notes hummed, I could feel all those knots of tension begin to relax—my growing fear of what Red might do next, my worry and pain over my mom's addiction, my guilt for leaving Jazz to deal with her alone. It was a lot to carry at seventeen. It felt good to lay my burdens down.

Church has often been one of the few places in America where Black people can feel truly free. On the Sunday that Pastor Taylor began to preach a sermon from Ezekiel, that's exactly how I felt: free. And feeling free made me know that I could get free. "It's clean-up time!" Pastor Taylor hollered, and on that day, his voice and message rang straight through to my soul. "It's not straighten-up time! It's not tidy-up time!" He paced to the other side of the pulpit, a sheen of sweat on his forehead, his voice lifting with each line. "You don't throw things under the bed, throw things in a drawer! No! You clean up! *All* the way up! And do you know what time it is now? Right now? Today? It's clean-up time!"

All my life I had felt this need, this urgency, to save people, to help heal them. But something in me realized that if I didn't act soon, I might be the one who needed saving. It was as though Pastor Taylor had written that sermon just for me. And I responded as though he had. I cleaned up.

Red was spending the weekend in Commerce with his family, so I was alone in the apartment. That night, I called my daddy, an hour away in Campbell. "Please," I said. "Just come get his stuff." Forty-five minutes later, I answered a knock at the door. There was my daddy, calm as ever, requiring no explanation. Relief washed over me. He opened his arms and I walked into them, burying my face in his chest, letting myself be his little girl for a few moments. Then I took a deep breath and stood up straight. Almost without a word, we quickly set to work, packing my dad's truck with Red's belongings. It was a huge step toward freedom, and I'm grateful to God and my family that I was strong enough to take it.

My experience with Red taught me how easy it can be for young women to fall into cycles of abuse—even confident, successful, strong young women. My abusive relationship became my own addiction. I was addicted to the intense highs and lows, to the intimacy you share with the one other person who knows just how bad things have gotten. And when you love the person abusing you, you have in-depth knowledge of the pain and brokenness that leads them to treat you in a damaging way. How will they ever heal, you think, if I leave? And as you worry about them, bit by bit your own sense of self gets broken down, too, so much so that being without the bond you share with the person hurting you seems impossible.

But I did it. With the kindness and quiet strength of Eleanore Murrell, the clarity brought to me by Pastor Taylor's beautiful sermon, the strength of my own family bonds—I broke up with Red. No more sweeping his abuse under the rug or hiding his outbursts in the closet. Cleaning up made me feel free.

THE AFTERNOON OF Jazz's high school graduation was typically gorgeous for late May, the fields around my grandparents' house in Campbell stretching away in shades of gold and green, the sun high and warm, songbirds competing with the lowing cattle from the dairy farm next door. I was outside, catching up with cousins, glad to have the break from school and work, glad to be home. With work and school I hadn't been back as much as I'd wanted, but I was excited to see everybody and to celebrate Jazz.

My uncle Gerald came out onto the porch, looking like my dad's twin in his sports coat and slacks, his aviators in hand.

"Daddy Sudie wants you, Britt," he said. I'd heard the same thing from someone else not two minutes before. In all the jostling about who would ride with whom to the ceremony, the jokes and the stories to catch up with, I didn't pay them any mind. My grandpa was getting older and sometimes obsessed over small things that he would forget about shortly thereafter.

Just as we finally began piling into the cars, I heard my grandfather calling me insistently from the front window. He sat there most afternoons now, laughing uproariously at old *Martin* reruns, no longer spending his days at the pond where I used to follow him down to fish. His shoulders were slimmer and his belly rounder, but he still had the full cheeks and commanding tenor of the family patriarch. I left the car and pulled back the sliding glass door to the living room.

"Yes sir?" I asked.

"Brittany, I need you to be careful."

"Daddy Sudie, we're just going over to the graduation! I'll be okay."

"Brittany, you need to be careful," he said solemnly. "You're going to Commerce and that boy's going to be there. I want you to be careful."

"C'mon, Brittany!" came the shouts from the car. "We got to go!"

Jazz was so happy that day, all smiles when she walked the stage, even more when she heard the yells and applause from all of us in the audience. Red's cousins were graduating in the same class, and he was in the audience, but we didn't speak. I nodded hello in the general direction of his family but made sure not to catch Red's eye. There was nothing more to say to each other—we were through.

We celebrated Jazz into the evening, and then I drove back down to Arlington with Sissy and my cousin Kawoina for company. It was so good to be with people from home. At one in the morning we were still sprawled out on the living room sofa, laughing and talking and having a blast. When the porch light outside switched on, it startled all of us.

Bam! Bam! Bam! Someone was pounding on the front door, kicking at it, throwing their body at it.

"Let me in, you bitch! Let me in this fucking house before I kill you!"

The rage in his voice was unmistakable. It was Red. My body pumped with fear and adrenaline. Sissy and Kawoina were looking at each other in disbelief. Somebody got up and turned out the front room lights, and we sat still in the semidarkness. The pounding and cussing at the front door stopped, and we listened hard, hoping to hear a car start and drive away.

Instead, the patio door that led directly to the living room shattered. Red stood there with his shoulders heaving, eyes as red as his name. The concrete block he'd heaved through the double-paned glass lay in the middle of the living room. Kawoina and Sissy screamed. Red started cussing and shouting again, moving steadily toward me, Kawoina and Sissy pulling on his arms, hanging on his shirt, pleading with him. "Red, stop! Stop! What the fuck are you doing?"

But I knew. I'd been a victim of Red's rages before. He was coming for me. "How you gonna leave me, Brittany? You think you too good for me?" he said angrily.

I backed as fast as I could into the bedroom, talking to him, trying to calm him down as he came at me. The ironing board was still laid out from where I'd ironed my clothes for graduation, and all I could think about was getting that iron out of Red's way. My body stiffened for the blows that I knew were coming. Red cussing and belligerent, Sissy and Kawoina screaming at him from behind, me winding that cord around the iron, talking as calmly as I could, desperate to put that iron up before Red could hit me with it, knowing now I should have used it on him.

And then he was coming after me. I could hear Sissy screaming, "Run, Brittany, run!" I was barefooted; even as a country girl I never went out barefooted, but now I took off. I made it out the front door and looked back to see Sissy and Kawoina holding on to the lanyard around Red's neck that held his keys, holding him back by that lanyard with all of their weight and punching him in the back of his head with their fists.

I was gone. I ran upstairs to a neighbor's apartment, taking the concrete steps two at time, banged on a door, two doors, begging to be let in. Nobody opened for me. I could hear Red raging and knew they wouldn't be able to hold him much longer. As I stood pounding at the third neighbor's door, I could hear the police sirens getting louder and louder, until finally their flashing lights animated the complex. It took several officers to take Red down.

Something happened within me after Red's attack that night. For many young women, being in an abusive relationship, even surviving one, forms emotional and psychological scars that can be crippling for a long time after the initial abuse is over. I can understand that and completely empathize with it. But for me, the opposite happened. Going through that relationship and emerging on the other side laid the groundwork for who I am now—and the ground it left me on is in no way shaky. I became very secure in myself, confident in who I was and my worth. Red couldn't take that from me, no matter how many patio doors he slammed through. Nobody could. I emerged from the confusion and despair of that experience with a strong sense of power and purpose. I knew who I was and what I would not tolerate. I was nineteen when Red last attacked me. In the next few years, I became stronger and more confident than I ever thought I would be.

Soon, I would need all of that strength. For my family, the hardest times were just around the corner.

IN THE SUMMER of 2004, just before my senior year in college, I moved from Arlington to Dallas. I didn't have a job, wasn't sure what I was going to do, but I knew I wanted a fresh start. I channeled my faith and my father's teachings to visualize what I wanted, to live my life with intention, to set those intentions and go toward them without doubt or reservation. Daddy taught me to write it down, everything I wanted, and then to picture it as if it had already happened. "You got to imagine it down to the smallest detail," he would say. "What are you wearing? What color are your shoes? Is the sun out or the stars? You have to bring it into being, BK! Put the universe in motion and it will align for your heart's desires." In Dallas, the power of intention worked. Within a week of moving, I secured a job at Comerica Bank in downtown Dallas, in their Heavy Equipment Lending Group. I worked every day, from eight o'clock to four thirty, leaving work to drive the thirty minutes to Arlington and attend a full load of classes.

We found Jazz an efficiency apartment nearby with low rent. I was making sixteen dollars an hour at Comerica and had a little financial aid from school to cover my own rent, so I was able to pay hers for about six months that year, just until she could get on her feet. Jazz found an assembly line job and started going to school, too. We lived humbly, ate our meals together, hit the dollar menu at Wendy's a lot. We did what we had to, and it worked out.

But when Jazz moved to Dallas to be near me, my mother's addiction hit rock bottom. Without Jazz, without me, my mom was left in Commerce to face her demons on her own. She lost. For the first time in our lives, she wasn't able to hold down any type of job. She would come to Arlington and stay with me for a few months at a time. She'd get a good nursing gig and things would seem fine for a few weeks. Then she'd get her paycheck, and the nightmare would begin again.

In May 2005, I graduated from UTA. No one but Sissy and my family knew what I'd gone through in my personal life in those four years. My mother made it to my undergraduate graduation, gaunt and deep in the throes of addiction. Still, she was there. No matter how badly the disease ravaged her body and mind, Mama always came through for the big stuff. We knew we were loved, unconditionally.

When I graduated with my master's a year later, I should have been on top of the world. I'd completed my master's in a single year and had a high-paying job waiting for me at the nation's top accounting firm. But when I proudly walked that stage to receive my degree, there was a gaping hole in my chest where joy should have been. Because for the first time in my life, my mother didn't attend my graduation. She couldn't. While I walked the stage in my cap and gown, my mother was on a hard cot in a concrete cell, stripped of her nursing license, her freedom—even her name.

Chapter 5

PULLING CHAIN

Tears flowed down my cheeks so heavy and strong I could feel them soaking through my shirt. It was a sweltering Texas July and I was sitting in my car in the parking lot of Woodman State Jail. Just two weeks earlier, in June 2006, a judge in Red River County had sentenced my mom to eight years in the Texas Department of Corrections. I was twenty-two years old.

The week before, when my mom called me collect from the Red River County jail, I didn't have the heart to tell her I couldn't afford for her to call me every day because I was helping Jazz pay her rent. We didn't have much to say anyway. My mom cried on the other end of the line, and I tried not to cry on mine. We were still processing the prison sentence she had received.

"I think I'm going to pull chain this week," she said nervously. Her voice seemed so distant through the phone. "Pulling chain" is jailhouse slang for being transferred from a local jail to a state-run prison.

"Wow, Mama. That's fast." My stomach turned in knots.

"It's good though, you know?" she said. "I mean, I can't come home until I leave."

My mom had failed her drug tests over and over again after being put on probation when I was in high school. Time after time, her dad would bail her out, or sometimes Billy. Each time she failed a drug test, the length of her felony probation was extended, and over the years she had accumulated ten years' probation time. Finally, her luck had run out. When she violated probation this time, the judge had had enough. The court sentenced my mother to eight years in prison.

The news stunned our family. Any semblance of normalcy was stripped from us in that one judgment. It was so obvious that Mama's problem was drugs. The only crime she committed was against her own body. It had been six years since her drug-induced encounter with a police officer that had led to her initial arrest and charge. There was no new subsequent criminal offense, only the snowballing consequences of her addiction in every failed drug test. But Red River County had no alternate drug courts, and so instead of the drug treatment she so desperately needed, the State of Texas was going to lock her away for a sentence that seemed like forever to us.

At night, I lay awake, trying to keep the shattering emotions that I felt in the pit of my stomach from taking over. The nightmares of my childhood returned, and sometimes I woke up in a sweat, my head pounding from a tension migraine. My logical defenses were vulnerable at that midnight hour, and I would give over to the pain. In the morning my eyes were swollen and my face red from where I'd pressed my hands into it. I held a cold compress to my cheeks and eyes before heading to work.

Mama was right about pulling chain: They moved her out of Clarksville that very week. From work and in between classes, I checked the Texas Department of Criminal Justice website several times a day, trying to find where they would place her. Finally she came up in the system at the Woodman Unit in Gatesville. I didn't tell Jazz, I didn't tell anybody. I just went. I had to go see my mama.

I wanted to hug her, to hold her, to have her whole self in front of me, not some number on the endless list of the Texas Department of Criminal Justice website, not a tiny voice on the other end of an impossibly expensive collect call, not the image of her in that archaic black-and-white Jim Crow prison uniform from Clarksville, locked in some cage.

I set out for the two-and-a-half-hour drive to Gatesville determined to make the best of the day, to be positive for my mom. The heat rose in waves off the blacktop as I cruised down I-35. I turned up the stereo and let the heavy bass of T.I.'s new album *King* run through me, trying to keep my despair at bay.

Gatesville is a small rural town near Waco with a population of fifteen thousand. Over half of that population are incarcerated in the town's six prisons, all but one of which were built between 1980 and 2005, during which time the prison population in the United States grew an astounding six hundred percent, and in my home state of Texas, twelve hundred percent. Five of the Gatesville prisons are facilities for women.

Finally I turned onto the road that led to the Linda Woodman Unit. Fields stretched on either side of the road, some with corn knee-high, others dry and fallow, the soil baked hard in the heat. I drove slowly, afraid I would miss the turn, passing one prison on my right, then another. Despite my tinted windows and the air-conditioning on full blast, the steering wheel was hot to the touch from the sun's relentless rays. In the field ahead of me, a large man in a cowboy hat and spurs sat astride a tall horse, both horse and rider silhouetted against the yellow fields in a quintessential central Texas scene. Busy admiring the sun rippling off the animal's muscled flank, I didn't see the rifle cradled in the man's hands until I was almost upon them. For a moment I was confused. Then I saw what he was guarding.

Just beyond horse and rider, three rows of women in white prison uniforms broke the soil with hoes swung in perfect unison. Sweat poured from their faces and soaked through their cotton uniforms as they struck the earth again and again in a perfect, terrible choreography. The man guarding them didn't turn his head as I drove by. His mirrored sunglasses flashed in the unflinching sun. I felt physically sick.

Later I would learn that I'd witnessed a Hoe Squad, a common labor practice for prisoners under the age of forty in Gatesville prisons since the 1950s. Women and men cropped all day in the fields, despite temperatures averaging ninety-six degrees. If a prisoner fell out of plantation rhythm, she risked being written up for an infraction. At the time, though, I just drove on and tried to shut the image out of my mind.

I had reviewed visitor rules on the Texas Department of Criminal Justice website again and again to make sure I was as prepared as I could be, that I met the dress code, that I'd be able to follow the rules, and now I tried to ease the hard pit of anxiety in my stomach by going over them in my head. I knew I would be able to hug and kiss Mama when I arrived and again when I left. I knew we'd have only two hours to visit and that we'd have to stay mindful of the time if we were going to be able to catch up on everything.

The Linda Woodman Unit was a low-security prison, but razor wire and dozens of tall security floodlights still marked the perimeter. The low-roofed building resembled a cattle barn. I pulled into the huge parking lot and into one of the many available spaces. Even though it was peak visiting hours, the lot was almost empty. I sat still in my car, motor off, no music, no A/C, just me looking at that blue tin building. Somewhere inside, I'd find my mama.

I couldn't wait to see her, had driven these two hours full of anticipation. But now that I was here it was like I was stuck in the car. This wasn't the little Clarksville jailhouse; that had been scarring enough. I didn't know what to expect, but if the scene in the field was any indication, I wasn't ready. The temperature in the car rose steadily, but still I couldn't move. The tears started, and then the sobs, wild, uncontrolled. I didn't want Mama to see me like that, wanted to be smiling for her, to be strong. But at that moment, I felt anything but.

I was so sorry for my mother—I knew she had a disease, one that she was not able to control, one for which, since that first trip to rehab when I was ten years old, and despite failing drug test after drug test, she had yet to receive treatment. I missed her deeply, but I had no idea what to expect inside. Being prepared, feeling competent and confident, was everything to me, but I knew nothing about prison.

And there were other emotions, too, ones I'm less proud of but that were just as strong, just as real. I was thinking of myself. I was in my early twenties, a selfish time in my life. I had done everything I was supposed to do, just like my grandpa had told me out there by the pond. Just a few weeks ago I'd felt on top of the world—I'd be making good money at PricewaterhouseCoopers, and I was about to be a certified public accountant. All of it—my degrees, my car I'd just paid off, my apartment, my job—all of it I'd achieved myself, despite whatever else was going on in my life. And I felt proud of that. A few short weeks before, I had truly believed I had everything under control. But now here I was in a prison parking lot, hanging on to that hot steering wheel for dear life, crying my eyes out.

Was my mama really in that place? Would they keep her locked in that blue tin box for eight whole years? Drag her out to these hot fields, hand her a hoe, patrol her on horseback like a slave? All the anguish I'd felt since my mom had first called from Clarksville swelled inside of me and would not be contained. The armor I'd worked so hard to build, an armor made from competence, confidence, the trappings of success, had been pierced by the arrow of my mother's incarceration. The shock of it was as strong as the pain.

When my sobs finally eased, so had some of my despair. I felt numb and tired, but also centered. The truth was, none of my professional success would shelter me from this experience. And why should it? Did I really believe that I should be exempt from the degradation of prison because I had a good job, a couple of degrees, a plan for my life? The older woman in the beat-up Dodge

Caravan across the parking lot straightening the dresses and smoothing the hair of the twin girls with her was no less worthy. And the two little girls getting ready to go in and see their own mama certainly weren't. Nobody is suited for the experience of having a family member locked away in prison. I wasn't special, and no amount of personal success would make me exempt from this struggle. The answer to my despairing "Why me?" was simple. *Why* not *you?*

I STEPPED OUT of the sweltering car into the even hotter oven-like air to walk toward the blue building that held my mama. When I hit the button outside the blue steel door a gruff voice crackled back through the intercom. I said I was here for a visit. When the door opened, I entered a cramped space with two long tables with bins leading to a metal detector. I placed a plastic bag with quarters I had read to bring and my keys in one bin, took off my shoes and set them in another. "Belt," barked the guard standing at the metal detector, and it took me a moment before I realized she meant me. I went back, got another bin, put my belt inside. "Do you have underwire in your bra?" the guard asked as I approached the detector again. I felt a moment of panic. Did I? I didn't know. What if I did? Would they send me home after I'd driven all this way? The woman's voice was still hard when she spoke again, but maybe she saw the stricken look on my face. "They have wireless ones down the street at Dollar General if you need it," she said, and beckoned me through. The detector didn't go off, and I went toward the bins, but before I put my shoes back on another guard made me raise one foot and then the other; she ran a wand along the sole of each, then had me hold my arms straight out and spread my legs while she patted me down. The assumption of guilt was present in every brusque word and pat doled out by the guards—as if by just visiting an incarcerated person, we were somehow less than human. I tried to fight off the creeping sense of shame I felt at that moment just for being there, for being in a position to be herded through security with the other visitors like cattle. I felt humiliated, as I'm sure is the intention of such procedures. Finally they released me into the visitors room. I exhaled a sigh of relief, not realizing until just then that I had been holding my breath.

Anxiously, I scanned the tables in the cafeteria-like room, looking for Mama among the few women in white who sat waiting for their visitors. I didn't see her anywhere. I felt that rising sense of panic again, made worse by the nervous and discomfited feeling from the search I had just endured, the close, stale air, the jingle of the guards' keys, the scrape of plastic chairs. Finally, I approached a guard sitting behind a solo visiting table at the front of the room.

"Who are you here to see?" she asked.

"Evelyn Fulbright."

"Name won't work, inmate number?" I stood taken aback for a second, even though I'd already committed Mama's number to memory. Everything about this place was dehumanizing.

"1374671."

The woman glanced at her computer and beckoned another guard over. "Dog pound."

Dog pound? I followed the second guard around the corner, away from where visitors and prisoners held hands across the table and embraced at the beginning and end of their visit, to a narrow hallway lined with chairs pulled up to six windows. Mama was on the other side of one of them, waiting for our visit. As I saw the windows, I realized that all my hopes of touching her and hugging her were for naught.

After pulling chain, incarcerated women in Texas are placed in virtual quarantine, known informally in prisonspeak as the "the pound" or "dog pound." At night they're warehoused in cells with up to twelve other women while they're put through a series of tests—medical exams, psych evals, and others—and inducted into their new lives as prisoners in an institution. Mama wouldn't qualify for a contact visit for another thirty days. She hadn't known this, and neither had I.

I tried to hide my shock and disappointment, but I'm sure it was written all over my face. Mama waved furiously when she saw me, her smile genuine but also crumpling as she fought back the emotions she'd been struggling to contain since she'd been locked up. Her skin was pale and sallow from her weeks without sun, and she looked so thin, so vulnerable. I sat down heavily in the chair across from her.

Mama was talking—I could see her lips moving, could see her saying "I'm so glad to see you, Britt." But I couldn't hear anything. We were separated by a cloud of thick, scratched Plexiglas, three feet from each other but completely isolated, each in our own world. That glass is deceptive. You might as well be on a separate planet from the person you're trying to see, to touch, to hold, to smell. I needed more but couldn't have it. It's a desperate, lonely feeling to see your loved one right in front of you and yet be unable to reach out and rest a hand on their arm, to hear their voice, to smell their hair, their skin, to feel their soft touch patting your arm or cheek.

As though she could hear my thoughts, Mama scooted up as close to the glass as she could. She raised her hand to it, pressing hard. She picked up her phone and I picked up mine. I rested my forehead on the glass and put my hand to hers, the battered Plexiglas between us a barrier to our maternal bond. Next to our palms was the smudged imprint of a tiny pair of lips where some other, younger child tried to reach their own mother before me. The sight almost broke me.

When Mama first said hello into the receiver, I still couldn't hear her. Prison phones are cheap. They sound like you're in a tin can, and if you don't speak right into the receiver and press the hearing piece to your ear, you can miss a lot. We got it straight after a few tries, but when I think of the hell of that visit, I remember the tension in my arm and shoulder as I pressed that phone to my face, not wanting to miss a second of the sound of Mama's voice.

"Have you lost weight, Mama?" I asked.

"I'm sure I have. It's hot as hell in here. You think Texas prisons have air conditioners? They got us packed in here like sardines in a can, all in these thick granny-like gowns. Thick like a burlap sack. Everybody loses weight up in here."

"But it's a hundred degrees outside! How are y'all surviving?"

"Brittany. You don't want to know. There's these big old fans at the end of the hallways, but they don't do much. Whenever we get a chance we wet our gowns—in the sink, in the toilet water, whatever. Wear them wet to stay cool. It may be nasty but better than roasting to death. But enough about this place. Now tell me how your little sister is doing. Tell me everything."

Mama and I did talk about everything on that visit. We cried. We laughed to keep from crying more. Mama had been there only a week and couldn't believe she was in prison any more than the rest of us could. She said she'd been to a revival service given by Mike Barber Ministries that brought her some solace, was excited that they gave each of the women a box of popcorn and a fresh bar of soap. The gifts and the sermon gave her some hope, she said. Otherwise the weeks had been sheer hell. I comforted her the best I could, told her everything was going to be okay. I had no way of knowing if it would be.

Daddy Sudie had a saying for whenever times got tough. He'd gather up his fishing gear and make me follow him out to the pond in the front of his house, where fat yellow perch swam in lazy circles and laid their eggs in the reeds. Daddy Sudie always brought a pole for me. As he baited the hooks, he'd hear out my complaints, intent on every word. Only after I'd exhausted them and we'd tossed our lines into the still water would he speak.

"C'mon, Big Girl," Daddy Sudie would say to me, "ain't nothin' but a step for a stepper! You just gotta keep on steppin'."

That man was always right.

As anyone with a loved one in prison will tell you, no one does their time alone. Jazz and I were doing time right next to our mom. But on the outside, we had to keep stepping.

Jazz had a better job and was taking classes at a community college. She'd come out as a lesbian in high school and was busy exploring her identity and community away from the confines of small-town Texas, away from the instability of my mom's addiction. The emotional wounds surfaced sometimes unexpectedly—Jazz put her fist through a pane of glass when Mama was in county, shredding her forearm to the bone—but in her own way, she was steppin'. And so was I. From the impression I'd made as an intern, I had scored a job in the audit group at PricewaterhouseCoopers in downtown Dallas.

PwC was a great firm and gave me all kinds of experience. I primarily worked with venture capital funds that were investing in start-up technology companies, mostly out of Austin. I loved the detail of the work. Working analytically with the inflow and out-flow of numbers, the nuts and bolts of their finances, I was able to learn the minutiae of the businesses we were auditing. It was fascinating to me and began my personal obsession with tech. Still, I felt restless.

I was thinking a lot about dreams deferred—my childhood fantasies of becoming a lawyer. I recalled my childhood insistence about the profession whenever anyone asked, how I'd written essays about it and put my entire class in Bogata on notice about my future as an attorney in my eighth-grade valedictorian speech. By college, I had lost confidence in that vision. And by now, the dream that had seemed so clear to me as a child had faded at the edges.

But it still lingered. As I hunched over my old friend and mentor Ken's borrowed books in my cubicle, studying for the CPA exam, the image of Clair Huxtable's power suit and handsome briefcase arose from the depths of my past and pressed on my consciousness. I wanted to be a powerful businesswoman, to follow in the entrepreneurial footsteps of my father and his father.

From my work at PricewaterhouseCoopers, I knew now that corporate law could be an avenue for just that.

At lunch with Ken one July afternoon, borrowing more of his used books—with my own rent and some of Jazz's, and the money I was sending to my mom for prison commissary, I couldn't afford new ones—I tentatively broached the subject. Ken always talked straight to me, and I knew he'd tell me what I needed to hear.

"Ken," I said, "you know how you're always saying that the key to advancement is to add value to whatever you're doing?"

"Ah! You remembered!" Ken said, delighted. "And to wherever you are. Yes."

"I've just been thinking," I began, "maybe with all I've learned working at PwC, maybe I'll have value to add elsewhere. I was just thinking that after I get through this CPA exam . . . maybe I'll try law school. I don't know. It's just an idea. What do you think?"

Ken's face lit up. "Go for it. Brittany, I've known you for years now. I've witnessed you excel with every step you dared to take. Why not this one? In fact, I'm doing the same thing! I haven't told many people yet, but I start at SMU in the fall."

I left that lunch with a newfound sense of purpose. I'd been shooing away thoughts of law school for a while now, chastising myself for being overly ambitious, especially now with all that our family was going through. But here was Ken, already on his way. He'd always walked the path right before me, pointing out next steps. If Ken could do it, I knew I could.

Two months after the humiliation of the dog pound, Jazz and I went to visit Mama together for the first time. It was supposed to be a contact visit, but we still couldn't hold her. If we touched her for longer than ten seconds, we'd be screamed at by the guards, who we'd already seen bark out reprimands to other visitors in the most humiliating manner possible. Mama wore a white prison top and bottoms made of a thick, coarse cotton. The shirt and pants were unevenly cut and hung on her thin frame, the neck low and loose, exposing her jutting collarbones. She'd tried to make a joke of it—*Can you believe they make us sew our own shit in here?* She laughed and we laughed, our laughter masking our deep pain and the fact that we were sitting in a visitation room talking about how prison uniforms were made.

We spent the whole hour talking over each other, trying to catch up on what we'd missed. We bought three flavors of chips from the vending machine and poured them on a napkin in the middle of the table so we could share, had peanut M&M's for dessert. "I have not had an ice-cold Coke since Lassie was a pup," Mama said and laughed, drinking hers as if it were the last one on earth.

At the end of the visit, we took a picture. I'm wearing a black T-shirt that says GIRLS JUST WANNA HAVE FUN. Jazz, in her oversized green polo, has a hand in her jeans pocket and a slight lean to the left, an attempt to look at ease. Mama stands between us, a hand on each of our shoulders, her chin raised unnaturally, her lips barely managing a grimace. All of our shoulders are stiff with the tension of the day. We wear forced smiles, but our eyes are blank, frozen. Stunned.

We laugh now at how awkward that photo looks; laughter eases memory's pain. But I remember standing in that visiting room, the way my cheeks ached as I tried to smile for the camera. How nauseous I felt after hearing my grown mother ask a guard for permission to use the restroom. The cold concrete, the clanging of steel on steel that kept the body constantly on edge. And how empty. Empty from crying, empty from the confusion. Months had passed, but still none of us could believe what was happening.

Every single month, Jazz and I went to see her. The long drive to and from the prison, the rudeness of the guards, their absolute power over our mother, and our silent tears in the bumper-to-bumper traffic on the way home took their toll. But on Monday morning after a visit, we set our emotions aside and went to work.

MY MOTHER WAS in prison, and I carried that knowledge with me every minute of every day. But I had to keep steppin'. Now that I'd decided to pursue my dream, I had to apply to law school. I didn't know a soul besides Ken who'd gone through the process, and by now he was buried in his first year at SMU. I needed help but had no idea where to look for it. The only law firm that I knew by name was Baker Botts, and that was only because they were housed in the same building as PwC. But it was somewhere to start.

Law firm websites are the best resource for an aspiring attorney. You can find pictures, detailed bios of attorneys, even tidbits about their personal life. Things like that have always helped me with the visualization my dad encouraged. As I scrolled through the Baker Botts attorney bios, my interest grew. So did my confidence. I can do this, I thought. But I still didn't see exactly what I was looking for. I didn't see a reflection of myself in those glossy, smiling portraits.

And then I did.

Christa Brown-Sanford. Young, smiling, confident, gifted, and Black. I knew nothing about her besides what I saw on that website. But I sent her an email that very day, and she wrote me right back.

We met at a Starbucks downstairs from both our offices. I wasn't easily impressed, then or now, but something about Christa's polished poise, her calm and open demeanor, captured my imagination. She was the first lawyer I'd ever met, my Clair Huxtable in the flesh. To this day, I'm amazed by Christa's generous offer of her valuable time in response to a random email from a girl she didn't even know. There wasn't an ounce of arrogance in her. Just kindness. As I sipped my latte and Christa her tea, I took a deep breath and spoke out loud the dream that I had almost abandoned: I wanted to be a lawyer.

Christa smiled at me as if she'd known me all her life. "I am so glad to hear that, Brittany. And I'm so glad you reached out to me! You are exactly what the legal world needs. How can I help?"

Relief washed over me. We spent the rest of the hour making a game plan. "Take real practice LSATs," she said. "Every single one you can get your hands on. I'll send you a link to where you can buy them online. And you're going to need a really strong personal statement, so start drafting that now." With every note I wrote, I felt a weight lifting.

Another hour passed before Christa finally said, "I'm so sorry, I have to go." As she stood up and put her sleek blazer back on, she turned to me. "I have a meeting with a partner on a new deal they've put me on. But are you free again on Thursday? We can work through more of the process." I nodded, still not believing that this complete stranger would extend herself so far to lift me toward my goal. "In the meantime," Christa said, "call me anytime if you have questions. I've got you. This is so exciting!"

I see it over and over again now. A young person tells an attorney they want to be a lawyer and are met with a litany of reasons why not to be. Crazy long hours, no work-life balance, not the glamour you see on TV, mountains of debt, jobs hard to come by. All these are true things, but they were not things I heard from Christa. She encouraged me from day one. And she didn't pay me lip service, either, smiling and nodding and giving me words of encouragement only to go back to her partner track at Baker Botts and never think of me again. She even recruited her sister, who was getting her Ph.D. in literature at the time, to give me feedback on my personal statement. Christa took my hand that day in Starbucks and never let it go.

THERE WERE NO phone calls in Texas prisons in 2007. Every week I wrote my mom a letter, and every week she wrote to me. I told her about my ideas for applying to law school, about my new boyfriend, Rico, about the ins and outs of life at PwC, and an idea I had to help younger girls get to the prison to see their moms and to mentor the girls in between visits. She wrote me about nasty guards, the stifling heat of the cells, her continued efforts to take advantage of the prison ministries and self-improvement programs. She was proud of completing the twelve-step drug addiction recovery program. I was proud of her. She even opened up about her regrets, the shame she felt about how drugs had made her disappoint her daughters and herself. It was the first time we had ever spoken so openly about her addiction. Those letters bridged the distance between us.

At the end of August 2007, Mama was transferred from Gatesville to the Lockhart Correctional Facility, a prison just outside Austin. Conditions were better there. The new prison had air-conditioning—temperatures in Gatesville had routinely reached over a hundred degrees—and more programs, parenting classes, classes in self-esteem building, as well as an opportunity for my mom to teach pre-GED classes to other women in the prison. But it was an hour and a half farther away, meaning Jazz and I would now have to drive four hours for just a two-hour visit. I had frequent-flyer miles from work, and Southwest had an eighty-eight-dollar roundtrip deal, so we devised a plan to start flying into Austin and renting a cheap car at the airport for a few hours. It would cost a hundred dollars more each trip but save eight hours of travel time. It meant some penny-pinching, but we agreed the sacrifice would be worth it.

We still had one last drive to Lockhart before we put our plane plan into effect. The trip began like any other: I had Jazz spend the night at my house so we could get out the door as early as possible, and we spent the evening relaxing together, catching up on our lives. We always kept the nights before our visits lighthearted, subconsciously building up for the emotion to come. Prison visits were similar—Jazz and I dreaded and looked desperately forward to them at the same time. Usually I nagged Jazz about every little thing, just as I had since the moment I could first grab her little hand and pull her along behind me, playing the bossy big sister to the hilt. I'd ask her a hundred times whether she'd brought her ID, paid her last light bill. She was twenty-one years old, and I'm sure it drove her crazy, but it was the role I'd always played and I suppose she'd grown to depend on it. That week I was distracted by something at work, and when I woke her at five o'clock all I did was make sure she grabbed her hoodie and a piece of toast so we wouldn't lose time on the interstate stopping for breakfast.

Five hours later, we pulled into Lockhart. I opened the trunk so we could lock everything inside but our IDs and quarters. January is the coldest month in Texas, and the air of a gray day stung my gloveless fingers. Jazz was still rummaging in her backpack. All I could see of her was the back of her neatly cornrowed head, her hoodie pulled up around her neck in a futile attempt to keep her ears warm, and the back of her baggy jeans.

"Let's go, Jazz!" I said. "It's freezing out here. What are you doing?"

When she turned around, she didn't even need to tell me. I could see the whole story on her face.

"Jazz. Don't tell me you don't have your ID. Please don't tell me that."

My little sister doesn't cry very often, but she did then. She looked so lost, standing next to the car with her shoulders sagging in defeat, tears streaking her cheeks the way they hadn't since we were kids. Jazz didn't like writing letters, preferred to save her news for their visits. Her last contact with Mama had been a whole month ago, when Mama had fussed over the scarring on her arm from the glass. I knew Jazz wanted to tell her how she'd been putting cocoa butter on the scars every morning and night like Mama'd told her to, to show her the improvement in her finger mobility so she wouldn't worry. Jazz needed Mama, and Mama needed Jazz.

I was furious, but also heartbroken to see my tough little sister so lost. We were already dealing with the recent devastation of Mama's parole denial. It would be a whole year before she'd come up for parole again. We'd been so sure she would be coming back to us.

"It's okay, Jazz. Maybe we could just lie and say you're sixteen? Then you don't need an ID."

"Will it get Mama in trouble, though? What if they find out and don't let us back in again?"

We agreed we couldn't risk that. We decided to tell the truth. Surely this happened to people sometimes.

"Please, sir," I said to the burly red-haired man gripping his clipboard like a rifle, "we drove five hours to get here. It was just a mistake. You can see that we always visit together. Isn't there another way we can confirm my sister's identity?"

"No ID, no visit. She can wait for you in the car," he said, his face immobile. I wanted to snap at him for being so rude and unfeeling, but I didn't want it to come back on Mama. Our pleas to the other guards at the visitor's gate also fell on deaf ears.

"It's okay, Brittany," Jazz said finally, her voice small. "I'll just wait in the car. I'll be fine."

"Turn the car on so you can keep warm," I said, handing her the keys. "I'm sorry, Jazz." I turned to the security line as she walked dejectedly across the parking lot. We'd been up since five and now it was almost ten. And Jazz would be sitting in the car for another two hours at least, not getting to see Mama at all. It was my worst trip through security since my very first visit.

"Where's Jazz?" was the first thing Mama said as I sat down in the visiting room. We tried to have a normal visit, but all we could think about was Jazz sitting alone in the parking lot. Like our mom, my sister was fragile behind her tough exterior, and we both knew how much she was hurting. We were quiet through a lot of our visit. I tried not to stare at Mama's hands. Even in Fulbright she had taken great care with her hands and with ours, making even Jazz sit still while she trimmed and filed our nails and pushed down our tiny cuticles with her thumbnail. Hers were soft and smooth from the shea butter lotion she applied every time she washed them, nails short, neatly clipped and rounded, buffed and shining. She took pride in her hands and was stern with nurses who didn't do the same. "How would you feel if you had to have those rough things rubbing on you all day? Our patients' skin is sensitive enough! For some of them, we're all the touch they got. The least we can do is keep our hands soft and nice!"

After over a year in prison, Mama's hands weren't soft and nice anymore. A hangnail had recently been torn off one thumb, leaving the skin there red and raw. Her nails were broken, cuticles jagged. And worst, her beautiful copper-brown skin was chapped and peeling—discolored, even, a dry, lifeless gray splotched with painful-looking red from her knuckles to her wrists.

"What's the matter with your hands, Mama?" I finally asked.

"They are a mess," she said, turning them over in front of her. "It's from washing dishes in the kitchen. That's my job now. On top of the tutoring. You wouldn't believe how big them damn pans are. You can actually stand in 'em."

"But why do they look so ashy?"

"From the chemicals in whatever made-up cleaning solution they got in there. It's so nasty it burns."

"You're working two jobs now. They should be paying you a little bit."

"You know they don't pay us shit in Texas. Not to work. Not in prison."

"That's modern-day slavery for real. Well, look on the bright side," I said, trying to joke, "at least they don't have you out there with the hoe squad."

"Right?" Mama smiled. "Can you imagine me out there in the fields? Lord have mercy. No. I'd rather go to the hole before I sweat a drop in those fields for these people."

We laughed at the image, laughed as we always did, this time under the heavy burden of picturing Jazz sitting out in the car. Mama's eyes were clear, and her skin had its beautiful sheen back. She had been sober over a year now, and no matter how demeaning the prison visit experience, being together, and seeing our real mama come back to us, was everything. I made a mental note to tell my little sister how good our mama looked.

At the end of our visit Mama hugged me tight. "Play Sade's 'By

Your Side' on the way home," she whispered, just as the guard told us to separate. "For Jazz."

Back in the car, I told Jazz what Mama had said about the hoe squad, how she was sick and tired of looking at naked bodies in the shower room, where there were no curtains. We laughed a little. We turned up Sade's unmatched voice as loud as we could stand and let it soothe and reassure us. When we stopped at a Whataburger a couple of hours later, Jazz looked at me, her face drawn and tired from the long hours of waiting, her deep brown eyes, so like our mom's, searching mine. "How did yo mama take me not being able to come in? Was she sad?"

"Yeah, she was sad," I said. "She looked real good, though. So beautiful and healthy. I told her we would be flying next time. And I'll make sure you have your ID."

It wasn't what she needed, but it was all I could offer.

MAMA TOOK ADVANTAGE of every rehabilitation program, every individual and group counseling opportunity, every parenting and recovery class that she possibly could. Until she did, she told us later, she was paralyzed by what she had done to us. After our visits she'd spend two days in a debilitating depression, unable to leave her prison cot. She was paralyzed by shame and embarrassment, haunted by the knowledge of all that had happened, of leaving us on the outside without her. A lot of women experienced this, she said. Visiting days brought a few hours of relief, of joy, and they spent that time showing their loved ones how much it meant to see them. Then the hours would be over, and the elation of the visit would slowly fade. The long wait between visits was the darkest.

My mother was plagued by dreams of our childhood, by vivid reels of me and Jazz growing up without her, left on our own as she spiraled into addiction. The guilt almost killed her, she said. It was the end of that road for Evelyn Fulbright. She wanted her family back, and despite the disease she found some reserves of that Fulbright will way down deep. And the loving siren call of her two daughters pulling her through. Somehow, in this darkest and most degrading of places, she found the strength to sit down and be still—to think, and to face herself. When she did, she found the strength to begin her recovery.

No one emerges from the indignity of incarceration unscathed. My mother was traumatized from her time in prison, and she should never have been there. She suffered a drug addiction and spent two years of her life locked in a cage because she was sick. Instead of treatment, she received punishment. Her decision to get herself sober while inside was hers alone. We punish addiction in this country, treating it as a moral flaw instead of an illness. Prison does not bring redemption, and it does not cure or treat addiction. That enormous victory belongs to Evelyn Fulbright, not to the institution that tried to break her spirit. My mother got sober despite the suffering she endured in prison, not because of it.

I SAT DOWN at my desk close to midnight. It was audit season at PwC, our busiest time of year, when all accountants were required to put in fifty-five-hour workweeks, which usually meant closer to seventy. But I wasn't burning the midnight oil to audit a client's financials. It was time to complete my personal statement for my law school application. I took a deep breath, staring at the laptop in front of me. I'd made a few starts, describing the encouragement of my dad and the incredible role model of my grandfather, who'd pulled himself out of a childhood spent sharecropping and a third-grade education to become one of the most successful contractors in a four-county radius. It was all true. Still, hands shaking and breath growing short, I highlighted what I had written and pressed Delete. I wanted to start over. I need to say something else.

By the time I'd written the first line, I was shaking all over. "Number 1374671 isn't just a number to me. Number 1374671 was assigned to my mother, a prisoner in a Texas women's facility." Several times while writing that statement, I almost quit. It was terrifying, and cathartic.

In part because of Christa's guidance and support, I, too, was able to do something I had never done before: I spoke candidly about my personal experience with my mom. I wrote about being a child of a drug-addicted parent and then being a young woman with an incarcerated parent. I had never spoken these words aloud, not even to those closest to me, let alone to complete strangers. Our family had an unspoken code of silence, and I didn't want anyone to feel sorry for me, let alone give anyone the wrong impression of us. But Christa encouraged me to speak my whole truth, to tell my story. She encouraged me to see my experience as a source of strength, power, and wisdom—not a weakness. For the first time, I put my whole story on paper along with my vision for a project I wanted to create, called GEM—Girls Embracing Mothers. I wanted to help girls like myself. Girls with mothers in prison.

Writing that personal statement was the first time I'd let myself really face the trauma I had sustained growing up, the first time I even admitted to myself that there had *been* trauma. When I finally went to bed that night, spent, I was grateful to my mom for facing her demons head-on, for showing me what absolute courage looks like. I was grateful for Jazz always being by my side through the storm. And I was grateful for Christa, who took my hand and said, "Leap. Leap, so you can fly."

MAMA WAS A fighter. A survivor. She survived every day with the same unflinching determination she had shown in Fulbright when she had two toddlers in tow and still earned her nursing license. My mother was released from prison in November 2008 during my first semester as a student at the University of Houston Law Center. She stepped out of that prison looking like the real Evelyn Fulbright. And she was. She pledged to do whatever it took to get her nursing license back and get fully on her feet again. "I swear on my life and all that is holy I will never go back to that hell again," she said to me and Jazz on three-way as soon as she could call, her jokes already having us laughing until our sides hurt. We knew it was true. We had our mama back.

Part Two

KNOCKING

One might have hoped that, by this hour, the very sight of chains on Black flesh, or the very sight of chains, would be so intolerable a sight for the American people, and so unbearable a memory, that they would themselves spontaneously rise up and strike off the manacles. But, no, they appear to glory in their chains; now, more than ever, they appear to measure their safety in chains and corpses. And so, *Newsweek*, civilized defender of the indefensible, attempts to drown you in a sea of crocodile tears ("it remained to be seen what sort of personal liberation she had achieved") and puts you on its cover, chained.

—JAMES BALDWIN

Chapter 6

PROXIMITY

The day of President Obama's inauguration, we were let out of Property Law early. I sat on the floor in the common area of the University of Houston Law Center. The lounge was packed with students and professors, the energy electric. Harvard scholar Henry Louis Gates, Jr., said of Black people that day, "We jumped, we wept, we whooped and hollered," and he was right. I wasn't in D.C. the day Barack Obama placed his gloved hand on the Lincoln Bible to be sworn in as the forty-fourth president of the United States, but my fervor and sentiment matched the overwhelming emotions on the faces of all of those who were. For months we had been on edge, urged into an extraordinary movement of hope, of change, of conviction that the impossible would be done. The Black Law Students Association held Obama watch parties to mark each speech, each debate. We wore our Obama T-shirts all over campus and let our hope be known. For many of us, it was the first time an election had stimulated our minds and kindled our passion. And now the historic moment had arrived. Obama was *our* president. When we elected Obama, we elected ourselves.

I loved every minute of the inauguration. When Aretha took the stage, resplendent in her Swarovski-crystal-studded bow, and lifted her angelic, soulful voice in a soaring rendition of "My Country 'Tis of Thee," I felt the old church hymns of my childhood in my bones. Michelle Obama was a queen in chartreuse. And the president-elect himself—impossibly young, impossibly handsome, impossibly Black. All of those Black faces on that stage and in the crowd, the joy, the pride. It was an extraordinary moment. In the shadow of a Capitol built by slave labor, on a Bible first used in the year 1861, a year when Black people were by federal law considered only three-fifths of a human being, a Black man was sworn in as our nation's president. A New Birth of Freedom indeed.

When President Obama stepped to the podium and looked over that extraordinary crowd, his face, so beautifully brown, seemed to me to hold all of the pain and triumph of our past. He was solemn, dignified—no longer the youthful senator rousing jubilant crowds on the campaign trail, but the commander in chief, ready to lead us through the perils of our present.

"My fellow citizens," the president began, in his distinctive tenor, "I stand here today humbled by the task before us, grateful for the trust you have bestowed, mindful of the sacrifices borne by our ancestors."

I clung to every syllable. As well as I knew the rhythm of my own heartbeat, I knew a simple truth: *We as a people can do anything.* Maybe it was the first time in my life that I really felt that, really embodied it: We can do *anything.* I knew I was watching a moment of profound spiritual velocity. Its momentum would fuel me time and time again in the years to come.

THE SUMMER BEFORE I transferred from the University of Houston to SMU Dedman School of Law, I got a troubling phone call. I was late to court, where I was interning for the summer. Even so, when I heard Mr. Mitchell's voice on the other end of the phone, I stopped walking and passed my latte to my other hand so I could hear him better. After what his family had been through, he at least deserved my attention.

I'd known Mr. Mitchell since I was in high school, as the father of my friend Keyon. Keyon had grown up in Paris, where we used to go to house parties and impromptu kickbacks at "the Corner," a four-way stop sign by the Paris basketball courts where people hung out, sitting on the hoods of cars, listening to music, being and breathing. The Corner was down the street from Mr. Mitchell's auto body shop. Everybody knew Keyon's dad. Everybody knew Keyon.

On the phone, Mr. Mitchell greeted me warmly and asked about my family. I could hear the strain in his usually smooth voice. "I'm guessing you heard the latest . . ."

"That they denied Keyon's appeal? I heard, Mr. Mitchell. I'm sorry."

"Brittany, I know you're studying hard, that you're not a lawyer yet. But I'm calling to ask you— If there's anything . . . a project, or a campaign, maybe get one of those professors over there interested in Keyon's case . . ."

"If there was anything I could do, I'd do it, Mr. Mitchell. I just don't think—"

"They took his life, Brittany. *His life.*" His voice cracked with emotion. "Just take a look at the case. You'll see."

When we hung up, I stood on the sidewalk for a minute before gathering myself to hustle into court. Keyon's situation had turned Mr. Mitchell, a respected community figure with twenty years at a local factory and a thriving auto shop in Paris, into an activist fighting to save his son's life. He'd done everything he could to help Keyon, gone through multiple lawyers, even organized street protests. He would have resorted to calling me only because he was desperate. Not being able to help stung. Mr. Mitchell was right. I wasn't a lawyer yet.

And I wasn't even interested in practicing criminal law when I did become a lawyer. I'd glimpsed the fruits of finance at PricewaterhouseCoopers, and my sights were set on joining the big dogs in corporate. It was what I'd always imagined—at first from the images of power and prestige I saw on television, and then through my own work at PwC. That was what I wanted—to be the very epitome of efficiency and capable power, to be the one calling the shots or at least guiding them.

But appeals like the one from Mr. Mitchell were already coming to me with some regularity, each one a desperate SOS from someone looking for legal help or advice that might free a friend or family member. Each time, I explained that I had just started school; that I was studying corporate law, not criminal law; that I didn't have a license; that I couldn't file a motion even if I wanted to. Each time, I could hear the disappointment in their voices, the kind of piercing desperation that hits the inner ear and ricochets to the heart. It was hard hearing it, but nowhere near as terrible for me as for the person on the other end of the line. This I knew from personal experience. My mama had served over two years in prison, and every day had felt like a decade.

And so when people like Mr. Mitchell called for help, I always listened. There wasn't anything else I could do.

But after I hung up with Mr. Mitchell, I couldn't stop thinking about Keyon. Charismatic, funny, good-looking, a successful student, Keyon had been the epitome of popular, the one all the girls had a crush on. We'd worked together one summer at a call center and become friends. He went to Texas A&M in Commerce and pledged Omega Psi Phi, a historical Black fraternity. The Q-Dogs threw the best parties, and whenever I drove down for one during my first year in college, I'd see Keyon flexing with his frat brothers, stepping in line to George Clinton's "Atomic Dog" in their royal purple silk jackets and gold boots, repping their organization with pride and exuberance. By 2005, he was president of his fraternity chapter and a spokesman for the local NAACP. Keyon was twenty-three years old, proud father of a little girl, and months shy of graduating from Texas A&M Commerce with a dual degree in criminal justice and sociology. But he never got the chance to wear that cap and gown.

On his way to one of the last classes of his college career, squad cars screeched onto the A&M campus in Commerce, sirens blaring, and blocked Keyon in on all sides. With his peers looking on, the police threw Keyon against a car and read him his Miranda rights. Eventually, he was convicted of conspiracy to distribute crack cocaine. Instead of walking the stage for his diploma, Keyon walked into federal prison with a mandatory life without parole sentence.

I was an undergrad at UT Arlington at the time of the verdict, and Sissy and I would sit on the phone in the evening after classes, trying to make sense of it all. We knew Keyon had probably dealt some drugs, but how could he get life? It didn't seem possible. This was someone we knew, who we hung out with. Growing up, Keyon was supposed to be one of the ones to make it, go to college, become somebody important. Keyon was no drug kingpin. He was a college kid with a bright future ahead of him. Yet some judge had determined that he was unfit ever to set foot into society again? It made no sense. We didn't have to know much about the case to know something was horribly wrong.

For a while Keyon's sentence was all we talked about. But although his family did everything they could to keep his name in the media, eventually the shock of the news faded and we went on with our lives. This is one of the effects of prison. People locked up are out of sight and often, no matter how unjust their situation, out of mind.

The summer that Keyon's father called me about his denied appeal, I was working as an intern in the United States District Court for the Southern District of Texas. I sat through all of Judge Nancy J. Atlas's sentencing hearings. The cases were already concluded, most often without trial. The defendants had already pleaded guilty, and the proceedings I observed would determine the length of their prison sentence. Most of the hearings were deeply disturbing. In case after case, I saw men who resembled my father, my uncles, my friends, stand before the court and plead for their lives. Often, their harsh sentences made as little sense to me as Keyon's.

To make matters worse, the judges I observed handed down sentences in months, not years: 120 months, 264 months, 360 months. I had a master's degree in accounting and it still took me a minute to compute the numbers in my head. I watched these men stand there, marked as prisoners in their jailhouse jumpsuits, hands cuffed in front of them, trying desperately to work out the math in their head. I saw the horror and pain on their faces as the months, divided by twelve, became decades of their lives. I will never forget that sight for as long as I live. *There is absolutely no reason for this,* I would think each time. No possible purpose but to strip these men of their dignity and humanity.

To see so many Black men led away in shackles as their families wept in the front row was profoundly troubling to me. I was witnessing mass incarceration at its height and could not help but be affected. It was all just too close to home. I was studying hard to be a lawyer. But in the federal courthouse in downtown Houston, the law, or at least its application, was beginning to seem very, very flawed.

One day, I had the opportunity to sit in on a full trial for a high-profile drug case. These were no small-time dealers being prosecuted, but members of an international drug cartel. The case seemed like an episode from *Miami Vice*. The men on trial had been charged with importing dozens of tons of powder cocaine into the United States across the Rio Grande border. I watched with fascination as the prosecutors built an airtight case. The feds had everything on these guys: surveillance video of cartel members sealing bricks of cocaine into tires that they stacked in waiting trucks; wiretap evidence; photographs of bundles of money changing hands. Guilty verdicts were guaranteed.

There was just one thing that didn't make sense: the sentences. The drug cartel had imported truckloads of drugs across the border into the United States, dozens of tons of pure cocaine. I'd seen pictures of the stuff, piles of it. Yet when the judge in the case finally read their sentences out loud, I couldn't believe my ears. The sentences of the men who had organized and run this multimillion-dollar international drug ring ranged from six to twenty-five years in prison. Nearly all the men I'd seen paraded in and out of Judge Atlas's court for crack got sentences twice that for far less quantities. And Keyon got life for two kilograms of crack— the same weight as a plastic bottle of Heinz ketchup.

In these courtrooms, the incredible sense of progress and possibility I'd felt in the wake of President Obama's election seemed nonexistent. The disparity in sentencing blew my mind. I began to wonder whether America's harsh drug sentences were tied to the drugs in a man's hands or the melanin in his skin.

Seeking answers for the disparity between the "post-racial" America being lauded by mainstream media and what I'd witnessed in court, I signed up for a seminar class at SMU that fall. Well, "sign up" doesn't exactly cut it. Professor David Lacy, one of the few Black professors at SMU, allowed only twenty students into Critical Race Theory. I knew the class was about examining the intersection between race and the law, and I hoped it might hold some answers to the questions that were beginning to feel incredibly urgent to me. But the class was always full, with a long waitlist. Short of staging a one-woman sit-in, I did everything possible to gain admission. Two or three times a day I would check to see if someone had dropped, making space for me. It never happened. I wrote emails. I appealed to the dean. Finally, a week before the semester started, I petitioned Professor Lacy himself to let me in, and, fatefully, he did. Taking that class would change the course of my life.

Professor Lacy had a salt-and-pepper goatee, waist-length dreadlocks down his back, and a fabulous collection of silk ties. He embodied that alchemy that seems so natural in great teachers, a simultaneous vigorous energy and calm, gentle demeanor that created space for sometimes difficult discussions. On the first day of class he paced in front of us, gesturing passionately. "Critical Race Theory takes as its premise that racism is ingrained in the fabric and system of the American society," he said. "That's not a question, and not up for debate in this class. The question is, *how?*"

I leaned in with my classmates as he tackled the taboo subject of race head-on. It was the most diverse class I'd taken at SMU, nearly fifty percent students of color, which in itself changed the classroom dynamic, opening space for voices so often silenced.

Professor Lacy took in our excitement and anxieties and let them weight and energize his words. "In what ways," he continued, "do our legal structures intersect with race and other forms of oppression, and how does that impact people's lives? How do our laws contribute to the experience of white supremacy in this nation? This course demands that we rigorously interrogate the very assumption that law itself is just. It will require not only a sharp and open mind but an open heart. For the class final, you will select a subject to interrogate and present to your peers, demonstrating how racial discrimination intersects with the law, and provide an argument for a way forward."

For me, Professor Lacy's class was a godsend. On the very first day of class, this dynamic, poised Black professor—my very first—laid out in the first moments as an inarguable premise something that by now I knew in my very bones: that race shaped all of our lives, brown, white, or Black, in both visible and invisible ways, and that our legal systems were inseparable from our sordid racial past.

While the topics of the course ranged far and wide, from bank redlining to employment discrimination, from public education funding to gerrymandering, each example more illuminating than the last, I knew almost from the beginning what I wanted to research for my final class paper and presentation. I wanted to grapple with what I had seen in Judge Atlas's courtroom, and to heed Mr. Mitchell's call to look more deeply into his son's case. I decided to write about the unjust difference between crack cocaine and powder cocaine sentencing and the disparate effect this had on Black people.

In 1986, Congress enacted the Anti-Drug Abuse Act, implementing mandatory minimum sentences for federal drug offenses. Federal law adopted a 100-to-1 ratio, treating one gram of crack as equivalent to one hundred grams of powder cocaine for sentencing purposes. The international drug cartel I had observed during my internship had been importing truckloads of pure, undiluted cocaine. My friend Keyon had been sentenced for two kilograms of crack—the very same drug in a diluted, cheaper form. But punished one hundred times more severely.

The online PACER (Public Access to Court Electronic Records) federal records system gives public access to electronic transcripts, and since Keyon's case was so recent, I could access his court transcripts that way. To prepare my final paper and presentation, I pored over almost a thousand pages of them. What I found blew my mind.

When a police raid in Keyon's hometown of Paris, Texas, led to the indictment of thirty-two individuals on drug charges in 2004, Keyon was sitting in his sociology class at Texas A&M in Commerce, where he lived and went to school. His name wasn't on the original indictment and didn't come up in any ensuing investigation. And for a whole year after a federal grand jury returned the indictment, it would stay that way.

But a year later, six of Keyon's childhood friends—whom I also knew from around the way, and who were facing serious time—suddenly produced Keyon's name as a key player in the drug game. Based on these men's word alone, Keyon was indicted and wrested from his campus life three months before graduation and charged with conspiracy to distribute crack cocaine.

Drugs were never found on Keyon, or even in his vicinity. Nor was any physical evidence presented at his trial. There were no large sums of money, no controlled buys, no surveillance of any kind to implicate him. The entire prosecution was based on the testimony of the six guys Keyon knew from the neighborhood, all of whom had extensive arrest records to their names. And it wasn't just the nonexistent evidence that was shocking, or the blatantly farfetched, self-serving ways that those on the stand tried to implicate Keyon. As I turned the pages of the transcripts, I couldn't believe what I was reading. In the nature of the questioning, and in its content, racial bias was on full display, so obvious as to be absurd.

A Black woman prosecutor used every racial stereotype she could muster to portray Keyon to the all-white jury as a beast, a slick kingpin drug dealer, the type of irredeemable, inhuman thug that exists only in America's racist imagination. In tones sometimes goading, sometimes mocking, sometimes sisterly, she asked witness after witness countless questions about their clothing, their jewelry, their shopping habits. She was particularly obsessed with Air Jordans, how many pairs the young men on the stand owned, how often they went to the mall to purchase new ones, whether they'd ever gone to the mall with Keyon, and which mall? I shook my head. Could an extensive collection of Jordans or throwback jerseys really be used as government evidence that someone was a leader of a drug syndicate? If the nearly thirty pages of official court transcripts devoted to the issue were any indication, the answer—in East Texas, at least—was yes.

The prosecutor's ridiculous line of questioning didn't stop there. Keyon's dad owned an auto shop and Keyon had customized cars his whole life, but according to the prosecutor, his newly installed woofers constituted evidence of drug trafficking—in spite of the fact that no investigation turned up an ounce of even so much as weed. His gold chain, too. Even after the defense established that he'd bought the chain used from a pawnshop for a fraction of its market price, the prosecutor tossed it around like a smoking gun.

Jordans, gold chains, and a subwoofer. The testimony of other young men who had accepted plea deals for turning on Keyon. This was the "evidence" that earned my friend a life sentence. I kept going back through the transcripts, thinking I must have missed something. But I hadn't. There was no evidence connecting Keyon to the two kilos. Unbelievably, the opposite was true for those who testified against him. We're talking videotaped transactions. Wiretaps. Individuals caught red-handed with drugs. Confessions. It didn't seem to matter to the court. For their trouble, the men who'd snitched on Keyon received a reward for their cooperation, lesser sentences of five to seven years in prison. And on no evidence but their word, Keyon Mitchell received a life sentence.

Keyon's trial transcripts shook me to my core. These were young men's lives at stake—not only Keyon's, but all the people caught up in the indictment. All of them Black, all of them from Paris, Texas, where the Klan had recently rallied to protest the city council's debate about potentially removing a Confederate statue. And while it's unlikely that anyone involved in the indictment—including Keyon—were one hundred percent innocent, the court's reliance on hearsay was beyond disturbing. I thought about what Professor Lacy had said on the first day of class—that racism was a part of the very fabric of our society, inseparable from the institutions that guide and shape our lives. As I read through Keyon's transcripts as both a student of law and a friend of the accused, nothing seemed more true.

At the time of Keyon's trial, the jury had to establish the quantity of drugs in question as well as the guilt or innocence of the defendant. Ultimately, the jury refused to go along with the forty kilos the prosecution was pushing, but they did find Keyon guilty of conspiring to distribute two kilos of crack cocaine. Under federal law in 2006, the punishment for selling two kilos of crack was the same as for selling two hundred kilos of pure cocaine.

The 100-to-1 ratio was the first extreme-sentence trigger for Keyon, and that was bad enough. But in Keyon's case—and most I would handle in the future—disparate sentencing turned out to be just the tip of the iceberg. Under federal law, a sentencing enhancement means more time. And the prosecutor in Keyon's case laid on the sentencing enhancements like there was no tomorrow. By the time the enhancements were added up, the judge couldn't have avoided giving Keyon a life sentence even if he'd wanted to.

———

I'M PRETTY SURE my fellow students in the SMU law library thought I was going crazy. My facial expressions and gasps while I pored through court documents must have been distracting for those trying to commit case law to memory. But I couldn't believe what I was reading. *How was any of this possible?* I kept thinking. Don't we have a constitutional right to a fair trial? Aren't we innocent until proven guilty—beyond a reasonable doubt? Isn't that the very basis of our nation's legal system?

Still reeling from what I had learned about Keyon's case, I dug into the history of federal drug legislation, trying to find justification for the clearly inequitable 100-to-1 crack-to-powder ratio. Surely there had to be some legislative history that explained lawmakers' rationale. But I found none. There simply was no precedent anywhere on the books for these laws. In fact, in its efforts to pass dramatic "War on Drugs" legislation before the November 1986 midterm elections, Congress seemed to have bypassed many of the typical deliberative processes customarily employed to prevent terrible legislation from being passed. No committee hearings were held to examine the cocaine sentencing scheme, and no report was produced analyzing the act's key provisions. Unbelievably, there was zero record of discussion about possible inequities in the ratio, or even the reasoning for it. The number is completely arbitrary with no rational basis.

What little legislative history there was suggested that legislators justified penalties a hundred times harsher for crack cocaine for reasons unsubstantiated at the time and completely debunked within a decade by the United States Sentencing Commission itself. In an effort to track what had led to the frenzied effort to pass laws that twenty years later had stolen my friend's life, I scrolled through the archives available in SMU's research database, searching for clues in articles and media coverage of the time. There I discovered a trail of propaganda that turned my stomach sour.

In the months leading up to the 1986 elections—the year the Anti-Drug Abuse Act mandating the 100-to-1 sentencing ratio was passed—more than one thousand articles appeared in major news outlets around the country focused on the devastation wrought by crack cocaine. There were cover stories from *Time* and *Newsweek,* front-page spreads from every major media outlet featuring endless images of thin, ravaged Black bodies. The accompanying articles played on age-old racist white fears of Black criminality, ignoring the fact that white Americans used cocaine at higher rates than Black Americans. "Less than a block from where unsuspecting white retirees play tennis," one article read, "bands of young Black men push their rocks on passing motorists, interested or not."

Every story played upon stereotypes of hypercriminal Black men and a morally degenerate Black community. In picture after picture, young Black boys and men crouched, tatted and lean in baggy jeans and gold chains, throwing up signs, looking every bit the part of pathological perpetrators of this pandemic. That some of the images were of rappers, not drug dealers, didn't seem to alter the message. The media treated them the same: Crack was not a public health crisis, it was a public safety crisis. The subtext was clear: Get rid of these ruthless (Black) thugs, or we (whites) are all in peril.

MY MOM WAS recovering from addiction. I had dated a drug dealer. I knew firsthand what drugs could do to a family and community. But these grotesque distortions of the racist imagination were as far away from the real people and communities that I knew and loved—that I came from—as any image could be.

I never shared my own experience with anyone in my class. But it was behind every argument I made. Our final paper seemed deeply personal and deeply urgent. I wanted to make my peers feel the issue as much as I did, not just see it as a topic of intellectual interest outside themselves. But I could sense it would be a challenge. Reading these misleading, hyperbolic stories from the height of the crack era was confusing and distressing, and I was doing it on purpose for a research paper and presentation, with an extensive personal and academic background in the topic. Many of my classmates were white and wealthy. As we moved through egregious examples of institutionalized racism, I was struck by how often my fellow students seemed interested in an abstract way, but not on a gut level. There didn't seem to be a connection between what we were studying in books and real human lives.

"But these are people!" I wanted to shout. "Not numbers! Not case numbers or statistics. Everything we talk about in this class is connected to a real, breathing human being, a mother, a father, someone's child."

I had to start by debunking the myths. Media coverage of the crack epidemic furthered the false notion that crack was more heinously addictive than pure cocaine and had more devastating effects on the user. In my paper, I explained the science showing that crack was no stronger than cocaine, was in fact a diluted version of the pure form, and that the effects were the same. The data simply do not support Congress's assumption that crack is significantly more addictive than powder cocaine. The goals of the legislation claimed to be to take down high-level dealers, drug kingpins, as opposed to low-level street dealers. But, I argued, if all crack is made out of cocaine, then every crack sale both relies upon and generates profits for powder cocaine distributors. Under the 100-to-1 sentencing ratio, relatively low-level crack dealers received higher sentences than the wholesale-level powder cocaine dealer from whom crack sellers originally purchase the powder to make the crack.

I had done my research, had all the data. But I needed more than that to make my classmates truly understand the cruelty of the drug war's senseless sacrifice of human capital. I would have to show my classmates the heartbeats behind the numbers. I wanted them to know Keyon as I did. And I wanted to find other cases that would remind us all that these were real people, real lives cut short for the same poor decisions that many SMU undergrads made every Friday night at the school's notorious frat parties.

I found one. Clarence Aaron's case was eerily similar to Keyon's.

In 1993, Clarence, a star athlete, was a twenty-three-year-old college junior at Southern University in Louisiana. Clarence worked his way through college, paying his own expenses and sending money home to his grandparents in Mobile, Alabama. His beloved grandfather's sudden diagnosis of terminal cancer and then rapid decline and death while Clarence was away at school left him distraught. He made a fatal mistake. For fifteen hundred dollars, Clarence Aaron introduced a high school football buddy to one of his college classmates. The classmate's brother was a drug dealer. With Clarence present, the two made a deal.

This was Clarence's sole foray into the drug world. Arrested and charged in the ensuing indictment, he went on trial for his first-ever offense. Just as in Keyon's case, there was no physical evidence presented at Clarence's trial. Just as in Keyon's case, the entire case against Clarence was based on the testimony of co-defendants who received significantly lesser sentences for their cooperation. The two dealers that Clarence introduced for fifteen hundred dollars testified that he had been a "middleman" of the entire operation. The prosecution sought multiple enhancements, and ultimately Clarence was convicted on three charges—possession, conspiracy, and attempted possession—with the intent to distribute twenty-four kilos of crack cocaine. His punishment? Three natural life sentences without parole.

Clarence's and Keyon's stories were both compelling, but would they be enough? I didn't think so. I needed one more human face to underscore what was beginning to look to me more and more like an absolute travesty of justice. And this time, I wanted a woman. In Google, I typed "woman, life sentence, drugs." The first hit was a YouTube video featuring Sharanda Jones.

SHE WAS FAMILIAR to me in every way, from her soft, slow manner of speaking to the stoic way she tried to cover her pain with a small smile to the prison number on her khakis that rocketed me back to the pain of my own mother's incarceration. Sharanda was forty-two years old, a mother, a former beautician and restaurant owner, serving a life sentence for conspiracy to distribute crack cocaine. At the time the video was made, Sharanda Jones had already spent more than ten years in prison. An entire decade.

When I wrote about Sharanda in my paper I tried to let the facts of her case speak for themselves. I presented my findings to my classmates and was encouraged by the discussions that ensued. Just seeing Sharanda's, Keyon's, and Clarence's faces on the Power-Point and hearing their stories did seem to bring the horror of life sentences more closely into view for my classmates. But for me, a deep pain had been triggered. Inside I was reeling, both from my own memories and from my sudden understanding of what exactly a life sentence in federal prison meant—for Keyon, and for Mr. Mitchell. For Sharanda, and for her daughter, Clenesha.

Mama had stayed in prison for two years and that had seemed like an eternity. She had been released on parole the year before and was working incredibly hard to get her life on track. Most important, she stayed sober. We were all so relieved that the dual nightmares of addiction and prison were over that any other issue paled in comparison. Still, the trauma of Mama's incarceration haunted us all. For me, it manifested in moments like these—a library, a paper, research, an image, a voice, a number. Each time, a gut punch. And if she had received life? I couldn't fathom it. I couldn't fathom it for Sharanda Jones, either. Now that I knew about her case, now that I had spoken her name aloud in my classroom presentation, I couldn't just let her die in prison. To let her waste away in there was unconscionable. I mailed Sharanda a card telling her that I was a law student and that I wanted to try to help her.

Her response was kind, but distant. A lot of people had offered their help, she wrote in a letter, the round swoops of her handwriting containing a calm and measured energy all their own. Sometimes they interviewed her and got a lot of grant money for this campaign or that one, but no one spent any time on the case. She thanked me and wished me the best in my future studies. Said she'd pray for me. It was clear she wasn't impressed by my statement of solidarity. But she could not deter me. I was thrilled to get her response, as cool as it was. I had never imagined myself ever setting foot inside another prison, and yet I found myself determined to do everything I could for this woman, whose story struck me at my core.

I think it probable that just learning about Sharanda would have been enough to make me intent on helping her in some way, any way. But there was something else, too. The thin line between us, a proximity born of circumstances beyond our control. I just could not let go.

And so I decided to pay Sharanda a visit.

Chapter 7

I Am Sharanda Jones

I sat nervously in the visiting room of the Carswell women's prison in Fort Worth, watching tearful reunions take place each time an unseen guard buzzed one of the doors that led to the cells. It was late fall and I'd driven down from Dallas after classes on a Monday evening. Usually weekdays are quieter, but maybe because we were so close to Christmas, several visitors waited in the line before me in security.

Just entering the stark grounds of a prison heightens your stress levels. A prevailing feeling of constant surveillance, of powerlessness, is impossible to evade. I warded off memories of visits with my mom as I waited in line. One flustered woman ahead of me kept setting off the metal detector with her underwire bra. She was an older Black woman with short gray hair and light blue slacks like the kind Mama Lena used to wear, and the third time the guards barked at her to go back through I could see her hands shaking. She apologized for making me wait, and I smiled at her as kindly as I could. "Don't worry," I told her. "It's happened to me before."

"Thank you, baby," she said, and the third time she made it through.

The visiting room looked out over a yard, where in the warmer months kids could play while adults visited. But it was cold now, and everyone was inside. At a child-sized table in the middle of a side room, a woman in a tan jumpsuit sat with two toddlers, drawing them a picture with a crayon as the children looked on. The other visiting stations were metal, with attached mauve-colored chairs, an effort to soften the place, the chairs attached in a line as in an airport, with small side tables between every four or five. Around the room hung canvases with homemade photo backdrops—a tropical beach scene, a mountain with a lake, pink with flowers in the corners, a Christmas tree, Santa. Later I'd learn the incarcerated women had painted them.

I'd found some free chairs in the corner. I kept glancing at the door that led to the cells, hoping to see Sharanda. I hadn't been to a prison since my mom was released, had forgotten the claustrophobic feeling—all that metal, the clanging echo of slamming doors, guards' keys, steel on steel cutting through the visiting room buzz. I had a plastic bag of quarters on the table in front of me for the vending machines, twenty dollars' worth—prison vending machines cost a fortune. I was nervous. I had never met anyone set to die in prison, and I had no idea what to expect.

Finally, the beige door buzzed and swung open, and there stood Sharanda, searching the room for me. We spotted each other at the same time, locking eyes and smiling wide. Sharanda was absolutely beautiful, just radiant, and as she wound her way across the room to me I was struck by her short, jazzy haircut, those deep dimples, her laughing eyes. Who could lock away this woman?

Sharanda opened her arms wide and gave me a big hug before we both sat down. I was relieved. I hadn't been sure she would be happy to see me, didn't know if the woman I'd meet would be bitter or sad. Under the circumstances I half expected it. But here was Sharanda Purlette Jones, warm and gracious as could be.

We'd written a few emails through Corrlinks, the prison email system, before this first visit. I'd learned Sharanda was the exact same age as my dad, and she'd grown up within an hour of both Greenville, my mom's hometown, and Campbell, my dad's.

"There's a white lady in here that knows your family," Sharanda said. "I was telling her about your visit and she was like, wait, Barnett? Like from Campbell? She told me to ask you if you're related to Leland."

"That's my dad!" I said. "What's her name?"

"Kim Wagoner. She said she grew up with him. She got fifteen years for meth." Sharanda shook her head. "So crazy. She just got in here a few years ago, so she's got at least a decade to go."

"It's mind-blowing how much time they give people," I said. "Like it's nothing."

"Tell me about it," Sharanda said, smiling, and I thought about how many decades stretched ahead of her. Her ability to find any humor in the face of her own sentence seemed to me a profound grace.

"Who cut your layers, Brittany?" Sharanda said, keeping the mood light. "They're gorgeous."

"I love yours, too. I wish I could pull off a pixie cut! Did you do it yourself?"

"No, but I am real picky about who I let touch my head," Sharanda said. "I can always tell who has blessed hands or not. Girl, I never would have guessed you were twenty-five."

"And you sure don't look forty-two," I said. "No way. I guess it's true what they say"—I smiled—"Black don't crack."

"You better know it," Sharanda said, raising her head and flashing her gorgeous smile.

Sharanda's quick laugh and familiar country accent put me so at ease. We talked as if we'd known each other our whole lives. About family, friends, what we'd done that day—everything.

The closest we came to discussing her case that day was in line for the vending machines. In all prison visiting rooms there are vending machines, often poorly stocked, sometimes broken. The women aren't allowed to approach the machines. There are yellow lines painted on the floor that they stand behind to point out what they want. Carswell was pretty well stocked; one machine even had cheeseburgers in plastic wrap you could heat up in a microwave.

"I'm sorry if I was a little cold at first," Sharanda said, as we waited for those ahead of us to make their selections. "I didn't know who you were working for."

"You were nice," I said. "Nice-nasty." We laughed. "What do you mean who I worked for? I told you I'm just a student."

"All these lawyers," Sharanda said. "They come in all excited, say they're gonna help me. As soon as I get the money together, they're back. It's like they work for the feds now. If you say this about this person, maybe . . . if you say that about so-and-so, it's possible that . . ." For the first time since our visit began, Sharanda looked upset. "That's just not in my heart, Brittany. I have a daughter. I believe in karma. How am I gonna have somebody in here suffering for something they didn't do? It's just not in my heart to lie like that."

We moved up a little in the line. "I'm gonna be free someday," Sharanda continued, looking at me intently. "I believe that. I'm not gonna die in here. That just can't be God's plan for me. But I'm getting out the right way, you know? These lawyers, they just want money. And then it's like they flip and work for the feds."

"I don't want your money," I said. "This is pro bono work. And I'd never ask you to do anything you're not comfortable with."

"I know," Sharanda said, looking at me with a sly smile. "That's why you're here." We shuffled forward. "From what I've seen," she said, "I don't even think most of these lawyers could get me out, regardless of what I did. Everybody just lying all the time. It makes you tired."

We were silent for a minute. Sharanda tried to smile, but despite her positivity, I could see that she was tired. She had been here ten years already. I couldn't imagine the strain of doing that kind of time. In front of us, a couple made their selections, and then it was our turn at the yellow line.

Sharanda pointed to the red hot Cheetos. "Those are my favorite," she said. "I'll take two, please." She watched me from behind the line as I put my quarters into the vending machine. Two red hot bags of Cheetos for her, a bag of Cheez-Its for me. Two Cokes.

"You know, you can use dollar bills in here," Sharanda said. "Look at you with all your quarters."

I smiled. "They only let you use quarters in State," I said.

"We fancy, huh?" Sharanda laughed. The rest of the visit we spent that way—laughing, teasing, talking about everybody and everything. I felt we'd known each other for years. It wasn't like I'd acquired a client. I had made a friend for life. It felt like instant family. It felt like home.

Sharanda and I communicated constantly after our first visit. We emailed and sent letters to each other, and I visited whenever my school schedule allowed. When I faced an exam or had a grueling month of coursework, Sharanda would send me an encouraging note on one of the beautiful cards she handcrafted in her cell, intricate stitched designs of thread and yarn so polished it was hard to believe they were handmade, let alone from the meager supplies available through the prison commissary. Our bond grew. I told Sharanda about my own mom, her incarceration, and even her struggles with addiction, which I normally kept so private. And Sharanda opened up, too, revealing pieces of her life to me in the form of vivid childhood memories and the more painful fragments of the months leading to her inconceivable life sentence.

SHARANDA'S GRANDMOTHER PEARLIE had just put the needle back in the groove of the Five Stairsteps' "O-o-h Child" when the police knocked on the screen door one night in 1970. Sharanda was only three years old, but she would never forget the sound of that knock, she said, or the sight of the large white police officer standing in the doorway, only partly obscured by Pearlie in the bright-colored kaftan she always wore when she was babysitting.

"Are you Ms. Pearlie B. Luke?" the policeman asked.

Her grandmother nodded, clutching her kaftan at the neck. "Your daughter has been in an accident," the officer said, his face white and serious. "You need to come with me to the hospital now."

Sharanda's mother, Genice Stribling, a twenty-year-old nurse's aide, artist, and mother of four, had been in a horrendous car accident. The collision fractured her spine and neck, severing her spinal cord and leaving her paralyzed from the neck down, apart from the partial ability to raise and lower her right arm and minimal muscle control in her wrists. Sharanda remembers being placed on the white hospital bed, the beep of machines, her mother's labored breathing, the sharp antiseptic air. The Genice that Sharanda knew was as beautiful as a movie star, full of jokes and games, always laughing. Now she lay still as a doll. Tubes ran from every part of her body, and huge metal hooks hung from a traction device attached to a steel band across her head. The accident left Genice a quadriplegic, bedridden for the rest of her life, apart from short stints in a specialized wheelchair.

It uprooted everything. Sharanda and her brother and sisters moved in with Pearlie. When Genice was released from the hospital a year after the accident, Pearlie, only thirty-nine years old, found herself the primary caretaker of her quadriplegic adult daughter and four grandchildren under the age of five: Sharanda, her older brother, Earnest, and younger sisters, Sharena and Tina.

With the help of home-healthcare nurses and their extended family of cousins, aunts, and uncles, Pearlie tended to Genice. She made Genice's disability and welfare checks stretch as far as possible, made a little extra money butchering and cooking game for hunters in the neighborhood, got the kids dressed and out the door to school. As Genice's wounds healed, her resilient spirit reemerged. She may have loved her kids from the bed, but she still loved them just as fiercely and wholly as she had when she walked.

"That must have been so difficult," I said to Sharanda on a subsequent visit, when she'd described the accident in more detail.

"If it was hard we didn't know it," she said. "That's just how it was in our family. We all pitched in and helped our mama. It never felt like a burden. It was just always a part of us, of our family. We were happy."

Genice's body may not have worked, Sharanda said, but her brain did. She was a bright woman, full of joy, with the same soft voice and dimpled smile as Sharanda, the same pleasant way of disarming people. She adapted to the confines of her accident in the same way she'd adapted to everything else in her young life— with good humor and grace. But she was no pushover. After her first tough years of healing had passed, she ruled the roost from her bed.

Genice had been an excellent cook before the accident and had no intention of leaving her kitchen to the whims of others, even her own mother. When she had a taste for something in particular, she'd send Sharanda to the kitchen for the ingredients. Sharanda would carry everything to her mother's bedside table, making however many trips to the kitchen were required. Genice liked everything lined up just so, and then she'd begin instructions for mixing. She eyeballed everything and taught Sharanda to do the same. "Another pinch of salt," Genice would say. "Not that pinch. A smaller pinch. That's right. Now black pepper . . . more garlic powder, too. A little handful. That's right. No, that's too much. Stir that in . . . a little more pepper . . . that's it!" When the seasoning was just right, she'd send Sharanda back to the kitchen, and together they prepared the meal, Genice calling precise instructions from her bed, Sharanda asking for clarification when she needed it. Everything Sharanda knew about cooking she learned from her mom.

Money always seemed a day late and a dollar short, but somehow Genice and Pearlie made holidays magical. Genice's friends would come over to do everybody's hair. The girls always got new short sets—matching for Sharanda and Tina, who delighted in being the same age for three days out of each year. At Christmas Genice got on the phone with Toys for Tots to make sure everyone had something to open. All four kids had bikes—where they came from, Sharanda never knew. She and her sisters played hopscotch and held double dutch competitions with other girls in the neighborhood. In the fall they would spend time in their backyard, collecting pecans off the ground from the trees, carefully inspecting the nuts before popping the bittersweet treats into their mouths.

Pearlie did her best to give the kids a normal childhood. But by the time Sharanda was eleven, Pearlie's new life as primary caregiver to her paralyzed daughter and four young grandchildren had taken its toll. Every day, the time for her glass of liquor got earlier and earlier, and the liquor overtook her more and more often. On those nights, Genice would call Sharanda over and explain what to do. From her bed, she taught Sharanda and her siblings how to help change her, do her hair, boil the water for her pan baths to sponge her down, feed her, administer her medicine, and tend to her bowels—an elaborate process involving two kinds of stool relaxers and manual massage.

In every way but age, Sharanda took the part of the oldest child, watching after her siblings, keeping her mom company, acting as Genice's hands and legs. The other siblings helped, too—Sharena, nicknamed Weasel, who took so long to grow but scrappily kept up all the same; Tina, always the prissy, girly one from the beginning, their mama's favorite, the girls always thought; and Earnest, who they called Cooter and whose gentle teasing and good nature lightened everybody's mood.

Genice's "friend" Mitchell moved in with them when Sharanda was in middle school. A tall, dark-skinned man, he helped the family out with his income as a construction worker. He could move Genice on and off the couch easier than anyone else, and he fell into the caretaking rotation with the rest of them. Mitchell was the closest thing to a dad they had, and his consistency counted for something.

Pearlie made sure the kids stayed on track. "Y'all have to graduate high school. Every one of y'all," she would declare after a few drinks. "After that, I'm done!" Genice hadn't graduated and neither had Pearlie, so to Sharanda a high school diploma seemed the ultimate educational goal. She was a solid student, but her teachers were uninspired and so was she. Every day after school she went home to tend to Genice, when she wasn't putting in evening shifts at her job, first as a cashier at the local cleaner and then at the Walmart photo lab. Nobody ever mentioned college and the thought never crossed her mind. Still, she dreamed of a life outside of Terrell, Texas.

Terrell was a small rural town of fifteen thousand people, about thirty miles east of Dallas. Its wide, tree-lined streets, mom-and-pop shops, and railroad tracks leading to deep thickets of pine trees were perfect for growing up, but not as fun for being grown. The actor Jamie Foxx, Sharanda's high school classmate, later spoke about the abject racism he experienced there as a young man. The tracks that were so fun to play on as a kid also separated white from Black and rich from poor—although "rich" in Terrell was relative, since the median family income was around $25,000. Sharanda wasn't sure what she wanted to do with her life, but she was pretty sure she didn't want to live it in Terrell. But she didn't want to be far from her mom—couldn't be. And Genice wasn't going anywhere.

One, two, three, four—Genice's children graduated, one after another, right on time, just as Pearlie planned, Sharanda in the class of 1985. For a few months afterward she worked nights at the photo lab and helped with her mom and Pearlie, whose drinking was taking a severe toll on her health. When her cousin Charlotte suggested Sharanda come stay with her in her Dallas apartment and experience the big city, she jumped at the chance.

To Sharanda, Dallas seemed ablaze with life. Her fun-loving cousin Charlotte was a "hot girl"—naturally beautiful and vivacious, much like Sharanda herself. It seemed to Sharanda like everybody knew Charlotte and everybody else wanted to know her. Dressed in tight jeans and tank tops, hair curled and edges laid just right, flashing those family dimples, Sharanda and Charlotte got to skip the line at clubs. They rolled dice in the VIP back rooms of Lady Pearl's After Hours and danced off the stress of the day. They let good-looking men in Adidas sweatsuits and Kangol hats or smoothed-out Big Daddy Kane suits buy their drinks: Long Island iced tea for Charlotte, virgin strawberry daiquiris for Sharanda—she wouldn't touch liquor, not after seeing what it did to Pearlie. It was the late eighties and the culture was unstoppable. Eric B and Rakim had dropped, and the funk-laced beat of EPMD's "You Got to Chill" blasted from everybody's speakers. Sharanda got a job at a shoe store and began saving her money to get her own place. Every other day, she drove back to Terrell to help take care of Genice—the sisters had developed a rotating schedule to save money on nurses. It felt good to be in both places her heart called her to be—with Genice, and in the midst of the generative culture and creativity of Black Dallas.

Charlotte began taking Sharanda to Jazz's, a popular hair salon in the Oak Cliff neighborhood. The owners, Gae and Pam, were legendary hairstylists, so much so that people could just look at your hair and tell you went to Jazz's. Sharanda, with her sweet smile, caramel complexion, and perfect curves in a five-foot-two-inch frame, was the perfect model for the latest looks. Being at Jazz's, watching two powerful Black women call all the shots in a thriving business they had built themselves, was transformative. With Gae's sure hands sculpting every strand on her head into a work of polished art, Sharanda listened to her friend talk about the independence and pleasure of owning her own salon. *I could do this,* she thought. *I could do this myself.*

Once Sharanda's entrepreneurial spirit began to blossom, she discovered a pleasure and excitement in work that she had never known. She found an old building in Terrell for $180 a month, far cheaper than anything in Dallas, and close to Genice. It was tiny and in terrible shape, but she had a vision for transforming the space with elbow grease and a good eye for style and a bargain. She borrowed some money from a boyfriend for first and last month's rent and rolled up her sleeves, determined to get the small space into salon shape herself. She was more interested in owning a business than in doing hair, but Gae urged her to get her cosmetology license as a backup: "What if all your stylists leave? How will you pay the rent?" Grateful for the guidance, Sharanda went to cosmetology school at night after her shift at the shoe store. There she discovered she had real talent as a stylist and came to love the artistry of it. Slowly, through hard work and her own keen eye for detail, the salon took shape.

"MY MOM WAS like, Chile, what have you done? Everybody and they mama is talking about you and that paint color!" Sharanda laughed and took a few M&M's from the napkin between us. "I was like, what are you talking about? I just knew I'd picked a classy design, ballet pink, black cursive for the sign: 'A New Attitude.'" Genice told her she better drive down and see for herself, and as soon as she finished doing her mama's hair, she did. She could see the little building she'd rented for her salon from two blocks away. They'd painted it pink, all right.

Hot pink.

Sharanda stood out front, her hand over her eyes to protect from the glare bouncing off the near-fuchsia facade. She took a deep breath.

"Well, it's a New Attitude for the ladies of Terrell. That's for sure!"

And a new attitude it was. The hot-pink exterior was unplanned, to say the least, but Sharanda couldn't afford a new paint job. She made it her own.

Over the next few years, hot pink and black became Sharanda's trademark color scheme. She used it on flyers and business cards she would hand out in Detroit where she traveled a couple of times a year to take classes at the city's renowned Black hair shows. Black hair is Black art, and stylists from around the country would travel to Detroit rocking the latest blunt-cut bobs, freezes, and asymmetrical styles so they could take classes, show off, and earn a name in the business. By the midnineties, Sharanda had rented space within her salon in Terrell to four other women; her own clientele was increasing faster than she could keep up with. She was doing well enough to make ends meet, though not with much left over. No matter how many new hairstyles she mastered, women in Terrell could not afford to pay much.

Still, for a first business she'd started at age twenty-three, she thought she'd done all right. And she loved the entrepreneurial part, the risk taking, the creativity. Money was always tight, with her daughter, Clenesha, now three, and her mom to help care for. And Sharanda had a vision for a new business, a way to incorporate her true passion, cooking. With Clenesha on her hip, she started hunting for a new venue. She found another small building and opened a takeout burger joint, hiring two people and cooking herself after closing up at the salon. Now she had two businesses, neither turning much of a profit, but all her own. And she was just getting started.

FOR A THURSDAY afternoon, the salon was slow when she got there, and Sharanda told the other stylist to go on home. Her client Alisha came in a few minutes late and greeted Sharanda warmly. Alisha always had all the gossip, and Sharanda knew she was about to get an earful.

"Sorry I'm late," she said. "Just ran into Baby Jack down at the Piggly Wiggly. He said what's up."

"Aww, how is Baby Jack?" Sharanda said, clipping a towel around Alisha's neck. "I haven't seen him in a minute!" She'd gone to school with Keith Jackson, called Baby Jack on account of his being the youngest of so many brothers and sisters Sharanda had lost count.

"He's all right," Alisha said. "Trippin' like everybody over this drought. I swear, it's been dry for weeks."

When crack hit Terrell hard in the late eighties, Sharanda hadn't paid much attention. She had been in Dallas starting cosmetology school, living life, dreaming of the very salon they stood in now. But Terrell was a small town, and she knew some of the people she grew up with were selling drugs. Even Cooter had gotten involved, getting arrested a few times for selling weed. She didn't think much of it. There weren't a whole lot of jobs out there, and people had to eat.

"You know Baby Jack usually gets his supply from his nephew. But he's got nothin'," Alisha said as Sharanda rinsed her hair in the basin. "Shoot, Sharanda—all those people you know in Dallas? Seems like there's a drought all the time these days. If you knew somebody with a supply for when times are like this—you'd do real well out here."

Sharanda stayed quiet for the rest of the afternoon while she worked, absently nodding while Alisha filled her in on the goings-on of mutual friends and acquaintances. The truth was, she'd been thinking about it. Another friend had said the same thing to her just the week before. People in Terrell would be steady complaining about a dry spell for weeks while the money was still flowing in the city. And she *did* know everybody in Dallas—she'd commuted to A New Attitude for a long time, reluctant to leave the pulsing energy of the city.

A drought simply meant that the drugs had stopped flowing from suppliers. Sometimes someone had gotten arrested up the line, maybe a major bust at the border. The flow of drugs from source to major supplier to midlevel supplier to street dealer to user would be affected. For a small town like Terrell, where people supplemented their income by selling a rock or a dime bag of weed every now and then to cover bills and groceries, or were grinding full-time like Baby Jack, dry spells hit hard. Lean times got leaner. Whoever could make the connection between someone who had dope and someone whose supply had dried up like Baby Jack's would surely make some quick money.

"If you think of somebody, call Baby Jack," Alisha said as she left the salon. "He'll hook you up good for a tip like that, for sure."

When Sharanda asked around about what Alisha and others were saying about business opportunities in Terrell, everybody said the same thing. "You gotta meet Spider. Even when Dallas is dry, Spider's always in action. Big-time here *and* in Houston, all over, really. He went to college a few years ago here in Terrell. He's cool. And if you get in with him, you're set."

Sharanda didn't doubt it. Everybody in Dallas knew Spider for the far reach of his game. He owned a nightclub in Houston, an even hotter strip club, a high-class hair salon, and more. He appeared at the hottest spots in town in his drop-top Jag.

The next time she went down to Houston, Sharanda asked a cousin to introduce them. Spider was dark skinned, slim, and saw the world through designer glasses. When they met he greeted Sharanda kindly, with a soft-spoken, familiar manner, and within minutes they were talking about mutual friends in Terrell and their mamas' hot-water cornbread recipes. In his burgundy sweatsuit and Air Max, he looked like he was still running track at Southwestern Christian College in Terrell. Spider took to her right away, said he knew he could trust her. Plus, he said, he admired her business spirit. He'd heard about A New Attitude in Terrell. Sharanda had spunk and fire, and he liked that.

When they parted ways, Sharanda had a new job. Later that night, she called Baby Jack.

"Next time you have a problem, just call me," she told him. "I got you."

The work was pretty easy. Baby Jack had a bunch of suppliers, number one among them his own nephew, so he called Sharanda only when there was a drought for real, once every three to four months or so. Sharanda and Spider were cool by then, chatting by phone on occasion about the running of his salon and her ideas for a small club in Terrell, the mini drive-through burger spot she'd gotten off the ground as her first cooking venture. When Baby Jack called she paged Spider, who told her when to come see him in Houston. She'd get the cash from Baby Jack to purchase a kilo of cocaine from Spider, usually about $17,000 to $20,000, then pick up a friend or have her little sister Weasel ride with her so she wouldn't get drowsy in the car.

Mostly, the four-hour drive down I-45 was monotonous, and

pretty soon after she got to Houston she'd be turning around and coming straight back. Still, she made a thousand dollars each time she went, sometimes five thousand if Spider was selling kilos for less than normal. She shared some of the money with the friend who drove with her, paid extra bills, covered gymnastics classes for Clenesha, did repairs, bought equipment for the hair salon, and helped her mom around the house. She didn't really think about the risk, never felt nervous. It was just something she did for some extra money from time to time.

In the months Baby Jack didn't need her, Sharanda never thought for a minute about getting deeper into the game. She had a vision for her life—expanding her hair salon, maybe even following her passion for cooking and opening a larger restaurant. When the work ended—when Spider went down—Sharanda was neither relieved nor discouraged. It was what it was. The side hustle had been good while it lasted. Clenesha was getting older, and Sharanda had started to think more about what would happen if she was ever pulled over on I-45. That part of her life was over.

FIVE O'CLOCK IN the morning, Terrell, Texas, November 17, 1997. It could have been a television show: dawn breaking, a dog barking, dozens of police cars surrounding a clapboard house, a baby wailing somewhere. And Chuck Norris—karate champion, action hero, star of *Walker, Texas Ranger,* and occasional reserve officer at the Terrell Police Department—standing next to a black-and-white police car, hand on the holster of a gun.

The scene seemed pure Hollywood. But it was real life.

In a timed paramilitary-style raid typical of those used to serve drug warrants in America, the DEA, local Terrell police, and Chuck Norris busted down twenty different doors. Guns drawn, shouting commands, threatening further use of violence, they forced sleepy, shirtless men, women, and children onto the floor, hands on their heads. One hundred and five people had been indicted, accused of selling crack in Terrell. Sixty-seven of those indicted were arrested, handcuffed, and thrown into paddy wagons that morning, all of them Black.

It was the largest drug bust in Kaufman County history, set in motion by the considerable financial incentives available to local police departments around the country to join the feds in the ongoing round-up and lock-down phase of America's War on Drugs. Similar raids were taking place all over the American South, including an infamous case in Tulia, Texas, a rural town of about five thousand people in the Texas panhandle. During the Tulia raid, ten percent of the town's Black population was arrested in a drug bust based solely on the false testimony of a single undercover cop who had a history of racial prejudice.

In Terrell, everybody knew somebody who'd been tossed into a paddy wagon. The police released all the names of those indicted to the public. Sharanda knew a few of the people from as far back as elementary school. And there were two names she knew very well: Keith Jackson and his wife, Julie Franklin.

The Terrell raid devastated the small, insular Black community. Many couldn't afford legal assistance or bail and sat in jail for months. Federal agents, local police, and prosecutors began approaching those indicted with plea deals to avoid lengthy prison sentences. There was one catch: The plea deals were available only if the person snitched—substantially cooperated with law enforcement and implicated others.

Sharanda worried about Cooter. In and out of jail over the years, he had become a street-level dealer in Terrell, selling small amounts of crack. Sharanda fussed at Cooter constantly, anytime she would hear that he was selling from Genice's house or storing his dope in Genice's backyard. Word was going around Terrell that people who had been arrested in the raid were now acting as informants for the police.

"I warned him," she said to me. "Told him he was gonna catch a case, keeping his stash at Genice's house like that. Hell, everyone in that house could get in trouble behind Cooter's mess. And by that time he had his own place across town. He might as well have been running a car wash, the way he had folks lined up to buy rocks like that. A mess for real."

"Were you worried they'd come after you?" I asked.

"Me? Not for a minute. I just wasn't dealing drugs like that. And I'd been out of it. I kept telling Cooter, though. Every time I seen him."

Sure enough, Cooter was picked up just a few months later on state drug charges after selling to a confidential informant. "I mean, of course we were upset," Sharanda said. "That's our brother. Genice's only son. But the way he was going, it was inevitable. We weren't surprised, I guess. We all had to just keep on going. It was the only thing to do. Look after our mama and keep on going."

NOT LONG AFTER Cooter's arrest, Sharanda was putting the finishing touches on a client's braids when her phone rang. Julie again. It was the third time she'd called this week. Sharanda sighed and picked up.

"Sharanda, look, we're really desperate over here. The kids need new shoes. Just a connect, that's all we need. Things are bad, girl. We need some help."

Sharanda sighed again. This woman really didn't get it.

"I told you"—Sharanda sealed the end of a braid as she spoke, trying not to sound impatient—"I'm way out of it. I don't know anybody who does that. I'm way out."

She felt bad. After being arrested in the raid and bonding out, Julie and Baby Jack had been struggling to get on their feet. They were having a hard time making rent, and Julie had been calling Sharanda off the hook, trying to get a lead on a new supplier.

Sharanda wanted no part of it. With the help of Clenesha's dad, she had purchased her first home a few years earlier. It was an older home, but she was no stranger to fixing up places and had made it her own. Now she was in the process of selling it and moving into an apartment closer to Clenesha's school, and she was set to make a nice profit. She planned to use the money to pursue her dream and passion—opening her own soul food diner. In fact, the dream was already taking shape. She and her business partner, a childhood friend from Terrell who was now a police officer, had found an old boarded-up diner near downtown Dallas on Lamar Street that had stood empty for years. They tracked down the owner, an elderly woman whose eyes lit up when Sharanda described her vision for home-cooked soul food, open every weekday to feed the lunch crowd from the office buildings downtown. The owner agreed to an exchange of services: If Sharanda and her business partner cleaned the place up at no cost to her, she'd give them the first three months rent-free.

Sharanda recruited friends far and wide to roll up their sleeves and turn that dusty, abandoned storefront into a place fit for the mouthwatering menu she had in mind. She kept doing hair to have money to invest in Cooking on Lamar, but she talked to the other stylists at A New Attitude about taking over the Terrell salon. In the process of setting up the diner, Sharanda had discovered something about herself. Food was her passion, and the restaurant was her dream—cooking for people, preparing Pearlie's and Genice's and her own recipes, seeing people come together to enjoy and savor her food. Getting the restaurant off the ground while raising Clenesha to have all that she never had was hard work, but for the first time in a long time Sharanda felt happy and complete.

All the while, Julie would not leave her alone. Sharanda had told her no every which way, but still, Julie called. "Look," Sharanda said one day, more to get her off the phone than anything else, "when I get done here I'll come by the record shop, okay? See how y'all are doing. But I'm telling you now, Spider's long gone, and I don't know nobody else."

At the record shop, Sharanda flipped through CDs as she talked to Julie. The sound system, usually the best part of the shop, was turned down low. And Julie seemed stressed. Even her voice sounded different.

"Sharanda, you gotta help us," Julie pleaded. "I know you know people."

"I know who you know!" Sharanda said, trying to turn the tone of the conversation. "Everybody from Terrell, mostly. And most of 'em locked up in the same raid that got you!"

She stood there for a while between the stacks, exchanging gossip with Julie about people from the neighborhood, how much time they'd gotten, where they were serving it, who was on house arrest, the debt incurred from hiring a lawyer. It was the same conversation everybody in Terrell had been having since the raid, same as in the salon. But Julie kept bringing it back to the question of a hookup.

"What about Big O?" she asked. "Or one of Spider's old people?" She just wouldn't let it go.

"I told you I don't know those people no more. Those numbers are long gone," Sharanda said, exasperated. And finally, to get Julie off her back, "But let me see what I can do."

Sharanda knew something was off by Julie's demeanor. What she didn't know was that Julie Franklin was wearing a wire. For Sharanda, those last eight words would mean the difference between freedom and a life in prison.

ON THE MORNING of April 7, 1999, Sharanda was in Dallas at Weasel's, getting ready to have a garage sale. She was bent over the kitchen table writing prices for the items on small stickers when the phone rang. Weasel picked up. "What? Mama, slow down so I can understand you," she said. She motioned to her oldest boy to turn down the TV. The tone in her voice made Sharanda stop writing and look up. "Mama?" Weasel said. "What's going on?"

Genice was stammering and upset. Police had raided her house on Rose Hill Drive before dawn that morning.

"Scared me half to death," Genice said to Weasel. "Practically broke down the door, guns out, everything. Tore up the whole house! They took Mitchell to jail and told me I am under arrest, too. They are standing here now and let me call you to come and get me dressed and take me to the station to turn myself in."

"I'm on my way now!" said Weasel, shaking as she hung up the phone.

Weasel rushed to get dressed to drive to Terrell while she filled Sharanda in on the news. They were both in shock and spoke in hushed tones trying to figure out what could possibly be going on. Sharanda stayed behind to watch the kids while Weasel went to Terrell.

It was a setup. Once Weasel arrived to take Genice to turn herself in, she was told there were two other names on their warrant, hers and Sharanda's. Weasel was under arrest, too, and would need to turn herself in along with Genice.

Genice, Weasel, and Mitchell were processed and released on a personal recognizance bond, a mechanism that allows low-risk defendants to be released from jail without having to put up any money. They were not interviewed by police that day, but law enforcement made one thing clear during their interactions: It was Sharanda they wanted.

First thing the next morning, Sharanda turned herself in. Sharanda and her entire family—Cooter, Weasel, Genice, and Mitchell—had been indicted on federal drug charges. She was fingerprinted, processed, and also released on personal recognizance bond.

Their family nightmare had begun.

SHARANDA HAD NEVER been in any trouble with the law, not even a traffic ticket. But now she found herself charged with six counts of aiding and abetting the distribution of crack cocaine and one count of conspiracy to traffic crack cocaine. She knew she had better get a good lawyer.

Her cousin Charlotte recommended James Murphy. "He's real

good," she told Sharanda. "Helped out a few people we know on state criminal cases. Don't cry to nobody else. He'll hook you up! He's legit. Matter of fact, I'll introduce you."

Her cousin was good as her word. And Murphy certainly looked the part, like a young Matlock—a little goofy-looking, with a thick handlebar mustache and protruding teeth that reminded Sharanda of a beaver and endeared him to her right away. He wore a nice suit to their meeting and treated Sharanda with the utmost respect and attentiveness, listening carefully to her side of the story, taking detailed notes—the way a lawyer is supposed to do, Sharanda thought.

At the close of their meeting a few weeks later, Sharanda asked Murphy straight out: "I appreciate you listening to me, I really do. But I just want your best legal advice. Do I have to accept this? Or do I have a chance to win?"

"Sharanda," Murphy said, leaning earnestly toward her over his desk, "if I thought you should take a deal, I'd tell you to. In my view it would be foolish to do so. The government really has no case. They have nothing on you. They don't have any surveillance or confidential drug buys. They haven't found any drugs or money in your possession. Look, we're going in with 'Show me the money!'"

This all sounded good to Sharanda.

With Clenesha's dad's help, Sharanda hired him. She would go to trial and would do so with the confidence that only a person naïve about drug laws could possess, a confidence that only finally deserted her the moment she saw the marshals coming into the courtroom to take her away to county jail to await a living death sentence.

I LEARNED SHARANDA'S story over the course of many letters, emails, and conversations. Again and again, I was moved and inspired by Sharanda's resilience, her devotion to her family, her stoic positivity in the face of the inanity of what she'd been through, and the grinding gray reality of prison life. Our bond continued to deepen. But our journey together began on that very first visit.

Before I left Carswell that first day, I leaned across the barrier between our chairs and took her hand. Outside the prison, a winter's dusk was approaching, and most families had already reluctantly said their goodbyes and shepherded crying children out toward the cars. Sharanda and I had spent all evening visiting together, our first of many, and still I too felt reluctant to leave. I was twenty-five years old and a second-year law student. I knew next to nothing about the way the law worked in the real world. The only thing I knew after that first visit was that Sharanda Jones did not deserve to spend the rest of her life in prison. That day, I spoke to her with all the passion and conviction of a budding attorney.

"I will get you out, Sharanda," I said. "I will see you free. Even if I have to take this case all the way to the White House."

Sharanda looked me in the eye and was quiet for a long time. Then she leaned toward me and smiled.

"Well," she said, "I guess I'm getting out, then."

Chapter 8

LOOKING FOR A KEY

In the quiet of a Tuesday evening in the spring of 2010, a long day of classes behind me, I knelt on the floor of my apartment before a large postal box, pausing before I split open the packing tape with my key. I wanted to mark the occasion, if only with a moment of stillness. Sharanda had sent me her trial transcripts. Even though I still had another year of law school and the grueling bar exam to go before I could officially call myself an attorney-at-law, Sharanda had granted me complete access to her case. Her trust in me was a great honor.

Taking a deep breath, I opened the box. One by one, I lifted out the six volumes of transcripts, each one ranging from sixty to two hundred pages. They were ten years old—the paper thin, the font bearing the uneven ink of a typewriter. Almost reverently, I carried the first volume to my kitchen table, where a brand-new yellow legal pad sat waiting. There was no question or doubt in my mind about the task at hand. Somewhere in these six volumes of transcribed testimony, I believed, was the key to Sharanda's freedom. The thought filled me with nervous anticipation and purpose. Eagerly I began to read, pen poised for the notes I couldn't wait to take.

By the end of the first volume of transcripts I was gripping my pen so hard my hand ached, my furious handwriting almost illegible on the page. Over the past few weeks and months, Sharanda had shared every detail of her personal story with me, including her decision to serve as an intermediary between Spider and Baby Jack and Julie—a bad decision, to be sure. But the case before me exaggerated her role to grotesque proportions. Federal prosecutors painted Sharanda as a queenpin drug dealer who called the shots. I had been offended when Keyon's prosecutor portrayed my old friend as a callous street thug, but the picture Sharanda's prosecutors had conjured was nothing short of unconscionable. There was no physical evidence for any of it. In fact, most of the prosecution's absurd allegations were discredited throughout the trial by their own government witnesses. The more I read and understood, the more incensed I became.

From the beginning, Aaron Wiley and Bill McMurrey employed a prosecutorial strategy I'd learned about from Professor Lacey called "stacking": Prosecutors add on charges in order to increase the odds of a harsher sentence and to bully defendants into accepting plea bargains. Here's the prosecutors' version of events: Sharanda was a criminal mastermind and a drug queenpin, who supplied the greater part of Terrell with crack and powder cocaine. Not only was she the primary supplier for Baby Jack and Julie but also for Cooter, Weasel, Genice, and Mitchell. The prosecution said that Sharanda delivered crack cocaine to her quadriplegic mother and to her brother in duffel bags, so that they could distribute and run a crack house out of her mother's home. Wiley and McMurrey even used Sharanda's law-abiding, industrious spirit against her, arguing that Sharanda filed her tax returns, ran her hair salon, managed and served as head cook of Cooking on Lamar, and earned professional certificates in cosmetology and culinary arts because she was "smart" and wanted to "appear legitimate."

"What the evidence is going to show," Wiley said at trial, "is that there was one person making money in this whole equation . . . it was her. The rest of the people are just doing the best they can. And she's using them."

I didn't understand how any ethical attorney for the government of the United States could stand before a court of law and argue that Sharanda Jones, whose role was to pick up single kilos from Spider and deliver them to Baby Jack and Julie, could be using Spider, who by his own admission was a supplier known throughout Texas. And unlike Sharanda, to whom not a shred of physical evidence was ever connected, Baby Jack and Julie had been caught red-handed with an entire apartment devoted to cooking crack, the packing wrappers from multiple kilos of cocaine, and forty thousand dollars in cash. It was common for the feds to use low-hanging fruit to flip dealers higher up the chain—I'd seen that often enough in the courtroom throughout the course of my two judicial internships. But here was the reverse situation—the Department of Justice was using three higher-up career dealers to prosecute someone far less culpable. It didn't feel like justice to me.

My incredulity only grew as I read through the pages of testimony from government witnesses. The trial was a circus, with one clearly self-interested or unreliable witness after another paraded in front of the jurors.

"What did the feds want from you?" I asked Sharanda after my second night of reading, note taking, and pacing in outrage at the injustice of it all. "They must have wanted something."

"They wanted me to flip on my friend," she wrote back. "The one I opened Cooking on Lamar with. She was a police officer in Dallas, and they wanted me to say that she was my partner in carrying the drugs. But it wasn't true. They had it all wrong. And I was so clueless at the time, I didn't even get it. I didn't even get that they wanted me to be a snitch. My mind just didn't work like that. I didn't know why they were putting all this on me. It wasn't until way after when McMurrey came to visit me in prison and asked about her again that I even realized."

"He came to see you in prison?"

"He sure did. They don't ever give up. All they want is for you to flip on the next person. Basically told me if I gave her up they'd reduce my sentence. But none of it was even true. And how am I gonna just hand my suffering to somebody else? They didn't know what they were talking about. Later my friend sued them for defamation and won. She's still on the force now. She didn't have nothing to do with any of it. And that's the God-honest truth."

The feds were ready to reduce Sharanda's sentence if she made up a story about her friend. How could they play with people's lives like that? And to what end? They had stacked Sharanda's case with absurd charges against her entire family just to get to a woman who Sharanda swore was innocent? Was Sharanda's life sentence simply a callous bargaining chip gone bad? My disgust was outpaced only by my determination. I kept reading.

The charges concerning Genice's house on Rose Hill Road were absurd, and from the beginning, so was the testimony surrounding them. Prosecutors dragged up a motley crew of drug users and petty dealers, all of whom were testifying in exchange for lesser charges and sentences of their own. Their testimony was so farfetched and inconsistent it would have been laughable, if not for the gut-wrenching stakes.

Cooter was the linchpin in this part of the prosecutors' case. He'd been arrested for selling crack on multiple occasions to an undercover police officer, and in the early days of his ordeal he had signed an exceptionally eloquent statement that claimed Sharanda and his mother were his suppliers—a statement he'd never read and did not write himself. On the stand he retracted the written statement completely, stating that he alone in his family sold drugs. I knew from Sharanda that prosecutors added time to Cooter's sentence for crossing them on the stand. And he wasn't the only government witness who testified that the feds had put words in their mouth. An old friend of Cooter's, Kevin Henderson, refused to agree to leading questions establishing that Sharanda supplied crack to her family members. Instead, Kevin was adamant that all the dope was Cooter's. Yes, he and Cooter went to Genice's house to pick up the dope, he testified, but it was stashed in the back of the house, in the doghouses of Cooter's pit bulls. No, he'd never seen Sharanda come to the house with dope. And when asked about Cooter's suppliers, he named Baby Jack and two other people.

For Sharanda, it was clear that the damning work wasn't done by these inconsistent, low-level witnesses, but by the testimony provided by the biggest dealers in the case: Baby Jack, Julie, and Spider himself.

After being arrested in November 1997 as part of the Terrell sweep, nearly two years before Sharanda, Baby Jack and Julie entered into plea agreements to cooperate with the government. Julie had begged Sharanda repeatedly to find them a new connection, but it was all a setup; whenever Sharanda went to see her at the record store, Julie was wearing a wire. Many of the recorded conversations had been entered into evidence and played at Sharanda's trial. In the majority of the tapes, Sharanda and Julie were gossiping about mutual friends from Terrell who'd been caught up in the same bust that had swept up Julie and Baby Jack. That portion of the transcript reminded me exactly of the conversations we'd have sitting in Sissy's front yard in the Hole, especially after the feds hit Commerce during the summer of 2000, busting down doors before sunrise, rounding up friends and acquaintances in paddy wagons: how much time they were looking at, who had their kids, how much money and drugs were found, who was snitching. Federal prosecutors twisted all of this street talk to make Sharanda sound like a hardened dealer talking about her trade. And Julie went along with it.

I asked Sharanda about the tapes once when I went to see her. "When I heard them before trial, I wasn't worried, and neither was my lawyer." If anything, she thought they exonerated her. "I told Murphy that's just how we talk," Sharanda told me, shaking her head at the memory. "Everybody talks like that. Go anywhere in Terrell right now, I said, and somebody'll be having the same conversation. It's not even about anything we did. How does that prove anything?

"The jurors were starting to look at me funny because of how the prosecutors were spinning it. When I told Julie 'Let me see what I can do,' I was trying to get her off my back! What else do you say to someone who you've already said no to a million times? But Murphy wasn't even worried about those tapes. I remember clear as day what he said—'Smoke and mirrors. Don't worry, they've got nothing. And the burden of proof is on them.' I believed him."

Baby Jack's testimony didn't go well for the prosecution, either. At one point, in Murphy's cross-examination of Baby Jack—one of his best moments in the trial, in my mind—Baby Jack basically gave up the whole reason for his testimony. Julie had testified that during the time of the indictment, Sharanda was their main supplier, even though that contradicted both her own and Baby Jack's testimony as to how often Sharanda delivered a kilo. Murphy pushed Baby Jack on this further.

"Isn't it true that Nathan Bivens is your nephew?" he asked.

"Yes."

"And so aren't you providing this testimony today in order to protect your nephew, who is in fact your main supplier?"

"Yes," said Baby Jack.

Nothing could have been more transparent.

On my next visit to Sharanda, I couldn't stop my questions. She was patient with me, although I'm sure it was hard for her to relive the trauma of that time. We sat side by side in the padded mauve visiting seats, twisted toward each other so we could make eye contact. I was filled with detail-oriented legal questions about the case itself, but I was also captivated by Sharanda's resilience and her positivity. I'd always been taken by this part of her character, but now that I'd had a front-row seat at the circus that led to her incarceration, I was even more impressed.

"Baby Jack, Julie, Spider—these were people you knew. How did it feel, sitting there and hearing them tell these lies on you? How did you stand it?"

"When Baby Jack walked in there—I mean, we've known each other since we were little kids, grew up together. We've always been cool. He just looked and shrugged at me on his way to the stand, like, 'It is what it is.' It hurt. It did. I just tried not to feel nothing. Just watching them lie on me like that, though—it was sickening for real. I try to understand it from their side. Someone offered them a lifeline and they took it. They hung me with it. I wouldn't do anybody like that, not even somebody I didn't know."

"And Spider?"

"He was slick with it. I mean, that's Spider. Smooth, always in control. But let me tell you what he said the feds did to him. Cooter saw him while they were both at the county jail and Spider told him straight-up that he was sorry for what he was doing to me. He told Cooter that the feds said if he didn't testify against me, they was gonna go after his mom, indict her for being a part of his drug dealings. Now ain't that grimy."

My stomach turned at the thought of the lengths the feds would go to obtain convictions. I thought about what extraordinary fortitude it must have taken for Sharanda to be staring a life sentence in the face and refuse such a possible pathway to freedom—especially after people she'd known for years had done the same to her. As I continued to study the transcripts and talk to her about them, my admiration for her strength and for her grace grew.

To THEIR GREAT credit, the jurors were also largely unimpressed, and unswayed, by the government's case. They found Sharanda not guilty on all six of the possession and aiding and abetting counts. But they found her guilty of the charge of conspiracy to distribute crack cocaine. I had come across conspiracy in Keyon's case, too, and was having a hard time getting my head around it. The law seemed so broad as to ensnare anyone charged. How could Sharanda be given a life sentence on a charge that seemed so all-encompassing?

I needed to understand federal drug conspiracy. I couldn't bear to read the sentencing transcript yet, not while still reeling and try-ing to process the trial itself. So I read through and studied dozens of drug conspiracy cases, trying to get a better grasp of what the law meant in practice.

Added to the books at the height of the drug panic in the late eighties, federal drug conspiracy laws exemplified everything that was wrong with the War on Drugs. The laws, I discovered, were incredibly broad. When I thought of drug conspiracy, I imagined vast international drug cartels, but Keyon's and Sharanda's cases painted an entirely different reality. A federal drug conspiracy has just three simple elements: (1) an agreement to traffic drugs in any amount (2) between two or more people who (3) join the agree-ment voluntarily. The government did not need to prove that Sharanda knew all the details of the conspiracy or even that she knew all the other people involved.

Still trying to wrap my head around the law, I sought help from the best source I knew. Professor Robert Udashen was one of the most sought-after criminal defense attorneys in Dallas. He served as an adjunct professor at SMU and I was taking his criminal pro-cedure class that semester in my efforts to better understand the criminal justice system. In his office, I conveyed the frustration I'd felt while reading those transcripts.

"If none of the other charges stuck, how could conspiracy?" I asked him. "I've been reading up on it, and it seems like the broad-est law in the world."

Professor Udashen nodded. "Your understanding is correct. No drugs, no money—no physical evidence is required. Drug conspir-acies are popular with federal prosecutors—it's their greatest tool.

Many conspiracy charges are based on the word of cooperating witnesses, who usually get lesser sentences in exchange for their testimony. The law is supposed to be used to catch the kingpins but usually ends up affecting people much lower on the totem pole."

"That's exactly what happened in Sharanda's case."

"It happens all the time," Professor Udashen said, with a tired smile. "I'm representing a young lady now who was indicted with twenty-three other people here in the Northern District. Her boyfriend sent her to Western Union a couple of times to pick up money someone was sending him for drugs he had fronted. She did it, didn't think anything of it. She just knew she was picking up money, didn't know the type or even the quantity of drugs fronted. Now she's charged with one count of drug conspiracy. The government is offering to dismiss her charges if she turns on the boyfriend."

"It's that easy?" I asked. "That's all it took was her picking up money? Even though she had nothing else to do with it?"

"That's it. It's why so many people convicted of drug charges plead guilty. It doesn't matter how minor their role is. As long as a defendant is somehow linked to a conspiracy, they can be held accountable for the greatest crimes of that conspiracy."

I thanked Professor Udashen for his time and walked briskly down the hall. I felt slightly sick. And it wasn't only about Sharanda. I was thinking about myself.

More specifically, I was thinking about how in my senior year of high school, I used to drive Red to the little clapboard house in East Dallas on the way to pick up Sissy. How I knew Red sold drugs. How I knew exactly what was in the plastic-wrapped package that he hid under my passenger seat. How we used to drive down Interstate 30—"Dirty 30," they used to call it, on account of the state troopers that lay in wait to jam up drug traffickers. *I don't have nothing to do with it*, I would have said if anyone asked. That was Red's business, not mine. But according to what my professor had just explained to me, driving Red to Dallas made me just as guilty of violating federal drug conspiracy laws as Sharanda Jones.

That night, I lay in bed, shaken. I imagined the headlines: PROMISING LAW STUDENT RECEIVES LIFE SENTENCE. BOGATA GIRL GONE BAD. I pictured the look on my dad's face as he was forced to sit through a trial at which guys I didn't even know testified that I supplied them all with drugs. I imagined my mom and Jazz and me eating Cheetos off napkins again in the visiting room—only this time it would be federal prison, not state, and they'd be visiting me. I thought about the extraordinary grace with which Sharanda met every inhuman challenge of her incarceration. I wondered if I had even an ounce of that kind of strength. By morning, I had been through every nightmare scenario in my head and talked myself out of most of them. But my new understanding of conspiracy made one thing very clear: I would fight for Sharanda's life as if it were my own, because it was.

I GREW OBSESSED with Sharanda's case, breathing it, eating it, sleeping it. In between campus interviews for summer internships and class, I would pull out a section of transcripts from my bag and continue my note taking. I continued to look up relevant case law as I went, along with scholarly articles that I thought might help me. It was time-consuming, but I was in too deep to turn back now.

The sentencing disparities in Sharanda's case might have been the hardest thing to swallow. Julie and Baby Jack ended up serving less than eight years each after providing testimony against Sharanda; they had already been released before I even started law school. Sharanda's entire family was sentenced for longer than that. The judge handed Mitchell five years, Weasel eight, Cooter eighteen and, unbelievably, Sharanda's quadriplegic mother, Genice, received a seventeen-year sentence in federal prison. The most insane sentencing disparity was with Spider, who testified that he supplied Sharanda with cocaine and admitted to selling more than

150 kilos of powder cocaine to various individuals in two states over the course of several years. Obviously, as the supplier—not only to Julie and Baby Jack through Sharanda but also to others—Spider trafficked significantly more drugs than anyone else in the case. And yet for his damning testimony against Sharanda, his sentence was reduced to nineteen and a half years, while the woman who acted as a go-between, carrying kilos for him to Baby Jack and Julie, was sentenced to life.

The disparity took my breath away. The feds had reduced the sentence of a big fish—a supplier—so they could take the entire natural life of someone who was barely even swimming. The injustice seemed so blatant I kept flipping back and rereading sections of the transcripts, my chest tight, to make sure my mind wasn't playing tricks on me. It hurt to read.

I needed to understand how the judge had come up with Sharanda's sentence. From my time interning for federal judges and observing sentencing hearings, I knew federal sentencing guidelines were used when calculating sentences in federal cases. Two categories, offense conduct and criminal history of the defendant, are put into a formula and adjusted based on sentencing enhancements.

At that time, federal drug sentencings were largely a formulaic exercise. In drug cases, the offense conduct is based on the type and quantity of the drug. The racially disproportionate 100-to-1 crack-to-powder ratio is embedded in the guidelines. At the time Sharanda was sentenced, 1.5 kilograms or more of crack yielded the highest base offense level possible in the guidelines—the same base offense level as 150 kilos of powder cocaine.

Although no drugs were found, the judge determined that Sharanda was responsible for the distribution of 30 kilograms of cocaine. The way he arrived at that number was mind-blowing. It was based solely on the testimony of Baby Jack, Julie, and Spider. To make matters worse and subject Sharanda to stiffer punishment, the judge determined that it was reasonably forseeable that the powder from Spider was going to be "rocked up," or converted to crack by Baby Jack and Julie, therefore holding Sharanda accountable for trafficking crack, not powder. Using what seemed to me an arbitrary formula presented by a DEA analyst, the prosecutor said that the 30 kilograms of powder was equal to 13.39 kilograms of crack cocaine. The judge agreed.

But it didn't stop there. The judge then added 10.528 kilograms of crack cocaine that the prosecutors said had been distributed in Terrell and was linked to Cooter. In total, the judge held Sharanda accountable for 23.92 kilograms of crack, triggering a base offense guideline level of 38.

Just like Keyon, Sharanda was being held accountable for "ghost dope." The legal term is "relevant conduct," but "ghost dope" is so much more accurate that even law professors use it. Basically, it refers to the calculation of drug quantity based entirely on testimony, often uncorroborated, in the absence of physical evidence. Prosecutors seek maximum quantities in order to trigger mandatory minimums, and ghost dope is a great way to get that number into the stratosphere.

Sharanda's sentence was made even more severe with a punishment tool introduced at the height of the drug war that allowed judges in certain cases to "enhance" sentences—that is, make them longer. During the trial, Sharanda's lawyer made a huge mistake. In his direct examination of Sharanda, when she took the stand to testify on her own behalf, Murphy asked her about her handgun license. As I read that portion of the trial transcripts, it was obvious Murphy thought that line of questioning would establish Sharanda's character as a hardworking, law-abiding citizen. His point seemed to be that if Sharanda had been so deeply involved in illegal activity as the government was saying, she wouldn't have gone through the rigorous steps to legally obtain a handgun, which she did for protection in her various businesses. Sharanda testified freely at trial to carrying her handgun. She said her business in the salon and restaurant was all cash-based, and that she carried a gun to and from work daily to protect herself, a woman walking to her car late at night carrying significant amounts of cash.

There was no testimony from any witness that they ever saw Sharanda with a gun, absolutely no allegations of violence.

But Murphy had introduced a weapon into the courtroom where previously there had been none. And prosecutors pounced. Since Sharanda said she never went anywhere without her gun and had been convicted on the drug conspiracy charge, she had to have had the gun with her on the trips to Houston. And "carrying a gun in furtherance of a drug conspiracy" was against the law.

Two-point enhancement.

Sharanda testified on her own behalf during trial. But because she was found guilty of drug conspiracy, the judge found she committed perjury on the stand while testifying in her own defense. And perjury on the stand was an "obstruction of justice."

Two-point enhancement.

Prosecutors portrayed Sharanda as the leader and organizer of drugs being sold out of her mom's house in Terrell, even though the people she was supposed to be "leading"—Cooter, Genice, Mitchell, Weasel—testified to the contrary.

Four-point enhancement.

Sharanda had no criminal history, so she was placed in the lowest criminal history category. But her clean record was no match for her total offense level after all the enhancements.

When Sharanda was sentenced, the guidelines were mandatory, so the judge had no choice but to impose the sentence predetermined by the federal formula. In Sharanda's case, her guideline sentence was not a range of numbers, but four letters: L-I-F-E. Mandatory sentencing guidelines had effectively reduced the federal judge to a mere calculator, unable to take into account the human being who stood before him. Unable to look beyond the numbers in the guideline calculation and see her heartbeat.

"Ms. Jones, it will be the judgment of the Court that you be sentenced to the custody of the U.S. Bureau of Prisons for a term of life imprisonment," said Judge Solis. "You are remanded to the custody of the marshal, Ms. Jones, to serve your sentence."

WHEN I LOOKED up from the last of the transcripts, I had to make a conscious effort to unclench my jaw, loosen my shoulders, breathe. I was furious, but I was also heartbroken. The system had failed Sharanda. Failed Clenesha. The judge took Sharanda's entire life, kidnapped her from Clenesha, condemned her to spend the remainder of her days in a cage. I thought of my own mother and could not imagine her so abruptly snatched from my life, for the rest of her life. I logged into Corrlinks and emailed Sharanda.

"Just finished reading the sentencing transcript. Your survivor-ship empowers me. How did you feel standing there after the judge sentenced you?"

Her response came in a few hours later.

"I felt numb," she wrote. "I had absolutely no understanding. When other women in here ask me my time, it's like I can't even fix my mouth correctly to let the word roll off my tongue. I refuse to believe I will die in here."

I refused to believe it, too.

I WAS DETERMINED to get Sharanda out of prison. Everything about her conviction and sentence seemed fundamentally flawed. So I spent nights and weekends in the law library, digging deeper into federal statutes and case law to see how I could get Sharanda's case back into court.

I came across the 2005 case of *United States v. Booker,* in which the U.S. Supreme Court held that mandatory federal sentencing guidelines were unconstitutional. Rigid and unforgiving sentenc-ing guidelines had tied the hands of federal judges for nearly twenty years. After *Booker* the guidelines were made advisory, re-storing some semblance of individualized sentencing discretion stripped from Sharanda's judge in 1999. *Booker* also instructed appellate courts to review all district court sentencing decisions for "reasonableness."

The U.S. Supreme Court then issued several decisions mapping out the advisory sentencing guidelines system that *Booker* created. *Kimbrough v. United States* seemed the most promising. Based on a categorical disagreement with the 100-to-1 policy, the Court ruled that federal judges could use their discretion in sentencing a defendant below the sentencing guideline range in crack cocaine cases.

Once again I couldn't believe what I was reading—but this time it was a pleasant surprise. In her opinion, Ruth Bader Ginsburg, my favorite Supreme Court justice, examined the disparate treatment of crack and powder cocaine in federal sentencing. She came to the exact same conclusion I had in my critical race theory paper. Disparate sentencing between crack and powder greatly harmed Black people.

"The crack/powder sentencing differential 'fosters disrespect for and lack of confidence in the criminal justice system,'" wrote Ginsburg, "because of a 'widely-held perception' that it 'promotes unwarranted disparity based on race.' Approximately 85 percent of defendants convicted of crack offenses in federal court are black; thus the severe sentences required by the 100-to-1 ratio are imposed 'primarily on black offenders.'"

This was it! I knew I could make the argument that Sharanda's life sentence was unreasonable. It was beyond the point of legitimate debate that Sharanda's permanent removal from society offended prevailing standards of human decency.

But as I read further, my heart sank. *Kimbrough v. United States* was not made retroactive. The decision would help people in Sharanda's situation going forward, but it couldn't undo what had already been done. In fact, under *Booker* and its progeny, I was procedurally barred from getting Sharanda back into court.

None of this made any sense. If a law is wrong today, wasn't it wrong yesterday? And shouldn't the people in prison because of it get another shot at justice? I had learned in law school that there was a limit to a lawyer's use of creativity. We were bound by the law. But increasingly, it seemed that we were bound by laws entirely outside the bounds of moral consciousness.

THAT SPRING, I interviewed with Winstead PC, a national law firm and among the largest business law firms in Texas, and received an offer to join as summer associate between my second and third year of law school. I spent the summer accompanying partners to meetings with clients, listening in on risk assessment conference calls, even analyzing a few cases. But even as I found renewed focus at work, I was determined to figure out how to get Sharanda out of prison. That summer, while I threw myself into corporate law by day, I spent four nights a week in a constitutional law course focused on cruel and unusual punishment, hoping to find a solution for Sharanda.

There had been some recent movement in the courts, and in Congress. In May 2010, the Supreme Court ruled in *Graham v. Florida* that it was unconstitutional to sentence juveniles to life imprisonment for nonhomicide offenses. Debates were heating up in Congress over a potential change to the law that would eliminate the crack and powder cocaine disparity. The Senate had passed a bill in the spring, and I was hopeful that the House would do the right thing by passing it as well. The Obama administration had encouraged Congress to adjust the 100-to-1 sentencing ratio to 1-to-1. In order to get both sides of the aisle to agree, they compromised to a ratio of 18-to-1. The Fair Sentencing Act was by no means perfect, but at least it marked some recognition by Congress that the draconian penalties for crack offenses they had codified in the 1986 Anti-Drug Abuse Act were unfair.

On August 3, 2010, the day before his birthday, President Barack Obama made history by signing the Fair Sentencing Act into law. In our emails to each other, Sharanda and I were almost giddy with anticipation. We were sure the new law would enable her to get back into court.

And it surely would have, had it applied to her. But the FSA had one life-shattering deficiency aimed directly at Sharanda and the thousands like her already serving excessive sentences for crack. Like *Booker*, it was not made retroactive.

We were devastated. I returned to Professor Udashen's office, seeking some combination of explanation and commiseration.

"It all boils down to compromise and convenience," he said. "Congress makes compromises to get a bipartisan consensus. And courts claim that retroactivity overburdens judicial resources."

"Freedom should not be a matter of compromise or convenience," I said, my voice unsteady.

"It shouldn't be," Professor Udashen said, shaking his head sadly. "But all too often in this country, it is."

In the months that followed, the U.S. Sentencing Commission retroactively modified the federal sentencing guidelines, reducing the base offense level used to calculate crack cocaine offenses by two points. The move was hopeful, as were all the changes that dramatically altered the federal sentencing landscape. Still, Sharanda's inflated ghost dope quantity exceeded the threshold for a reduction. Even under all the hopeful changes, her sentence could not be amended. But Keyon Mitchell's could. And if I could do something to help Keyon, I was going to. Using cases and sample motions I found in Westlaw, and with Sharanda's encouragement, I drafted a twenty-eight-page sentence reduction motion for him based on the guideline amendment. There was just one problem: I was not a lawyer yet. I couldn't file the motion with the court on my own.

Keyon suggested I reach out to Bruce Cobb, a lawyer who had tried to help him with an appeal a few years before. Already familiar with Keyon's case, Bruce was more than happy to help. He reviewed my work and filed the motion with the court.

Relief was immediate. Only one week after Bruce filed the motion, a federal judge reduced Keyon's life sentence to the low end of his new guideline range: 384 months. That was thirty-two years. Keyon and his family were elated. Mr. Mitchell called me three times in one day to thank me over and over.

On the phone with Mr. Mitchell, I tried to sound excited. I was glad Keyon's sentence had been reduced, but in truth, I was underwhelmed. Keyon still had a quarter of a century left to serve. He was still looking at more time in prison than he'd even been alive.

There had to be more we could do.

But the more I learned about the law, the less it seemed I would be able to help him. And the prognosis for Sharanda was even worse. As much as I hated to admit it—refused to admit it—a legal remedy through the courts for Sharanda simply did not exist. I worried that I had earned Sharanda's trust just to let her down.

I needed to find another legal tool, one that would give Sharanda a fighting chance. Then, one day, the tool I needed found me.

A Knock at My Door

In the fall of 2011, I walked through the glass doors into Winstead PC's marble-floored lobby as a bona fide attorney. I'd set my sights on corporate law, and here I was. After three rigorous years at SMU, it felt amazing. At the end of my time as a summer associate, I received an offer to join the firm after I completed my final year at law school. For me, the vibe at Winstead was just what I was looking for. They were fast-moving and ambitious, but a lot less formal and stuffy than some of the other firms who had offered me positions. It was just my kind of place.

I joined the firm's Finance and Banking group, representing and advising banks in complex commercial lending transactions across a wide array of industries: telecom, natural resources, technology, healthcare, and beyond. There was a learning curve, but my experience in banking and accounting at Comerica and PwC ensured it wasn't as steep as for some of my peers. No two days were ever the same. Finance and Banking was a high-stakes world where our legal advice could have multimillion-dollar consequences for our clients. The hours were long, and many weekends

I found myself at work drafting credit agreements or tackling the dreaded and monotonous junior associate task of performing due diligence for an acquisition financing deal.

For weeks, I missed Sunday dinners at Mama Lena's, becoming engrossed in big-firm life. Within my first year I second-chaired a billion-dollar finance deal. Melissa Stewart, an equity partner and one of the firm's rainmakers, was lead counsel, and I worked side by side with her. A brilliant attorney and incomparable negotiator, Melissa showed me what it meant to leave it all on the table for a big deal. We regularly put in sixteen-hour days, working closely with the client to develop financing structure and strategy. The art of the deal fueled us. This was the life I had always dreamed of.

Once the deal closed, I finally had a Sunday off to have dinner at Mama Lena's. Jazz was excited to ride with me, not just so we could catch up but also because the week before, I'd traded in my beloved Mitsubishi Eclipse for a new Silver BMW 5 Series. Jazz had a great new job as a pharmacy technician for a company that provided kidney dialysis to outpatient centers. We turned the music up and laughed and talked nonstop all the way to Mama Lena's. It felt good to shed my professional poise and just be my whole self. Jazz's carefree spirit always seemed to give me permission to do just that.

"How's Sharanda doing?" Jazz asked.

"She's doing good," I said. "Her spirit is amazing. Nothing gets her down."

"Anything new on her case?"

There hadn't been. And it wasn't for lack of trying. I had set up Google alerts for updates in federal sentencing reform, followed criminal justice reform organizations like Families Against Mandatory Minimums (FAMM) and the ACLU on social media, scoured articles and legislative news feeds, hoping for some legal shift that would give the tiniest crack of light. For now, there was nothing.

"I know it probably seems hard, but if anyone can get her out, you can, Sis," Jazz said. "You know what Daddy Sudie would say."

"Ain't nothin' but a step for a stepper!" we said at the same time, laughing.

It was so good to be home. Mama Lena's front door was a gateway to a mansion full of love and belly-deep laughs. My spirit swelled as we pulled into the driveway. Mama Lena had cooked beef tips and rice, chicken breast with her special mushroom sauce, greens, and my favorite candied yams. Not to mention two cakes. My dad was there with the hug I needed. And my aunt Felicia and all my cousins were there to tease me to death about being Mama Lena's favorite.

"Mama, you have seven kids and dozens of grandkids," Felicia said as we heaped our plates with Mama Lena's cooking. "Why do you only have a picture of Brittany on your TV stand? And why is she in between your pictures of Jesus and Barack?" My family cried laughing.

As we cleaned up after dinner, my cellphone rang from a number I didn't recognize. Usually I sent these to voicemail; for some reason, on this day I answered. When I heard that sweet Southern voice on the other end of the line I smiled, glad to have picked up. "De-Ann! How are you?"

"Hey, Brittany, it's been a minute! Mama Lena's been bragging on you. She says you're a lawyer now! We're all so proud of you."

"Thank you so much," I said. "I'm at her house with the fam right now. What are you doing these days?"

"I'm doing good! I'm the general manager for a mobile home sales company. Girl, can you believe they letting me run shit?" she said, laughing. "I got blessed with this job. They have no idea about my background and I pray every damn day they don't find out. Terrified they would fire me. It's too damn hard to find a job with a felony, ya know? I don't take any of my freedom for granted. Not after as close as I got to living out the rest of my life in a cell."

I'd known Loretta De-Ann Coffman all my life. She jokes now that she used to change my diapers, and I'm sure it's true. De-Ann grew up in Campbell with my dad and his brothers and sister, and as a teenager she and my uncle Ricky dated hot and heavy—

so much so that her family disowned her for having a Black boyfriend. Mama Lena took her in, at least emotionally, and De-Ann
practically lived her senior year in high school at our house in
Campbell. I was five years old then, and I remember her sweet,
joyful presence. She would play with me and Jazz outside, teaching us how to turn cartwheels. Always stylish, she looked like the
iconic Demi Moore in the movie *Ghost,* petite with a short haircut,
sharp chin, and brown eyes. Her huge, open smile was matched
only by her feisty temper. De-Ann didn't take mess from anyone,
but she had the biggest heart. She was family.

After high school, De-Ann graduated from VTI vocational
school with a degree in business administration and management.
She moved to Dallas with her friend Sophia, and started looking
for a regular job, but they were hard to come by. So instead, she
found her own path. Every weekend, Sophia and Sophia's husband, Gregg, drove her up to a couple of local nightclubs to strut
her stuff in their bikini contests. First prize paid about three hundred bucks. De-Ann won so consistently she didn't even need a
regular job.

On the Fourth of July that year a friend invited her to a boat
party on Lake Ray Hubbard, where she spent the evening sitting at
the bow beneath the fireworks, listening to Keith Sweat and flirt-
ing with the boat's owner, Mike. A tall, broad-shouldered twenty-
seven-year-old from the big city of Dallas, with sloe eyes and a
magnetic smile, handsome and fly in his bright yellow and purple
fit, Mike Wilson caught her attention and held it. By the end of
that summer of 1991 they were a couple. De-Ann quit her bikini
contests at Mike's urging and moved into a lakeside condo. Mike
paid the rent.

A little over a year later their romance would be cut short when
Mike, De-Ann, Mike's older brother Wayland, their cousin Terry,
Donel Clark, and four others were indicted on federal charges that
included conspiracy to distribute cocaine, crack, and marijuana.
None of them had ever been in trouble with the law before. After
a two-week trial, Wayland, Donel, and Terry received extreme

sentences for their roles in the conspiracy. Like carnival mirrors, prosecutors had a way of distorting how people looked and making them appear larger than life. I'd seen them use this trick against Keyon and Sharanda. Mike and De-Ann were no exception. They were portrayed as leaders in the conspiracy and sentenced to life in prison without the possibility of parole.

I was only nine when De-Ann was sentenced. I remember Mama Lena accepting prison calls from her, trying to sound cheerful and upbeat. I didn't understand the details then, only that she no longer came around the house. I heard Mama Lena talking about it with my daddy and uncles in grave tones; they said she'd been sent away under the new crack laws. No one could make sense of De-Ann having to spend the rest of her life in prison. She was only twenty-two. I just knew it felt like someone had died or, more accurately, was living through the nightmare of their own death. The grown-ups all shook their heads in sorrow and disbelief. I didn't know what that meant, not then. But I missed De-Ann—we all did.

De-Ann served eight years of her life sentence before President Bill Clinton, who ironically had bolstered the very laws that sealed De-Ann's fate in his devastating 1994 Crime Bill, granted her clemency in 2001. She was the only woman in the case who went to prison with these guys, the only white person. Mike, Donel, Terry, and Wayland were all Black men, and when De-Ann called me at Mama Lena's that day, it looked for sure like they'd be spending the better part of their lives in human cages.

Eleven years after her release, De-Ann was still desperate to find support for her friends. From the moment she got out of prison, all De-Ann could think about was freeing her codefendants. She had reached out to dozens of lawyers over the years to help the guys, even shelling out her own money for legal fees when she could. Most of the lawyers charged too much money, or simply just strung her along. But De-Ann was unrelenting in her fight to see her codefendants freed. In typical De-Ann fashion, she would fall down seven times and get up eight.

"Mama Lena told me you were a lawyer," said De-Ann, "and I

was hoping you might be able to do something for these guys. The law has changed since we went in, a few times. I think that might help. Even if it doesn't, though, there's clemency. After they deny all your appeals, clemency from the president is the only chance. It's a long shot, but shoot, if I got it, why can't they?" She paused a minute. "I mean, I know I'm white. And racism is real. But still. We gotta try."

"I hear you, De-Ann," I said. "But I'm a corporate lawyer. I don't have much experience at all with criminal law."

"Brittany, you've got to help me," De-Ann said. "You gotta help them. Here I am, out now for more than a decade. Meanwhile, they're still locked up in that hell, set to rot. They been in there twenty years. *Twenty years.* And Mike's sick. He had a stroke last year and they are not even trying to help him in there with his medical needs." Her usual joyful, laughing voice was filled with pain and desperation. "It just ain't right. Brittany, if we don't do something, they're gonna *die* in there."

I got off the phone overwhelmed. I was still searching for an avenue for Sharanda while shouldering a heavy load at Winstead. I felt ill-equipped and unqualified to take on a case in which the lives of four men hung in the balance. But this was De-Ann asking. And there's no way I could say no to Auntie De-Ann.

In the hours following that call, a single thought kept spinning around in my mind. Clemency. Why hadn't I made this connection before? President Bill Clinton had granted De-Ann clemency. I hadn't known what it was then, and I didn't much care; I was just thrilled to see De-Ann again, a loving face from my childhood. But now, as it all came rushing back to me with the sound of De-Ann's sweet country twang, I felt an idea stirring. A kernel of new hope began to germinate and seed.

IN THE MEANTIME, I had work to do. In the space of a single phone call, I had more than doubled my pro bono clientele. I knew that if I was going to take on the Wilson case, it was going to be all or nothing. I wasn't going to play. I would have to get to know each man as intimately as I knew Keyon and Sharanda. I didn't know how to approach the work any other way, and I wouldn't have wanted to. These were people's lives in my hands, and I never wanted to forget that. I needed to get a full picture of their lives in Dallas before they caught the case and after so that I could better understand the situation, and build the relationships and trust it would take to go up against the beast of draconian drug laws.

Over the next few weeks I took advantage of the brief lull between deals at work and dug into the case. I had more calls with De-Ann and, when we could, with the guys themselves. When De-Ann gave me the name and number of Mike's former attorney, I couldn't believe it.

"Robert Udashen?" I said.

"Yes, Mr. Udashen. He represented Mike. He was real good, too," De-Ann said.

"That was my law professor!" I said.

De-Ann and I had a good laugh over that. "No such thing as coincidences in this world," she said.

Professor Udashen met with me in his office once again to go over what he recalled of the Wilson case. "It's been nearly twenty years, but I'll never forget that case," he said. "Mike was a good person, and now he would die in prison. You never forget a life sentence. I'm so glad to hear you're on this. I still have all my old case files archived in storage. I'll have my assistant request them for you. All of the trial transcripts are there, too."

Unlike Sharanda's, which came through snail mail in a single box, the Wilson transcripts and case documents were neatly filed and tightly packed into several legal boxes. I lugged them all to the car and into my apartment. Late at night, after completing my Winstead workday, I sifted carefully through the files, determined to get the best and most comprehensive picture possible of my newest clients' stories.

———

I HAD NEVER met Mike Wilson back when he was dating De-Ann, but I knew about him. Laid-back and generous to a fault, he loved chilling at the lake with some lawn chairs and a cooler of Miller Light, spending hours at the water's edge, dreaming up new details for souping up the latest old-school car he'd salvaged. When I first talked to him on the phone, his vibe was exactly that—soft-spoken, low-key, and gentle. Not the voice of a man who should be spending the rest of his life in prison.

By then, Mike had been locked up nearly twenty years, and the time had taken a terrible toll. His stroke made speech difficult, and there were long pauses as he tried to get his thoughts into words. He was patient with himself, but I could sense the underlying frustration, mixed with what was likely embarrassment. Mike was locked up in Victorville, California, nearly fifteen hundred miles away from his brother, Wayland, who was serving his time in Texarkana, Texas. Their mother's only two children and two years apart, they'd been super close their whole lives, much like me and Jazz. By now they'd been separated for twenty years. It was like losing their other half.

"De-Ann has told me so much about y'all," I told him on the phone, "I feel like I know you already!"

"Man, it feels so good having a lawyer willing to help us," he said slowly. "You just don't know. When De-Ann said you weren't going to charge us, I couldn't believe it. Even if I never give this life sentence back, just the fact someone fought for me is a victory. Thank you."

"It's my pleasure, Mike. Truly. Thank *you* for trusting me with your life. My approach is a little different than some lawyers'. I really want to know your story. There's always more to the story than what the transcripts say."

Mike's voice relaxed when he talked about his childhood in South Dallas, and when he talked about his parents, I could hear his love through the line.

Thomas Earl and Dorothy Wilson raised their boys with pride, pinching pennies to send them to St. Anthony's, a nearby private school. A guidance counselor for the Dallas Independent School District, Dorothy doted on her sons. Her husband, Thomas Earl, was a hard man with particular ideas about making his sons men, but a devoted father. He worked for the railroad and as a coach at St. Anthony's—a one-man show, he coached basketball, football and track, girls and boys, and ferried the athletes in the school bus to and from their games. After their divorce, Thomas Earl and Dorothy coparented, stressing the importance of education and hard work.

Mike's brother, Wayland, the older of the two boys, shared his sibling's easygoing ways but was the quieter, more introspective one. In prison, he'd become a jailhouse lawyer, counseling other incarcerated men on their cases, even writing successful briefs. He could be serious, focused, and intellectual, but then break out in a rumbling chuckle. He had a remarkable ability to find humor in anything.

As a kid, Wayland worked steady jobs all the way through high school. He attempted a semester at junior college before deciding to work full-time, loading and unloading buses at Continental Trailways from '81 to '84. He got his commercial license and drove for a couple of years for Schepps Dairy. In 1987, while loading newspapers for the Dallas *Times Herald* before his new route, an excruciating pain seared down his left leg, so intense his knees buckled. He'd crushed two discs in his lower back, resulting in tremendous chronic pain and a lack of mobility that restricted his ability to drive.

As compensation, Wayland received a $45,000 cash settlement. He bought a fourplex on Peabody Street near Pennsylvania Avenue, living in one unit and renting out the others. Eventually he had enough money saved to buy a small house with his wife, Jacqueline, who worked in merchandising for Coca-Cola and with whom he had two children, Reggie and Regina. In 1991, with money left over from the settlement and income from renting all four of the units in his complex, he started Motor Market Unlimited, an auto dealership that sold used luxury cars, listing his brother Mike as co-owner.

Wayland's chronic back pain continued to plague him. He didn't like the foggy, numb way the hydrocodone pills prescribed by his doctor made him feel, so he started smoking marijuana to manage the pain. Didn't mess with his stomach like the opioid, either. Wayland sold weed as a side hustle, largely to support his own habit. He sold a couple of pounds a month, smoked about a pound. It was a low-key business that he didn't think about too much. The car dealership he ran with Mike was doing well, car sales steady, and it kept him busy, as did managing his rental units.

Just as laid-back as his brother, Mike Wilson was popular in school and generous with friends and family alike. He was a natural leader, with the type of quiet confidence that made people follow him, believe in him. Tall and broad-shouldered, with deep-set eyes and a wide, easy smile that thrilled all the girls, Mike ran track and played football and had success in both. Sports and the firm hand of his parents kept him on the straight and narrow, although all around him the neighborhood was changing. White folks rolled through and interrupted pickup games to ask Mike and his friends where to buy drugs. The police were a constant presence, too, creeping through the streets in their black-and-whites, accelerating dangerously around corners, harassing young Black men, regarding every small Black child as a potential subject—even though all the children in South Dallas were Black. It was as though the neighborhood was under occupation.

Getting out of the city seemed like a good plan, so after high school, in the mideighties, Mike left to attend and play sports for Kilgore College, a community college a couple of hours east of Dallas. Kilgore was a small town where the local police station still flew a Confederate flag. Eighty years before, it had been the site of race riots sparked when white residents lynched a young Black man for having a relationship with a white woman. If things had changed in Kilgore in the years since, it was only on the surface.

At Kilgore College, Mike started dating a girl named Bonnie, who would eventually become the mother of his two sons, Mike Junior and Marc. Bonnie was a white girl, a local. Her father forbade "that nigger" to call the house or come by and had his friends in law enforcement harass Mike on his way to class. "You messing with that white girl, boy? Keep on and we're gonna run your ass all the way back to Dallas," the officers warned. Mike wasn't intimidated; he thought the whole thing was nonsense. He continued to go to class, determined not to let a couple of racist white men ruin his first year at school. But when Mike's parents got wind of the harassment on a visit down to Kilgore, they delivered their son a clear message. "No diploma from Kilgore College is worth your life," Dorothy told him. "You need to get on out of here."

Mike listened to his mother and headed back to Dallas; he wasn't going to take it much longer from any white man, police officer or not. He eventually became an apprentice mechanic at Petrick's Automotive while attending Cedar Valley College. About a year into his apprenticeship, Bonnie came up to meet him for lunch. It turned out Dallas wasn't immune to the race prejudice that lingered in Kilgore. The friendly shop banter cooled down considerably after Bonnie's visit, and a few days later, Mike was fired. All he could do was shake his head and laugh. The only way to avoid these white folks, he thought, is to work for my damn self. The most lucrative business in South Dallas in 1989? Crack cocaine.

A friend of Mike's from high school had been dealing for a while. "You better come on over here and see what's going on," he'd told Mike for years. Busy with school and work, Mike had resisted the call. But now he faced facts. Nobody in the hood living straight was bringing in much money, and they worked dawn to dusk for that. Mike didn't want to be at the whim of some white boss who cared more about who he dated or what he said than the quality of his work. He wanted to be his own boss. In South Dallas, it was clear where the money was, and with that money came freedom.

He began as a courier, driving and picking up packages of cocaine, and just for that made five hundred dollars a week, much more than he'd ever made as a mechanic. Fairly quickly, he got deeper into the game, purchasing kilos of powder himself and cooking it into rock to distribute.

Young and fun-loving, with a passion for the lake life and a soft spot for helping out friends in distress, Mike spent the money as soon as it came in, and sometimes even before. By the end of the summer of 1991, he had a seventeen-footer out by the lake, Jet Skis, and enough income to put his cute new girlfriend with that sweet country drawl up in her own condo.

He was still generous to a fault. He'd always looked after his little cousin Terry, whose mother was struggling to make ends meet, buying him clothes for school and giving him money for food. When he caught wind that Terry was dealing drugs out of his mother's house on one of Dallas's roughest blocks, Mike went and got him. "I wish you weren't doing this at all," he said. "But if you gone do it, you better come over here and do it with me." The same thing happened with his old school friend Donel.

For a while, business was going pretty well. But then somebody snitched, and the Dallas police rolled up on De-Ann's condo. The game was up. Mike wasn't shocked when he was picked up, though it was odd timing, with drug buys over the past few months so slow they'd considered scrapping the whole operation. But risk was par for the course, and none of them considered the bust that big a deal, at first. All the police had was a single kilo of cocaine in a cooler sitting in a breezeway outside De-Ann's condo. There were no huge stacks of cash, no piles of drugs—they didn't exist. The evidence was so weak that at the state level there was barely a case.

Then the feds took over.

"As soon as the feds came in, the whole thing changed," De-Ann told me. "It was like they would do anything to make the story line up with the one they had in their heads—even when it clearly didn't fit. They were gonna get their convictions no matter what. It wasn't an investigation to them. It was a done deal!"

However nasty or unprofessional the agents on the case got behind closed doors, the feds moved forward with charges with marksman-like precision, using every prosecutorial weapon at their disposal. Again, stacking charges. Again, ghost dope. And again, the almost unbeatable count of conspiracy.

By early fall, they'd built their case. On September 22, 1992, a thirty-one-count superseding indictment was filed charging eight defendants with conspiracy to distribute cocaine, crack, and marijuana, the use of a communication device to commit a felony, and money laundering. Mike, Wayland, De-Ann, Donel, and Terry were all named in the indictment. So were Bonnie, Mike's former girlfriend; Linda Lane, Wayland's girlfriend; and Koda Cook, Jr., a crack user who occasionally acted as a courier for Mike. In a related indictment, Leslie Calvert, De-Ann's best friend since elementary school, was also charged. With information gathered from confidential informants, agents alleged that Mike and Wayland headed a cocaine and marijuana distribution operation in Dallas.

Information from informants led to a three-week wiretap before the bust, and agents argued that conversations from the tap substantiated their informants' findings. Mike purchased cocaine in large amounts, they said, which he converted to crack. The government further alleged that Wayland "handled marijuana distribution." The legitimate car dealership owned by the brothers, Motor Market Unlimited, was portrayed by the feds to be a money-laundering front. The feds maintained that a single kilo of cocaine produced $48,600 for the "organization," a figure that would have been a market miracle; most sources estimate the profit from a kilo at the time to be closer to $9,000. The government claimed that the organization was responsible for selling over fifty kilos of crack cocaine that yielded them more than $2 million, all over the course of a ten-month period.

Mike and the others found the allegations ludicrous. They were all guilty of selling drugs, sure, but not that many or for anywhere near that much money. How could the charges stick when there was no evidence? And how could there be evidence when there was no way in hell they'd been moving that amount of dope? Two million dollars? Where was the money?

Working with the head FBI agent on the case, federal prosecutors dangled plea deals, urging them to snitch on each other or on "bigger fish" in exchange for reduced charges and time. "You better come down here and take this ten years before it's off the table," the agent would say to Mike, at least initially. The feds offered the others plea deals, too, each offer contingent on their rolling on one another or others, sometimes on people they'd never even heard of. Mike laughed in disbelief when his attorney, Robert Udashen, informed him of the government's ten-year plea offer. "Ten years? For these lies? You've got to be kidding me. If it was a fair offer, I would take it. But come on, man, I ain't moved that type of weight. Hell no."

Unaware of the tremendous power and leeway federal agents and prosecutors wield in drug cases, everyone charged in the case assumed they were innocent unless proven guilty. And how could the prosecutors prove an amount of crack and cash that never existed? Convinced they were being railroaded and could beat the charges, Mike and the others made a joint decision. They would exercise their constitutional rights and go to trial.

FROM THE BEGINNING, the case was tainted with good old-fashioned Texas racism. All the women in the indictment were white, all the men Black. The same prejudice that influenced Mike's decision to leave college and led to the dissolution of De-Ann's family in Campbell was fully present in their interrogations from the beginning. Bonnie, whose father's friends had driven Mike out of Kilgore, and whom Mike had recently left for De-Ann, flipped for the prosecution, agreeing to testify to whatever they wanted.

From where she was sitting, De-Ann had a pretty decent understanding of the fed's approach with Bonnie. "Brittany, they were *mean*," she told me. "I've never been talked to that way in my life." From the first interrogation, two of the agents on the case went at De-Ann on the question of race. "You gonna go down for a nigger?" they jeered at her. When De-Ann was locked in county jail, the feds called her parents, who had disowned her as a teenager for dating Black guys; the parents drove up to the jail and used the same racist language to try to persuade her to testify against Mike, Wayland, and the rest of the guys. De-Ann wouldn't budge. But Bonnie, who was seven months pregnant at the time by her new boyfriend, did, as did Leslie and Linda, the other white women in the case. These three were richly rewarded for rolling on their friends and exes. All three pleaded guilty to the one charge of the indictment that didn't carry with it a mandatory minimum sentence—use of a communication device—and received no prison time, only three years probation.

During the trial, the feds played phone call after phone call of wiretapped conversations between Mike, De-Ann, Donel, and Terry. Jurors—the ones who were awake; a few dozed off early and often—listened to hours of tapes. Mike would call De-Ann and ask her to check on the status of a single kilo. She'd call Donel and ask about the same kilo. Donel would call Terry. Terry would call De-Ann to report back to Mike. By the time the round of calls was over, the feds had turned a single kilo into five or six. They did this repeatedly. The number of kilos kept creeping up. De-Ann wanted to jump up in the middle of an agent's testimony and shout "That's a lie! We were talking about one kilo, the same single damn kilo, not five!" But the cruel paradox of the system was that no one on trial could say a thing without admitting culpability. They couldn't challenge the amount because to do so would admit to having dealt *some* amount.

In one call, De-Ann said, she'd called Motor Market Unlimited from a burger joint. "What y'all want?" she asked, taking their orders. "A quarter pounder? Fries or onion rings?"

"They're talking street code here," the agents testified. "Burger is code for kilo. That's a quarter kilo that Mr. Wilson just said he wanted."

De-Ann remembered looking at Donel in disbelief. Surely the

jury didn't buy this shit? But it was 1993. This was no jury of their peers. Why wouldn't this almost all-white jury from Dallas, Texas, one of the most segregated cities in the United States, believe federal officers from the United States government as they literally transformed beef patties into kilos of crack cocaine?

While I was researching the Wilson case, I came across an interesting story about Jennifer Bolen, one of the lead federal prosecutors in the case. Two years after the Wilson trial, in 1995, a federal court would sanction Bolen for gross prosecutorial misconduct in another drug case, concluding that "the record paints a picture of a prosecutor determined to obtain a guilty plea from the defendant, even if through improper means." That reckless aggressiveness sounded very consistent with the Bolen I was learning about through the Wilson trial transcripts. Unable to persuade any of them to cooperate, Bolen seemed determined to seek the stiffest punishments possible. From the beginning, she wanted life sentences: for Mike and, when she refused time and time again to flip as the rest of the white women on the case had, for De-Ann.

In addition to the creative mathematics the feds played with the phone calls, the prosecution claimed that they'd found ledgers with drug amounts written on them in the possession of both De-Ann and Donel. De-Ann's was a half-filled-in computer spreadsheet, listing "18 out" at the bottom. An agent testified that this was hard evidence that 18 kilos of crack had been moved by the conspiracy. The "ledger" they attributed to Donel was even more dubious. In a drawer in his kitchen they'd found a piece of paper with handwritten lines on it, much like a spades scorecard. Each line, they argued, was a kilo of cocaine. The eight rows meant that Donel was directing "eight to ten" street dealers to move the kilos indicated by his in-pencil line markings. At trial, an IRS special agent stated during cross-examination by Wayland's defense attorney that these records were not sufficient to be used as a basis for making a correct computation of the drug quantity or dollar amount. But his expert testimony didn't seem to matter to the judge. To determine the quantity of crack the members of the conspiracy would be held accountable of selling, the "expert" presented by the government—one of the agents originally assigned to the case—took the exaggerated numbers from the three weeks of intercepted phone calls, the numbers indicated on De-Ann's spreadsheet, and Donel's kitchen drawer "ledger" and added them up. They even multiplied some of the numbers by the number of weeks they alleged the conspiracy went on. Over a ten-month period, the prosecution argued, Mike, Donel, Terry, De-Ann, and Wayland had sold over fifty kilograms of crack cocaine. More than enough to trigger fundamental death sentences.

"Brittany, I just couldn't believe it," De-Ann said as we sat in my apartment one day not long after our first call. "I was numb. First off, they gave us the sentences in months. Wayland, four hundred and forty-four. Donel, four twenty. Terry, three forty-eight. We just sat there trying to do the math in our heads. One by one it would be like—*Oh my fucking God that means thirty-five years in prison?* And then it came to me. *Life,* the judge said. *Life!* And for Mike, too. I mean, shit, they were all so long, they might as well have all been life sentences. The whole time I just thought, *This cannot be happening.*"

For a first-time drug offense built on a questionable case, every single one of my new clients had been handed a sentence longer than the number of years they had been alive.

THE EXTREME DIVERGENCE in the work that filled every waking moment of my life was leading to an almost surreal double consciousness. On the one hand, I continued to excel at Winstead, working on deals that were all-consuming—that is, until I got home and immersed myself in federal drug law and appellant processes, my emails from Sharanda, or potentially relevant articles or cases sent to me by Wayland, who really was a hell of a jailhouse lawyer. I hadn't lost sight of my career path, which continued to develop as I got to see more women like Melissa Stewart in action. I had set a new goal for myself: to make partner.

Black lawyers make up less than two percent of partners in big law firms. Winstead was no exception. In fact, their numbers were even worse: zero. Perhaps sensing my intention from my drive at work, two women partners took me under their wings. Emeline Yang and Jennifer Knapek had both been at the firm for nearly twenty years. They personally coached me as I assumed more first-chair roles on deals, helping shape my confidence to take charge of negotiations, positioning me for advancement. With the help of these generous and passionate women who were determined to reach back and help younger women lawyers like myself climb the ranks, I set my sights on navigating the eight-year partnership track.

The sky was the limit. At least that's how it felt to me. But I was also keenly aware that for my clients there was no sky, only the water-stained, concrete ceiling of their prison cells. The weight of their sentences was like a chain I carried with me, out of view, under my growing collection of business suits. It was with me all the time. Until they were free, I would not truly be, either. No matter how intense the demands of corporate life, I had to push forward, to find the key to unlock these human cages. There was no turning back now.

And maybe, just maybe, the same call that had connected me to the Wilsons would be the key I needed. What I had already learned about the criminal justice system had shown that even a lawyer with deep experience would need a miracle in order to obtain relief in the courts. I had chipped away at Keyon's sentence, but we needed a fast track—the same one that De-Ann had taken. I started to wonder, if De-Ann could get clemency, why couldn't Mike, or Donel? Or Sharanda? I remembered the surge of hope I felt on President Obama's inauguration day, that sense that anything was possible. Could the first Black president of the United States be our saving grace? I could work the courts, sure. But increasingly I was thinking about a new strategy: going straight to the commander in chief.

Chapter 10

GIRLS EMBRACING MOTHERS

The ACLU calls Carswell Federal Medical Center a "hospital of horrors"—and for good reason. Women are sent there with diagnoses requiring urgent medical care and then are routinely denied treatment. Prescriptions are thrown out upon arrival until new tests can be ordered—tests that are often put off for months, at which point the woman's health has declined to the point of no return. Carswell is the only medical facility for women in federal prison, but from the beginning it was obvious the prison hospital was ill-equipped to handle a situation as severe as Genice Stribling's.

Within days of her arrival, the untrained prison aides assigned to help Genice rolled her out of bed incorrectly and broke her ankle. A day later, her toe. They put her in a full-body lift-sling and hoisted her high in the air onto a cot, but didn't fasten the sling correctly; Genice fell out and broke her tailbone. Prison doctors deemed treatment unnecessary, as Genice "couldn't feel it anyway." Her body swelled so severely they kept her in a compression brace for twenty-four hours a day, rushing her to an outside hospital only when the swelling compromised her internal organs. When she was released back to Carswell, medical staff refused to use Genice's method to move her bowels despite their method not working. Utterly dependent on her caregivers, Genice went for weeks without a bowel movement.

"Ms. Stribling," the prison doctor who oversaw her first traumatic months at Carswell leaned over and whispered in her ear, "we cannot care for you here. File the compassionate release paperwork and I'll recommend you for home confinement." But when Genice's attorney reached out to him for the recommendation, something had changed. The doctor just shook his head. "I'm sorry, I can't do it," he said, and refused to comment further. Another doctor quit after three weeks on Genice's unit after unsuccessfully arguing that they couldn't possibly meet her needs. "Nothing they're doing at that prison is ethical," she told a family member later.

Carswell's reputation extended well beyond its walls. "I took an oath. Just being in that place betrayed it," Kathleen Rumpf of the Catholic Workers Association lamented. "I have never seen anything like the corruption and cruelty at Carswell Women's Prison Hospital." A former medical officer at Carswell, Dr. Roger Guthrie, even filed a formal complaint with the U.S. Office of Special Counsel in which he detailed substandard care, medical mistakes, and delays in treatment leading to numerous cases of prisoner death and endangerment. He documented repeated incidences of falsified medical records and documents, the rape and sexual abuse of women prisoners, and misappropriation of funds intended to provide medical care for incarcerated women.

Even the media had found their way to the story. "If I have to stay in here," Genice told one reporter investigating prison hospital conditions, "I'll probably end up dead."

None of this made it any easier for Sharanda, who was halfway across the country from her family, serving her sentence 850 miles away in Tallahassee, Florida. Weasel, housed at Carswell's low-security camp across the street from the medical center, heard of

Genice's dire condition through the prison grapevine and updated her sister through letters. Caring for Genice had been one of the defining responsibilities of Sharanda's life, and even a life sentence wouldn't change that. Still numb from the shock of her sentencing, only one thing made sense to Sharanda: She had to get to Genice.

Sharanda spent her first year in federal prison desperately writing letters on her mother's behalf. From her concrete cell in Tallahassee, she wrote to the warden at Carswell, to Judge Solis, to journalists, to the ACLU. She sent lengthy instructions to the medical staff at Carswell, explaining how to turn her mother without causing damage, how to move her bowels, the therapy exercises required to keep her blood from clotting. She endured the cruel taunts of the guards as she petitioned the prison administration for a transfer to Carswell to be nearer to Genice. "Keep on writing, Jones," they told her. "You ain't never seeing Texas or your mama again."

When she wasn't advocating for Genice, Sharanda studied in the law library, where she slowly learned that the judge had handed her a virtual death sentence. In the federal system, life was life. All Sharanda could do was live in the present and pray. Every day, she spoke to Clenesha on the phone for ten minutes, trying to keep from screaming in grief as she listened to her nine-year-old recounting schoolday adventures. Back in her cell, she focused on getting her mother the care she'd helped provide since she was four years old.

She'd been inside for almost a year when the news came. "Jones, pack out," a guard said. "I don't know how in the hell, but you're going to Texas. Maybe now you can stop writing those damn letters."

The following day, Sharanda was chained, black-boxed, and transported in the same animal conditions she'd experienced when she first pulled chain. Only this time, she sat tall all the way, despite the digging metal of the black box, the chafing chains around her wrists, ankles, and waist. In the hell of the past year, even this dreadful passage counted as a small victory. Sharanda Jones was on her way to Carswell Federal Medical Center to be reunited with her mother.

IT WAS ALMOST too late. Sharanda arrived at Carswell on a cold night in 2001 to find her mother in alarming condition. Genice's face was discolored, her legs obscenely bloated despite her severe weight loss, her skin covered in a sheen of cold sweat. Well aware that complaining would get her nowhere but solitary, Sharanda began to nurse her mother back to health. This required every bit of ingenuity she could muster. Genice was on the fourth floor of the main hospital building, reserved for those with chronic conditions, so Sharanda got a job in cosmetology on the first. She took a second job in the laundry, located in the basement of the same building, so she could deliver sheets to Genice's floor. She made sure she was in charge of hair in that unit, too. In between work-sanctioned visits she would sneak up to Genice's bedside, timing her elevator rides to miss patrolling guards. Orderlies admired her devotion and turned a blind eye.

Under Sharanda's care, Genice's swelling went down, her sweats eased, and she gained color in her cheeks through a nutrition plan Sharanda concocted with what she could scrap together in the prison commissary and carefully monitored. Within a few months, Genice could make it outside the unit in a motorized wheelchair, where she met Sharanda on the yard and spent a recreational hour breathing in the fresh air, the sun on her face. If they went to the right place on the yard, they could even wave through the chain-link fence to Weasel, who was winding down her eight years at the low-security camp.

Despite Sharanda's growing realization that the attorneys she and her family continued to pour money into were not going to help her, she found reserves of courage and strength within herself that she didn't know she had. Committed to her mother's care, she made a pledge. "God is not going let you stay like this forever," Sharanda told herself. "But you are here right now. You can't live for the outside. You've got to be fully present. You've got to live here. In this moment. In this place."

With that commitment, Sharanda endured, even as Weasel was eventually released and it was just her and Genice. When I came to Sharanda a few years later, inexperienced and naïvely optimistic, she had nothing left to lose.

"And besides," she said, "I believed in you."

OVER THE NEXT several years, as I graduated from law school and threw myself into my corporate career, I visited Sharanda whenever I could. We hardly talked about her case on these visits. Unlike at Texas state prisons, where visiting sessions were a strict two hours, Saturdays with Sharanda could stretch all day. I got to know many of the women of Carswell and their stories through Sharanda. There were other lifers at Carswell, a few, like her friend Alice Johnson, also in for drug charges. In addition to those with medical needs, Carswell also housed women in maximum security, and some on death row. Sometimes Sharanda would point out women in the visiting room convicted of the most gruesome crimes—aggravated child abuse, kidnappings, murder. Most of them had a release date. Sharanda Jones did not.

The characters who peopled the visiting room were colorful, to say the least, their stories eye-opening and intriguing. There was the wonderfully personable Chyann Bratcher, who took our photo each time I visited; I'd been puzzled as to why I recognized Chyann, but Sharanda reminded me that she'd been featured on the TV show *Snapped* for allegedly conspiring with her mother to kill her husband and split the life insurance proceeds. Sure enough, I'd seen the episode. Chyann was beloved in the visiting room for the kind and careful way she helped children and family members prepare for the prison photos that the incarcerated women cherished so much, photos that said "I'm still here! I'm alive, I exist, I am loved!" She treated every family as though they had paid for a professional photo shoot. They *had* paid, of course—the prison charged the women for everything—but everyone respected and appreciated her careful diligence.

One paraplegic woman spent every visiting session passionately making out with her boyfriend when the guards weren't looking. The public displays were a bit much, but in prison privacy is not an option, and we all tolerated it good-naturedly enough. Their story was certainly dramatic, at least according to the other women in prison—she'd been shot by her husband after being caught in bed with this same lover and been paralyzed for life. Twenty years later, these two still couldn't keep their hands off each other. "That woman can write with her teeth!" Sharanda told me. "Perfect penmanship. Pristine!"

There were also more difficult stories. During one visit Sharanda asked me to help advocate for a few women whose horror stories of medical malpractice seemed almost beyond belief. "Ashly is so young, Brittany. There's no reason for her cancer to have gotten this far. She is so talented, sings like an angel, but they've put her through hell. And all for nothing! She got a mandatory minimum ten-year sentence for meth. There must be some kind of way to get her compassionate release or something. And she's not the only one."

It was just like Sharanda, facing a living death sentence herself, to advocate for the women with whom she'd formed family bonds. Her empathy and urgency inspired me, as always. I corresponded with some of these women in order to share their stories with Mary Price, General Counsel of Families Against Mandatory Minimums, who I knew was interested in compassionate release cases. Ashly wrote me a letter detailing her ordeal so that I could advocate for her, but when I received the envelope, it was empty, its contents censored, confiscated by Carswell officials. We finally connected via Corrlinks and her story broke my heart. At thirty, Ashly was only a few years older than me, but due to medical malpractice and negligence while incarcerated, she'd already had both breasts removed, would be unable to bear children, and would endure chemo for the rest of her short life. Diagnosed with Stage 4 breast cancer long after it was too late, her already draconian ten-year mandatory minimum sentence for drug possession had become a death sentence.

Another woman I corresponded with had been admitted to Carswell pregnant with twins. Locked in a cell without medical care for several hours, she began bleeding profusely. The guard on duty refused to take her to medical for another forty minutes despite having her pregnancy papers in hand, and when he finally did, he ordered her to take the stairs instead of the elevator. The distressed woman hemorrhaged at the top of the prison stairwell and was rushed to the outside hospital, where she spent the next three days before being readmitted to the prison hospital with explicit and detailed instructions for the care of her high-risk pregnancy. What followed is almost too gruesome to recount here. Doctors failed to inform her when she lost the first twin, then left the dead fetus and a metal clamp on her umbilical cord inside her for three days. Weeks later she lost the second baby. Parts of her placenta and a piece of the umbilical cord were left inside her for weeks, leading to infection. When the woman later filed for early release, citing the physical and emotional trauma of losing her twins due to medical malpractice, the attorney representing the prison warden argued that her motion was "frivolous."

The stories of these women and their resilience and dignity in the face of unimaginable suffering moved me deeply. Through visits and emails, Sharanda regaled me with lively stories of her life on the inside—horribly repressive, controlled, often heartbreaking, to be sure, but also filled with the complexities of living, the humor and pleasure and joy of it. Despite trials and tribulations, the women behind the razor wire did what they could to maintain their humanity in the face of an institution that so often seemed designed to strip them of it.

———

PRISON IS TORTURE, but for those with long-term sentences, it is also home. Throughout her incarceration, Sharanda devoted herself to making her present as full as it could be. From the beginning, she was determined not to be a burden on anyone on the outside, and at any rate it had always been Sharanda who looked out for everyone else. With the exception of the meager income incarcerated men and women make doing prison labor—for Sharanda just twelve to eighteen cents an hour for her jobs in laundry and cosmetology—most are dependent upon their families and friends outside for support.

Almost everything in prison, including food, has to be purchased through the prison commissary. Nutrition in Carswell prison had become notoriously poor, and women depended upon items from the commissary to supplement their diets and help ease the psychological burdens of imprisonment. Both to keep her mind busy and to make commissary money, Sharanda threw herself into what had given her such pleasure as a child and through high school—crafting. She knitted quilts, hats, and wall hangings, perfected cross-stitch. She purchased yarn and thread from the commissary and designed elaborate greeting cards, first for friends and family, and then to order on the prison's black market. Sharanda dyed yarn with coffee grounds to match skin color, and worked from photos provided to her by other women so that the portraits she stitched on the cards resembled as closely as possible the recipient and her loved ones. Her artwork took her hours and served as a form of meditation, allowing her to escape the closeness of the walls, the daily indignities of sharing a tiny box of a room with first one, then three other women as the years of her incarceration stretched on and prisons became more and more overcrowded. Sharanda sent me a card for every occasion, meticulously designed and constructed, as polished and pretty as any card purchased from a gift shop. I kept them all.

When she wasn't crafting, Sharanda was cooking. Prison cuisine is an intricate process, and to earn a reputation as the best

Carswell cook, as Sharanda soon did, is no small feat. The ingenuity it takes to make anything edible—let alone a delicacy—out of the junk food sold at the commissary with the rudimentary appliances available cannot be overstated. After Carswell took away all but a single shared microwave for several units, Sharanda constructed her own makeshift crockpot of sorts using a thermal cup and plastic bags. With this, you could cook any number of items simultaneously by mixing ingredients in the plastic bags, tying them tight, and dropping them in. In a pinch, a hot iron worked wonders as a grill. The real magic was figuring out how to break down processed foods in order to transform the ingredients. Sharanda ground corn chips into meal for her famous tamales, melted the insides of Oreos and used juice mix to make frosting; she broke down cookies to make a crust for a creamy cheesecake, made the filling with vanilla pudding, coffee creamer, and lemon juice, using ice in mini trash bags as a makeshift freezer. She whipped up a hell of a cranberry sauce from assorted jelly packets, and her meatballs had women lined up around the corner. Her chicken and dressing were famous, as was her gumbo.

"But how do you do it?" the women asked. "Please give me the recipe!" Sharanda was generous with her food but not her culinary secrets—those she shared not even with her mother, the only woman in that whole prison of eighteen hundred who Sharanda believed could outcook her. From her bedside, Genice had taught young Sharanda to cook elaborate meals as a child. Now, the two had a friendly competition going; Genice found someone on her floor to mix her ingredients for her. In this place where nothing was under your control, where there was zero privacy, and every small humiliation was on public display for the whole prison population to whisper about, it was important to hold on to some best thing, some private joy, for yourself. Sharanda's renowned recipes were hers alone.

For the most part, Sharanda cooked for pleasure, but daily, women knocked on her cell door asking to buy her food. When unending requests for her tamales inspired her to put them on sale (one tamale for a dollar's worth of stamps), she had three hundred orders by the end of the day. She hired two women she trusted to help her, one to mix, one to work the microwave. Sharanda assembled the ingredients and folded the tamales. She was two hundred down when another woman came over to her and whispered, "That officer said you better send him some tamales."

Sharanda froze.

"It's legit," the woman said. "He's hungry."

Sharanda laughed. "You better tell the officer to send over some tamale money!"

Sharanda never believed she would die in prison. She couldn't. To do so would be to succumb to a hopelessness and despair from which she might never emerge. Instead she threw herself into the everyday things that brought her joy and a sense of meaning—her card making, her culinary creations, caring for and mentoring other women on the unit. She taught cosmetology, did hair in the prison salon for women in maximum security or in the cells of those on hospice care. She dedicated herself to personal growth and development. As a "lifer," she was automatically dropped to the bottom of the list for prison classes and programs. Still, she signed up, and when finally admitted, took full advantage. A five-month office technician program, a keyboarding and data entry course, banking courses. Determined to prevent the younger generation from following in her footsteps, Sharanda joined the prison's SHARE Program, aimed at deterring at-risk teenage girls from a life of crime. She completed a comprehensive eighteen-month faith-based program called Life Connection, in which she participated in activities to help bring reconciliation to the community.

Women often succumbed to terrible depression in prison. The Carswell Admission and Orientation Handbook warns incoming women of this on page one, and includes instructions for what to do if they or a cellmate becomes suicidal. On any given day in any unit, several women would be on suicide watch. Often, prison staff asked Sharanda to mentor women who were having the hardest time adjusting to life inside. Sharanda nurtured and coached them, cajoled them to bathe and eat, did their hair, mentored them in their jobs so they wouldn't find themselves in further trouble and into the dark hell of solitary confinement. Her quick smile and positivity eased the burden of incarceration for many. Staff and prisoners alike adored her.

In the spring of 2012, as Sharanda and Genice entered their twelfth year of incarceration together, I was trying in earnest to get Girls Embracing Mothers off the ground. My conviction of the importance of its mission had only grown since I first conceived of the program when applying to law school. Though Mama was out and doing well, Jazz and I still struggled with the emotional trauma of having had a parent in prison, and the growing realization of the unending punishments society inflicted on those, like Mama, who had already served their time.

Clenesha, Sharanda's daughter, nine at the time of her sentencing, was now a beautiful twenty-one-year-old with her mother's dimples and infectious smile. Over the years, she had become like a little sister to me, and I knew the pain her mother's incarceration caused. At lunch one day, Clenesha agonized over whether to attend Texas Southern University in Houston with her friends. "I can't leave my mom," she said. "I want to go, but if I stay in Dallas I'm only thirty minutes from my mom." Her decision process was so like the one Sharanda had made in her youth to stay close to Genice. It was a sacrifice I knew all too well.

I had established GEM as a nonprofit in law school, assembling a diverse group of incredible women for the board of directors. To get it off the ground I searched the websites of universities for social workers and criminologists—much as I had done to find Christa Brown-Sanford—and sent random emails to strangers who agreed to hear out my vision for GEM. With no grant money, I invested money from my Winstead salary to kick us off. I started where I was, with what I had, and walked forward. My mom couldn't wait to help out.

But we couldn't run GEM without the full cooperation of a prison. Although we planned from the beginning to support the girls in their outside lives as well, structured and enhanced visits between mothers and daughters inside the prison were at the very heart of our vision. I sent emails and called wardens at both the state and federal levels, hoping to find a location for our pilot program. One of my most enthusiastic responses was from Chaplain Robert Danage, a kind, devoted, and sincere man—who just happened to serve as head chaplain at Carswell. He organized a meeting for me and GEM board member Dr. Jaya Davis, a criminology professor at the University of Texas at Arlington, to meet various staff at Carswell to discuss the possibility of monthly visits for a small group of incarcerated mothers and their daughters.

I liked Chaplain Danage immediately. Round-cheeked and jovial, he had the enduring positivity required of a job as emotionally taxing as prison chaplain. He believed in redemption and sought every opportunity to aid the women in his care. He supported our vision wholeheartedly, and thanks to his enthusiasm, our meeting with Carswell staff went well. I was elated and excited for next steps. But then, as we were getting ready to leave, Chaplain Danage kindly offered to give Dr. Davis and me a tour of the prison grounds. This presented a problem for me: I hadn't told him or anyone else at the prison about my advocacy for Sharanda, or my visits. It wasn't the chaplain himself that concerned me; Chaplain Danage was the polar opposite of some of the cruel, power-hungry guards I encountered when I came to the prison as a visitor. His face lit up when he talked about the programs they offered, and the changes he'd implemented since coming on board. But I knew my relationship with Sharanda might count against the program with prison officials rather than speak to its need. Nervously, I agreed to the tour, saying nothing to Chaplain Danage and hoping I wouldn't run into Sharanda.

I'd been to Carswell so many times at that point, passed through the razor wire, stood in line with families outside the visiting room, been brusquely patted down by the guards, endured the humiliations of the security procedures with a mind to the far greater ones Sharanda was subject to on the other side of the steel doors. I went through metal detectors and got a patdown, but for every visit she was forced to strip naked in a line of other women in front of several guards, bend over, spread her legs and buttocks, lift her breasts, cough as many times as ordered to ensure she'd hidden nothing on her person, and passively endure whatever verbal abuse or taunts were thrown her way by the guards or risk being sent back to her cell. She blanked it out, she said, and anyway it was worth it for the pleasure of an outside visit, the hours we spent catching up and laughing, in our own little world—away, for a few hours at least, from Carswell. Visits were the incarcerated women's greatest nourishment, a balm to the wounds inflicted by the daily indignities of prison existence, the promise of light that made the darkest moments bearable. My understanding of this had led me to found GEM in the first place. Now Chaplain Danage politely pointed out corners of the prison whose inner workings I already knew about in great detail from Sharanda.

For the most part, the Carswell women were allowed to move freely. After the years visiting my mom in state penitentiaries, where she and the other women walked single file along a yellow line painted on the ground, hands behind their backs, it was odd to see the women walking casually or sitting on benches in groups after a long day at their various jobs. I knew the horrors Carswell held, but at this hour the women seemed almost relaxed, talking freely, greeting Chaplain Danage as we strolled by. He called many women by name, pausing in his description of the history of the prison, which had once been a military hospital, the cells hospital rooms.

"We have to stop by the multipurpose building," he said. "The women there are hard at work on their Easter production. You can meet some of them." I was totally unprepared for the scene that I encountered when Chaplain Danage opened the door to the building. A hurricane of activity filled the room. In one corner, artists bent over cardboard and banner paper, drawing and painting elaborate scenes from the Bible. Across the room a pair of women intently discussed how to best stabilize three huge wooden crosses so that they could stand on their own.

Then, a loud clap.

"Quiet!"

When I turned, I saw a regal-looking woman with perfect posture, her hands still raised. With total command, she had brought the entire room to attention. Next to her, a timid-looking white woman was standing as if frozen to her spot. "I don't think I can do this," she said. "Maybe you should give my part to someone else."

The face of the woman who had clapped quickly softened, and she began to speak encouragingly to the actor. "Yes, you can. This is *your* part. I know you can do it. Come on, shake it off and show them what you showed me at your audition."

Not a thing about this buzzing, industrious, and professional-looking production indicated that it was taking place in a prison—except the women's khaki and gray uniforms, and the guards leaning against the walls, paying scant attention to the bustle of activity around them.

"I want you to meet some of the women responsible for what you are seeing," Chaplain Danage said. He led us up the aisle where women swished white sheets in buckets filled with dyed water and seamstresses worked busily to complete costumes. In the midst of this organized chaos, a woman intently inspected finished work. As we approached, she turned around, startled at our interruption. It was Sharanda.

She looked shocked to see me, and behind the chaplain's back I pressed my finger to my lips.

"This is our costume director, Sharanda Jones," said the chaplain. "You should see what this woman can do with a pot of glitter and some coffee grounds!"

Little did he know I had samples of her handiwork on display all around my apartment. Sharanda shook my hand and flashed her dimples at me as though she had never seen me in her life.

"And this is Alice, our resident playwright!" Chaplain Danage said, waving over the woman who was putting the actors through their paces.

"She's our female Tyler Perry for real," Sharanda said, laughing.

"It's a team effort," Alice said, before rushing away to urge more emotion from a hapless actor, her rich voice echoing around the building. "This is a *pivotal moment*! You must draw us into your pain. Make us feel it! Come on, *bring it!*"

Alice Johnson, Sharanda Jones, and I would learn much more about team efforts in the years to follow.

WHEN FINALLY WE launched GEM it wasn't at Carswell but Gatesville, the very prison in which my mother and I had pressed our palms together through that hateful Plexiglas in a futile attempt to break the barrier with our bond. Carswell officials had found out I represented Sharanda and had delayed their decision on the program, citing a conflict of interest, just as I had feared. But Gatesville's warden, a woman with three daughters of her own, was sold immediately on my proposal. "Well, Mama," I joked as we unpacked the van in the prison parking lot, "you said you'd never come back here!"

"I sure did," she said. "Never thought I would. But to go in now through the front door with no shackles—and with GEM? It's a beautiful thing."

Punishment for those imprisoned in our system doesn't stop after they leave the prison gates. After her release, Mama quickly learned that in many ways her trials were only just beginning and that she still had a long, hard road ahead. All the while, she fought to overcome the challenges of recovering from addiction. She'd discovered the futility of filling out a rental application with a criminal record—her apartment was in my name. She had been hesitant to reapply for her nursing license, afraid of being rejected, afraid of learning once and for all that she would never practice nursing again, afraid of what that knowledge would do to her fragile recovery process. We filled out the forms together, and she was reinstated, and overjoyed to find a job nursing again, but after a year and a half on the job, paying for her own mandated drug tests once a month, the nursing board suddenly announced they were suspending her license until she was off parole. We fought their absurd decision, but my mother, having painstakingly built herself back up, was once again stripped to nothing.

Evelyn Fulbright never gave up. She appealed the nursing board's decision, gathering letters of support from every single one of her former employers, and spoke on her own behalf in front of the Texas Board of Nursing. Showing that same incredible grit and determination from when she was a young woman making a life for her girls back in Fulbright, my mother fought through the red tape and bureaucracy and got her license back again. And she didn't stop there. Facing addiction head-on, Mama became an intake nurse at a drug rehabilitation center, providing care and counseling to those taking their first steps to recovery, seeing them through the throes of detox.

That courage was on full display as she stood before the mothers and daughters at our first GEM workshop. To see my mother on that day, handing out art supplies to moms and daughters so they could participate in the activities, comforting a woman overcome with emotion after helping her daughter decorate a pillowcase with fabric markers so she could sleep with a piece of her mom every night, sharing her own experience coming to terms with the guilt of her addiction and incarceration with the other mothers—it was painfully beautiful.

I knew from firsthand experience that the suffering of children with parents in prison is unspeakable, and the threat of lasting damage from that trauma—emotional, social, personal—is very real. Through GEM, I wanted to create space for intergenerational healing for girls and their incarcerated mothers, one that could break the cycle and build the bond between mothers and daughters. I wanted to create programming that gave girls a chance to create a relationship with their mothers that could withstand incarceration while instilling in them the strength they needed to make wise choices in their mothers' absence. Above all else, I wanted to recognize the humanity of this marginalized part of society and work to empower young girls directly impacted by maternal incarceration to face adversity in a positive way. I wanted them to believe in their personal power to become leaders.

My mom and I made ham and turkey sandwiches for mothers and daughters to eat together and loaded the bus with supplies for guided art therapy sessions. We had a curriculum that stressed life skills and helped facilitate difficult conversations between the girls and their moms. The impact of these enhanced visits was immediate, the structured hours spent together transformative in the most powerful ways. The girls' guardians reported improved school performance and behavior between visits, and the moms couldn't stress enough how much hope and perseverance the chance to hold their daughters in their arms meant for their ability to keep their heads up inside.

Our four-hour structured visits were full of joy, but departures were difficult. Daughters and mothers clung to each other, reminded suddenly that their time together was finite, and the exception. My mom and I were often overcome with emotion, thrust back in time to our own experience, the afternoons when Jazz and I would get back in the car for our long and painful drive and Mama would head back to her cot, alone again until our next life-giving visit. But at GEM, my mother was a model of strength, supporting the other mothers through their goodbyes, taking a knee beside Ariel, a nine-year-old slumped over in despair after her mother had gone back to her cell. With remarkable skill and an empathy earned in the hardest way, she reminded us all that the pain of separation would soon be eased again by the loving embrace of our next visit.

GENICE'S BODY WAS breaking down. Sharanda could see it, plain as day. Midsentence, Genice would break into heavy sweats. Her usually animated face would contort with pain, and afterward her skin would remain ice cold for hours. For weeks, Sharanda pleaded with the guards to do more than check her blood pressure. Eventually, Genice's legs started swelling so much that doctors were forced to take her to John Peter Smith Hospital, where a new doctor began to investigate her symptoms more aggressively. She found metal clamps stitched into Genice's stomach, carelessly left there during a surgery she'd had in Terrell eighteen years before.

Genice was in the outside hospital for almost a month after the clamps were removed, and during that time Sharanda received no updates concerning her mother's health. She couldn't sleep from the worry and stress, and prayed continually for her mother's healing. She kept herself busy with work and helping Alice with her theatrical productions. On a crisp, clear day, Sharanda and Alice were sitting on the bench outside, scouting talent for the next play, when they spotted staff carrying a blanketed woman on a hospital gurney into the medical unit. Without even seeing who was on it, Sharanda screamed out, "That's my mama coming back in!"

And it was.

"I feel so much better," Genice told Sharanda when she snuck up to the fourth floor to see her. "I swear, I'm a new woman!"

Keeping her emotions at bay was critical for Sharanda's survival inside, but that day, she let herself feel them all, especially relief. The thought of facing life at Carswell without her mom— well, it wasn't a thought she could bear.

She would soon have to.

Chaplain Danage called Alice first, to be there when he broke the news to Sharanda. On December 19, 2012, after twelve years of incarceration with her daughter, Genice Stribling died of a staph infection that she'd been harboring since her surgery a month before. Overcome by grief, Alice collapsed on the floor. This was losing a family member. When Sharanda arrived at the chapel and saw her friend broken down crying, she knew immediately that her mother was gone.

Sharanda was devastated. Her time at Carswell had been devoted to her mother's care. What was life without her daily visits to her mother, without Genice's sharp wit, her loving humor, the model of joyful resilience she provided to those in her company?

The entire prison community mourned Genice's passing, even some of the guards. While Sharanda sought solace in her cell, her prison family worked behind the scenes to give Genice the honor and respect in death she had rarely been granted in prison. Alice took over the preparations for the memorial service, determined to make it as beautiful as possible. She decorated the display table in regal purple, gold, and silver, and Chaplain Danage allowed her to borrow an elaborate gold frame to hold a picture of Genice. Other women prepared and printed an obituary with photos of Sharanda's family in it. The prison anticipated such a large crowd for the service that officials authorized the use of the multipurpose building.

The choir sang as Sharanda and the processional entered the building. A volunteer pastor, who conducted services that Sharanda and her mother attended in prison, was allowed to deliver the eulogy—a first in Carswell's history. Alice and the praise dancers performed "I Can Only Imagine" as hundreds of women—more than Sharanda had ever seen at a memorial service—gathered together to pray, grieve, love, and comfort each other.

Prisons often grant furloughs so that incarcerated men and women can attend a parent's funeral outside the prison. Sharanda begged officials to allow her to say goodbye to her mother, but she was denied, her "lifer" status cited as the excuse. Sharanda's family videotaped the funeral and sent the tape to the prison for her to view. She saw her family grieving and finding comfort in one another as they laid Genice Stribling to rest. The only one missing was Sharanda.

Genice's death marked the beginning of the most difficult phase of Sharanda's incarceration. She broke down for the first time a few days later while working in the prison laundry and had to be guided back to her cell. Always social, always busy, now she lay still on her cot except for work hours, when she went through the motions in a numb silence. She'd never been a crier, not when Weasel was released, not after Clenesha visited, not even when she was sentenced to life. But now her eyes were slits, her face swollen from the tears. Alice visited her in her cell, helped her up, made her walk around a little in an effort to keep her busy, to lift her out of her grief, but it felt like swimming against the tide. Every day Sharanda spent in prison had been devoted to her mother's care. She'd structured her life around that purpose. In her mother's absence, the hope Sharanda had maintained against all odds faded fast. For the first time since I'd met her, she was unable to maintain her positivity.

"I miss my mom so much," she said on my next visit, looking crushed. "Now it's just me here. This is starting to hurt, Brittany." For Sharanda, that statement was tantamount to a scream for help. I knew I needed to act. There was no time to wait for more changes in the law, to hope legislators would see the light and put people over politics, to enact retroactivity so that Sharanda could be freed from her virtual death sentence. My friend was nearing the end of her incredible endurance. She needed out, and I was determined to get her out. Even if, as I'd told her the very first day we met, I had to go all the way to the White House to do it.

Chapter 11

PLEA FOR MERCY

"Clemency is where justice meets mercy," said Sam Sheldon. "And it's all about telling your client's story in a way that makes it impossible to ignore."

We'd been talking for over an hour, and my hand hurt from scribbling pages of notes on one of my legal pads. It was eleven o'clock at night. I'd left the office just two hours earlier, and exhaustion was bleeding into my penmanship. But what Sam had to say about clemency, I needed to hear.

After my last visit to Sharanda, when her grief was so palpable I could feel the weight of it, I'd called De-Ann. "There's nothing else to do," I said. "There are no avenues of relief left through the courts for Sharanda or the guys. I think we should look into clemency. I just have no clue where to begin. Do you think your former lawyer could help?"

De-Ann connected me immediately to Sam, who'd represented her when President Clinton granted her clemency in 2001. De-Ann was Sam's second clemency success, and my late-night calls and emails with him were becoming routine. He took me under his wing, selflessly and patiently guiding me through the clemency process over the phone and via email. I'd get home from Winstead, have a quick shower, eat some dinner, and read anything I could get my hands on about clemency, trying to understand every aspect of the process.

"The Constitution gives the president of the United States sole and unchecked power to grant clemency," Sam told me. The clemency power granted to the president is supposed to correct injustices that the ordinary criminal process seems unable or unwilling to consider. But the process itself was secretive and extremely subjective. The lack of transparency made it difficult to determine whether any set criteria were used to identify the most likely candidates. Bureaucratic hurdles made the process even more daunting: A petition filed with the Office of the Pardon Attorney has to make it through no fewer than four levels of review within the Department of Justice. If there is a favorable recommendation from the DOJ, the petition then goes to the Office of White House Counsel and hopefully from there to the president's desk. But DOJ has no obligation to provide reasons for denial of clemency or to reveal aspects of the decision-making process.

"The essential thing is the story," Sam explained. "How can you get your client's story to stand out? How can you move them with the narrative so they'll see the human side of it? You want to show tremendous rehabilitation efforts they've made in prison, plans upon reentry, support from family and the community. I always reach out to the judge and prosecutors to see if they've had a change of heart over the years. You should also show disparities in sentencing. But don't relitigate the case. You have to swallow every ounce of irregularities in the trial. The goal of the petition is to show they are deserving of mercy."

Show they are deserving of mercy. Sam's advice echoed in my head after our call. My clients had all been incarcerated under drug laws that had since been deemed unfair and unconstitutional by the very system that now asked them to prove themselves exceptional. That they were still standing, still psychologically and emotionally intact, after what they'd been through, seemed qualification enough. But I had to follow Sam's blueprint. This was our only hope.

"You remind me a lot of myself, Brittany," Sam said one night after an hour of hashing through the process on the phone. "A young corporate lawyer with a humble background trying to do right. Anything you need, don't hesitate to ask. Clemency is a long shot, but you can never make the shot you don't take."

In January 2013, when I began to seriously pursue clemency for my clients, the chances of its being granted were slim to none. Presidential clemencies had diminished greatly over the past twenty-five years. Scholars attributed the diminished role of clemency to a justice system that had become inhumane and politicized through a "tough on crime" agenda. Clemency petitions started to pile up, and the processing time increased from months to years.

There are two primary forms of clemency: A *full pardon* forgives the defendant and completely absolves the person of the crime. A *commutation* is a narrower grant of clemency used to simply reduce their prison sentence. I was seeking commutations for my clients. President Reagan had granted thirteen commutations, President George H. W. Bush only three. There was an uptick under President Clinton, who granted sixty-one commutations, including De-Ann's, but the number drastically declined under President George W. Bush, down to just eleven. President Obama had been vocal about the need for criminal justice reform in a way that raised hope and expectations for many, but to date his clemency record was the worst of any American president. To put it mildly, the odds were not in our favor.

And filing for clemency was an arduous process. While balancing the demands of firm life, there was no way I could submit petitions for all five of my clients at once. At the moment, I had the capacity to prepare and submit two petitions simultaneously.

Sharanda's, of course. And one additional client from the Wilson case. But which one?

There were no criteria available from the Department of Justice as to who would be the most likely candidate for clemency. Following Sam's initial advice, I needed to start with the person whose story would stand out in the hearts and minds of the government lawyers who would read the petition. It seemed sick to me that I had to cherry-pick. All of my clients were worthy of getting out. Still, I had to choose. The person should clearly accept responsibility for their actions, and to show, like Sharanda, that his time in prison had been used for self-improvement. While every single one of my clients continuously sought to better themselves, at least on paper the choice was obvious. Slowly, painstakingly, seeking guidance every which way and writing each word with utter conviction, I began to prepare clemency petitions for Sharanda Purlette Jones and Donel Marcus Clark.

"Hey Donel, get over here and help me unload the meat truck."

Donel bit his lip in frustration. It was the fourth "Come help me" order of the morning, which almost always meant "Do it yourself." Meanwhile, his own department, frozen foods, once manned by a team of four workers led by himself and now by himself alone, suffered. He hadn't gotten to a single task in his own department all morning, though he'd been working since five. He had stocked Kroger bread from ten-foot-tall bread trays, stacked the shelves with canned corn, and unloaded the dairy truck. His own to-do list was way behind.

Donel sighed. He couldn't afford to say anything. Not now, not with the new house and a mountain of bills. He noted his manager's latest request meticulously in his notepad and then went out back to start unloading. The meat department employees were on their lunch break, and he worked alone, lifting packaged slabs of beef from the truck onto a dolly, wheeling it over to the butcher section in the back, and stacking the beef in the freezer before returning to the truck. He figured he'd get at least his inventory done before going to lunch himself, but he hadn't even reached the shelves before Ray paged him on the intercom to assist at check-out.

If people took advantage it was because Donel was a get-it-done kind of guy, as by-the-book as they came. Always had been. Donel was just ten years old when his mother suffered a back injury that prevented her from keeping her job at the post office in Dallas. The government salary had helped her enroll Donel and his brother at St. Anthony's Catholic School in South Dallas, where he became friends with Mike and Wayland Wilson. But when his mom lost her job, Donel knew that paying for the school he loved would be an impossible burden for her. So he and his little brother met with their two older sisters and made a pact—as much as they loved St. Anthony's, they'd volunteer to go to public school to lighten her load.

Life still wasn't easy—their mother had entered into an abusive relationship, and their home life was fraught with the collateral damage of domestic violence. Even so, Donel and his mom and siblings attended church regularly and enjoyed a close-knit family bond. In an act of tremendous courage, his mom left her abusive husband, and things got better again for a while. But three years later, she lost a grueling battle with leukemia. She was only thirty-seven years old. Donel moved with his siblings into his grandmother's house on Malcolm X Boulevard, down the street from St. Anthony's, where he rejoined the Wilson brothers briefly for his eighth-grade year before returning to public school. Donel worked all through high school to help out his grandmother and siblings, and even then he built up enough credits to graduate early, in the class of 1982.

At Donel's graduation barbecue, his sister's husband gave him the closest thing to fatherly advice he'd ever had. A cold beer in one hand to toast his young brother-in-law's accomplishment, Ricky put an arm around Donel's shoulders. "You gotta get the good things in life, Donel," he said. "Get a job, get two jobs if you have to, meet a nice woman, get a house, raise a family. Those are the good things. Don't you forget it." That sounded about right to Donel.

He got a job at the Kroger grocery on Henderson and Ross, and a few years later took on a second job as a night manager at a liquor store in South Dallas. At twenty-four, he married the love of his life, Ceyita, and they soon had a son. Ceyita had a child from a previous relationship, and Donel proudly supported both kids, as well as his son with an ex-girlfriend. At twenty-five, he bought his young family a house. A homeowner with two jobs and a thriving, happy family, Donel Clark could not have been more on track.

For the first couple of years everything was fine. He'd been made frozen foods manager at Kroger and worked well for a while with the team of four under him. But little by little they cut back on his team until he was the entire department, and then called him away constantly to do extra work in other areas of the store. When his own department tasks didn't get done, the new manager, Ray, jammed him up about it. Tensions between the two of them rose steadily, and finally Donel filed a formal complaint. Word got back to Ray quickly and he put him on night shifts.

"I can't do night shifts, man," Donel said. "I got a second job. You know I can't leave it. I just bought a house."

"I don't give a shit about your other job," Ray said. "I care about this store. You're on the night shift starting next week."

Frustrated, Donel kept working his liquor store night shifts, refusing to show up at Kroger. Three weeks later, he was fired for abandoning his post.

Bills got tough to keep up with, and then behind. At the liquor store, he asked for more hours. "I can't afford it, man," the owner told Donel. "Things are real tight as it is."

When his old friend from St. Anthony's, Mike Wilson, came through one Friday night, buying cases of Miller Genuine Draft for a party on the lake, Donel saw the jet skis on a small trailer hitched to the back of his truck, the pretty Demi Moore–looking girl in the front seat, the bottles of champagne Mike grabbed at the last minute to add to his purchase, already several hundred dollars. It was like a solution had just pulled up in the parking lot.

"Mike," Donel said, "you gotta hook me up, man. I need some work. Let me come help you out. Just until I can get caught up."

Mike shook his head, smiled at Donel. "This life ain't for you," he said. "You're not cut out for this." A few weeks later, Donel saw Mike again, this time at the carwash. "You gotta let me work for you, Mike. The liquor store is closing. I'm gonna lose the house. Let me do something. Just till I get on my feet. If it's not you, I'm gonna have to work for somebody. I'd rather it be you."

Mike tried to deter his friend again, but Donel pleaded with him until he agreed. Mostly, Donel cooked, staying up all night, rocking up powder cocaine. He'd almost leveled up on his house payments after just a few short months. He was grateful to Mike for helping him out when he needed it most. Not many would take a chance on someone as green as him.

After a few months, Donel worried about getting too comfortable in the business. He knew he didn't want to get trapped in the game forever. He was up to date on his payments, no longer in danger of losing his house. Forever was short in the drug business, Donel knew that. And he was still a square, in truth. He went to see the union, hoping to get his job back at Kroger, bringing his meticulous records of all the times he'd been pulled away from his job, all the times he'd requested additional assistance and been denied. The union lawyer was blunt. "Man, if you'd brought this to us at the time, you would've had these guys over a barrel. But too much time has passed. It's policy. There's nothing we can do for you now."

When Donel looked into other supermarket jobs, the pay rate wasn't even half of what he'd been making at Kroger, let alone his weekly earnings working for Mike. He still owed the hospital for bills incurred during his son's birth. He had three dependents, and house payments that would be a lot easier to fall behind on than they had been to catch up. And Mike had just doubled his salary to a thousand dollars a week, three times more than he'd been making at Kroger. So Donel kept cooking.

For Donel, as for all of my clients, an error of judgment turned into a virtual death sentence. He and Mike and the rest of the crew were picked up two years later, in May 1992. Mandatory minimums, conspiracy laws, ghost dope, and ruthless prosecution by the federal government sealed his fate.

I decided to pay Donel a visit. Previously, I'd communicated with him, Mike, Wayland, and Terry through Corrlinks email and phone calls. With De-Ann's help, I had gotten to know them each as individuals this way. Now I wanted to meet Donel to discuss strategy with him in person. Donel was always thoughtful in our phone calls and email exchanges, always impressing me with his incredible memory for nuance and detail, but it was important to me to meet my clients face-to-face. How could I make certain that the Office of the Pardon Attorney and the Department of Justice understood Donel as a whole, unique person if I didn't truly know him that way?

There was another reason, too. Donel had essentially put his life in my hands, ignoring my relative youth and inexperience, and the fact that I wasn't even a criminal lawyer. In truth, I had no idea what I was doing in regard to clemency, and I suspected my clients knew that. I wanted to let him know that I would be putting my heart and soul into his petition, that I felt honored to be trusted in this way. And I wanted him to be able to look me in the eye when I told him so.

When I visited Donel at Seagoville Federal Correctional Institution just east of Dallas, he'd already served twenty years of his thirty-five-year sentence. My first impression of him was one of impeccable neatness. In his late forties, he entered the visiting room in his neatly pressed khaki prison uniform, his deeply waved hair cut low and clean, hairline razor-sharp. When he shook my hand, his eyes, set deep in his acorn-brown face, were as gentle and kind as his manner.

"Thank you for coming, Brittany," he said as he sat down across from me at the small table. "I'm not the greatest fan of lawyers, but in your first email to me, you signed off with 'And this too shall pass.' You just don't know what that simple sentence did for my morale. I thought—this woman is different." He spoke with confidence, his manner calm and collected, but I could still feel the weight of the past twenty years behind every word.

"This is a privilege," I said. "Thank you for trusting me."

Donel's face broke into a wide smile. He seemed so familiar to me, calm, avuncular. The rest of our meeting felt natural and relaxed.

"I need to be up front with you," I said, leaning forward over the table. "Clemency is a long shot. Maybe a really long shot. But we can never make the shot we don't take."

We talked about ways to make his clemency petition stand out. Following Sam's advice, I wanted to reach out to prosecutor Jennifer Bolen to see if she would write a letter supporting clemency. Donel winced at the mention of her name. "That's a bold move," he said. "That woman was relentless."

"I'm willing to do whatever it takes to get you free. I'm going to let her know about all the classes you've taken in here. And your disciplinary record is spotless." Donel had gone two decades without a single disciplinary infraction, an almost unheard-of feat in prison, where guards handed out infractions for any perceived act of insubordination, large or small.

"I just try to stay busy. Keep my head down and concentrate on my faith," he said. "Is she still at the U.S. Attorney's Office?"

"You won't believe this. She's not a prosecutor anymore. She works as a consultant for opioid pharmaceutical companies."

"So she's a drug dealer now." Donel leaned back in his folding chair and put his arms behind his head, eyebrows raised, before letting loose a deep, low chuckle.

As our visit came to a close, Donel and I discussed more casual topics—my corporate law career, the work he was doing editing a book for his cellmate, our families. He was still devotedly married to Ceyita. His sons were now adults with children of their own, but they still made the twenty-five-minute drive from Dallas to visit their dad as often as possible.

As I left the prison, I thought about how familiar Donel had seemed, how easily he could have been my dad or one of my uncles. His humble intelligence, his gentle manner and confidence—these were the antithesis of the endless negative images and messages about so-called drug dealers, about all Black men, really, that we're forced to consume daily. Donel refused to be defeated by his suffering. The same was true for all of my clients. Each of them might be trapped in the same heinous system, but every life was unique, valuable, singular. Every person had their own distinctive heartbeat.

MY OWN LIFE at this point couldn't have been more removed from the repressive and inhuman conditions under which my clients bore out their days. Winstead had recently relocated from downtown to their own building with stunning new offices: rich, dark wood floors, white leather Bauhaus chairs, conversation nooks accented with stunning art, and a sleek conference room with floor-to-ceiling views of the Dallas skyline.

By day I wore a power suit and heels, dined with partners, got high on the thrill of the deal. But at night I hunched over my laptop on my couch, surrounded by cardboard boxes stacked full with legal documents, and worked to put together clemency petitions for Sharanda and Donel.

First, I had to humanize their story, to be sure that decision makers would not be able to ignore the living, breathing person whose life was at stake behind the legal document before them. I had to construct briefs that pointed out all of the ways Donel and Sharanda would have been eligible for sentence reductions had changes in the law been made retroactive. I wrote lengthy reports on their rehabilitation efforts in prison and on the unlikelihood of recidivism. This meant ensuring they had jobs lined up upon their release, as well as letters of support from the community at large.

Sharanda used to joke that we were both "doing our time"—me at Winstead, and her in prison. In truth, the fast-paced and lucrative lifestyle of corporate law could make it very difficult to conceive of doing anything else. And there I was finding success. In 2013, one of my colleagues, Robert Ivey, a senior associate, nominated me for the prestigious Texas Outstanding Young Lawyer Award. Partners at the firm and even my clients themselves wrote letters on my behalf, praising my work ethic, my abilities, and my efforts in my clients' cases, my efforts to make a way out of no way. I felt humbled to receive so much praise. And yet I felt ashamed, too. Sharanda was still in prison. So were the rest of my clients. How good a lawyer could I be?

In the end it was my mom who helped me see the bigger picture. "These awards aren't even about you, Britt," she told me in her matter-of-fact way. "This is way bigger than you. Winning just gives you a bigger platform to share your clients' stories, to tell the truth about what's going on in the criminal justice system. And to shine the light on GEM, so you can get the resources those women and girls need. You need to take yourself out of it."

I knew Mama was right. Her words gave me the encouragement to push myself even further outside my comfort zone in an effort to garner support for Sharanda's and Donel's clemency petitions.

Through my almost daily contact with my clients' family members, I soon realized that they were desperate to help their loved ones in prison—they just didn't know how to. So part of my plan became figuring out ways to help activate them. Clenesha took charge of gathering letters of support for Sharanda, and Donel's sister Barbara led the efforts on his side. Soon we were flooded with loving, supportive, and deeply personal letters from friends, cousins, in-laws, uncles, aunts, sisters, brothers, former employers, sons, daughters, friends of sons and daughters—all of them pleading to President Obama to have mercy and grant clemency to Sharanda and Donel.

I reached out more formally, too, to the former judges and prosecutors on the cases, asking them to weigh in on the harsh sentences that, under new sentencing guidelines and laws, would no longer be mandatory if the cases were tried today. Sharanda's prosecutors and judge were nonresponsive, but to my great surprise, Jennifer Bolen did respond—and wrote a letter on Donel's behalf. "I always thought his sentence was too harsh based on the evidence of his involvement," she wrote. "But under mandatory minimums, our hands were tied." In some ways, Bolen's admission was twenty years too late. Still, I was extremely grateful for her letter, and for the time she took in order to help right that wrong.

I also sought public support. I sent emails to national and local news outlets, print media, late-night show hosts, and radio stations, outlining the details of Sharanda's case and asking them to devote some airtime or column inches to her story. No one bit. Clemency wasn't popular, and nobody seemed interested in my clients. I worked with Clenesha, who was notoriously shy but beginning to seek avenues to be a more vocal advocate for her mom. She wrote a beautiful letter that we used to start an online Change .org petition as a means of garnering more public support. Every signature we received was empowering. Each one represented another person who knew about Sharanda's case and was moved by it.

I reached out to my pastor at Friendship-West Baptist Church in Dallas, which had a congregation of over twelve thousand people. Pastor Frederick D. Haynes III had always been committed to community transformation and social consciousness. His sermons on social and economic justice always rejuvenated me. I was extremely grateful when Pastor Haynes invited me to speak during both services that following Sunday to raise awareness of my clients' cases.

On the Sunday of my speech, I sat in the third row between my mom and Clenesha and listened to Pastor Haynes introduce me to a packed audience, his voice booming through the far reaches of the megachurch. I made my way to the pulpit and looked out over the sea of black and brown faces before me. It felt so good to be able to address my own community, to be able to share stories I knew they would recognize, to speak truth to power in the halls of what has for centuries been the hearth and foundation of our fight for justice—the Black church.

Afterward, people lined up in the foyer to sign letters of support for Sharanda and Donel. I collected over a thousand signatures that day. We had begun to gather up our belongings when an older Black woman in an eggshell-blue suit and matching hat approached me, tapping my hand gently but insistently in a gesture I recognized from my own grandmother. She held her Bible in one hand and her purse over the crook of her arm. With her free hand, she pressed a trifolded twenty-dollar bill into my palm. She was a petite woman and must have been in her eighties, her walnut-brown face etched with time, but her smile conveyed a pride and strength that radiated through me. I politely declined the bill, but she wouldn't hear of it. She wanted to help. Saying no too many times to the tapping hand would be disrespectful, so finally I took the money.

"I promise I'll use this toward the petitions. Thank you so much."

"You keep doing what you're doing, young lady. We love you."

Moments like that kept me going. For every day like the one at Friendship-West, there were long stretches of time when nothing seemed to give. But then, in March 2013, an email I had written the year before to Michelle Alexander, the author of *The New Jim Crow,* asking her to take note of Sharanda's case, paid off for my clients in a huge way. Michelle put me in touch with Ezekiel Edwards from the ACLU, who passed on Sharanda's and Mike's stories to his colleague Jennifer Turner. Jennifer was preparing an extensive report on life without parole sentences for nonviolent offenses that would eventually be titled "A Living Death." The ACLU planned to distribute the report to members of Congress, state legislators, and journalists in an effort to reform state and federal sentencing laws. Jennifer reached out to me and I sent her detailed information on Sharanda's and Mike's cases.

To meet an ally as deeply committed and thoughtful about the work as Jennifer meant a great deal to me. Young, passionate, and super sharp, Jennifer shared my core belief that humanizing those lost to draconian drug sentencing laws was key to transforming the issue. Her final report was an incredible document that highlighted the injustice of life without parole sentences in a profound way.

When the report was published in November 2013, I was moved and delighted to see that Sharanda's was the second profile featured and Mike's came soon after. Sharanda had reached out to Jennifer herself to make sure her friend Alice Johnson's case was included as well, in what proved to be a tremendous turning point for Alice. The report contained beautiful portraits of incarcerated men and women within its pages, including a great picture of Mike and his sons from the late nineties, the boys and their half-brother hanging off their dad's strong arms, Mike's smile splitting the sky. Sharanda and Clenesha beamed from its pages. With the report's appearance, Mike's and Sharanda's and Alice's plight received a huge boost from one of the most renowned social justice organizations in the nation.

AFTER SEVERAL MONTHS of working on both Sharanda's and Donel's petitions, they were almost ready. Still, I'd been holding off on submitting them. I was hyperaware of my own inexperience, of how much I didn't know. I wanted to keep adding and adding to the petitions, wanted to make sure that anyone reading them would feel the outrage I did when confronted with these cases. To me, their stories were compelling enough. But I had always felt pressure to get one more signature, one more letter of support, to reword that sentence one more time. Now, finally, that feeling had eased. Sharanda's clemency petition was as polished as it could be, and I was waiting on just one more document for Donel, an updated progress report from the prison.

One night in mid-November, about a week after "A Living Death" was published, I checked the mailbox after a long day of work and found the report I had been waiting for. It was thorough and glowing, evidencing Donel's dedication to self-improvement since the day he had entered prison. As I paged through I felt the fierce urgency of freedom. I was going to get these clemency petitions finalized and filed. Tonight.

I hopped in my car and headed back to Winstead. Just as I reached the office, my colleague Robert texted me, telling me he was about to cook his first dinner at home in weeks. We had both been clocking long days and late nights at the office. "Back at work," I replied. "Donel's progress report came. I'm going to finish these petitions TONIGHT!"

"I'll be there in twenty," he texted back. And he was, with takeout dinner for us both. It meant so much to me that he came. He could have been home, but he stayed with me for several hours as I prepared the petitions for printing. I had been holding them close, typing every word with as much love and intention as I could muster, just as my dad taught me. That night, I stood in the doorway of Robert's office, which was next door to mine, and prepared to let them go.

"Okay," I said, "they're ready for you to proof." Robert was known for his meticulous editing, and even though I knew in my heart they were ready, I needed a second pair of eyes on them. "But Robert," I added. "Typos *only*."

In the morning, I had both petitions printed with laminated covers and spiral binding, so that they would stand out when received by the Office of the Pardon Attorney in D.C. I printed a second, unbound version in case they needed to make copies. With the lengthy memo, supporting exhibits, and all of the support letters I had gathered, the clemency petitions were over two hundred pages long.

At the last minute, I had gone back to my office to grab my wallet. In one of the pockets, still folded in thirds, was the twenty-dollar bill that the older woman had pressed into my hand that day at Pastor Haynes's church several months prior. I held it in my hand for a moment, remembering that woman's smile, the warmth of her touch, the pride in her voice as she insisted I take her offering. There's a proverb that says "I am because we are." At moments like these, I felt all the love and support of my community. I paid for the binding on Sharanda's and Donel's petitions with that folded twenty-dollar bill.

I was proud of those clemency petitions. The final copies looked professional and worthy of the Pardon Attorney's most intensive scrutiny. I had faith in their contents and faith in the integrity of President Barack Obama. In my heart, I knew that we could not fail.

Still, when my assistant, Deborah, proudly took those packages herself to the mailroom to send them to the White House, my believing heart was in my throat. The weight of what the packages would carry was immeasurable. Two lives, to be lived in freedom or buried alive behind razor wire and concrete. Out of my hands, and into those of the president of the United States. I shut the door to my office and tried to breathe. In and out. Just breathe.

All we could do now was wait.

A MONTH LATER, six days before Christmas, President Obama finally exercised his executive power and announced eight clemencies in time for the holidays. Neither Sharanda nor Donel was among them.

I had submitted the clemency petitions only a month before, but of course I was disappointed. Still, that Obama had granted any clemencies at all was progress. Even more hopeful, the clemencies were targeted—all eight people who received commutations had been sentenced by what Obama described in his announcement as "an unfair system," namely the 100-to-1 sentencing disparity between crack and powder cocaine offenses. While eight clemencies was a woefully small number in comparison to the twenty-three thousand people serving time in the federal system for crack cocaine convictions, it was better than nothing. Whatever criteria had been used to select what the media soon dubbed "the Obama Eight," both Sharanda and Donel met them.

"If they had been sentenced under the current law," President Obama said of his eight clemency recipients in a press conference he gave to mark the day, "many of them would have already served their time and paid their debt to society. Instead, because of a disparity in the law that is now recognized as unjust, they remain in prison, separated from their families and communities, at a cost of millions of taxpayer dollars a year."

To hear the president of the United States—*my* president—give voice to the same argument I had just used in Donel's and Sharanda's clemency petitions energized me. It helped to mitigate the disappointment I felt over my clients' being overlooked.

If the news hurt Sharanda, she didn't let on. Just over a year had passed since her mother's death, and her heartbreak seemed to be lifting. When I visited her after the announcement, she was brimming with her usual positivity. I was so relieved to see her almost back to her vibrant self, those dime-like dimples punctuating every smile. At the end of our visit she gave me a huge hug. "Merry Christmas, Brittany! This is our last one in here, I promise! I'm getting out!"

A guard standing near to us snorted in derision. "You been saying that forever, Jones," he sneered.

Sharanda gave me another squeeze. *"Haters,"* she whispered, before turning to be buzzed back inside, where I knew guards waited to strip-search and insult her. She flashed her beautiful smile at the sneering guard as she passed him. "I'm getting *out,*" she said over her shoulder to me, then disappeared behind the thick steel doors.

I kept my head up, too, following Sharanda's lead. But the guard was right. It had been almost four years since Sharanda had come into my life, almost four years since we'd been saying this together. And Sharanda had spent ten years in the hell of prison before I'd even come across her name. *Please,* I prayed on the way home from the prison. *Please let my clients be next.*

On April 23, 2014, the Obama administration announced the historic Clemency Initiative to restore vigor and integrity to the clemency process and a sense of fairness to the heart of the justice system. In particular, Obama and his administration had been concerned about people serving decades in prison who were convicted of drug crimes during the height of the "tough on crime" era and who would get shorter sentences if they committed the same crimes today. Congress had the opportunity to make the Fair Sentencing Act of 2010 retroactive but failed to do so. And as far as the Obama administration was concerned, people still serving time under the outdated law were in prison as an accident of history.

Under the new initiative, the Obama administration invited people in federal prison to submit clemency petitions if they met all of the following benchmarks: "They must be (1) serving a federal sentence in prison and, by operation of law, likely would have received a substantially lower sentence if convicted of the same offense today; (2) are non-violent, low-level offenders without significant ties to large-scale criminal organizations, gangs, or cartels; (3) have served at least 10 years of their sentence; (4) do not have a significant criminal history; (5) have demonstrated good conduct in prison; and (6) have no history of violence prior to or during their current term of imprisonment."

Federal prisoners were notified of the project, and more than twenty-five thousand responded by submitting surveys to begin the process. Clemency Project 2014 launched after the Obama administration asked the legal profession to provide pro bono assistance to people in prison who met the president's clemency criteria. Thousands of lawyers signed up to assist, including myself. Jennifer Turner, the author of the "A Living Death" report, was a member of Clemency Project 2014's founding working group, and she asked me to serve as a member of the screening committee. In this volunteer role, I performed extensive legal analysis of hundreds of federal cases to determine eligibility for clemency. I also trained and supervised the work of pro bono attorneys to help shepherd cases to the White House. After reviewing so many cases, I had a completely different understanding of the sheer magnitude of the problem. Reviewing hundreds of cases put everything into perspective.

I also immediately filed supplemental petitions for Sharanda and Donel through Clemency Project 2014, specifically highlighting that my clients easily met the criteria. For sure they would be in the next round of clemencies. I imagined that after launching his initiative with so much fanfare, Obama would go bold, granting hundreds at a time.

That summer, I took a big leap in my own career, moving on from Winstead to serve as assistant general counsel at ORIX Corporation's U.S. and Latin business hub in Dallas. ORIX, headquartered in Tokyo, was a leading international financial services firm with global reach. Typically, attorneys work at least five to seven years at a firm like Winstead to become an attractive candidate to transition to an in-house counsel job. I had just three years' experience when ORIX offered me a position in its legal department. I enjoyed my new job, though I can't say I worked any less. I loved having a longer-term, more interactive relationship with a client. I was able to understand the bigger picture to advise ORIX on not only the law but business strategy, and to see every legal opportunity or crisis, big or small, through to the very end. Working in-house was a great fit for my skill set, and professionally, I was challenged, stimulated, and happy.

But outside work, as I continued to review petitions and got deeper into volunteering with Clemency Project 2014, I was frustrated by the pace of Obama's commutations. Because there weren't any. As summer turned to fall, there was no news from the White House. It didn't make sense. Why announce a big project and then slow-roll the actual decision making? Why build up the hopes of so many people only to keep them on tenterhooks?

Then, on December 17, 2014, President Obama granted clemency to eight more people. While this was welcome news, it was crushing for my clients and for the hundreds I'd helped to screen who were not in that number. At the time, the U.S. Pardon Attorney's Office had received 15,646 petitions for commutation since 2009. In 2014 alone, the Pardon Attorney received 6,561 applications. Yet throughout Obama's time in office, a total of 6,596 petitions had been denied while only eighteen, including these eight, had been granted. It was underwhelming, to say the least, and my joy was restrained.

On the afternoon of the last day of March 2015, I was sitting in my office at ORIX reviewing a stock purchase agreement when my phone lit up with a number from the 202 area code: Washington, D.C. I had been expecting a call from Cynthia Roseberry, Clemency Project 2014's project manager, to discuss one of the cases I was screening, and I was looking forward to digging in with her.

"This is Brittany," I answered, but the voice in response wasn't Cynthia's.

"Is this Ms. Brittany Barnett, attorney of record for Donel Marcus Clark?" My breath caught in my throat. Had something happened to Donel?

"Ms. Barnett, this is Kira Horstmeyer. I'm an attorney with the Office of the Pardon Attorney. I'm calling to inform you that President Barack Obama has granted executive clemency to Mr. Clark. The prison term he is serving is now set to expire on July 28, 2015, leaving intact any original terms of supervised release imposed at sentencing."

My hands shook with excitement as I took notes from the call, careful not to miss any detail. "Oh my God! My God! Thank you!"

"You are welcome, Ms. Barnett, congratulations. We have pre-arranged a call with the prison for you to give Mr. Clark the news. Please contact Seagoville FCI at two o'clock P.M. and ask to be transferred to Mr. Clark's case manager, who will facilitate the call."

"Of course!" And then, in an instant, my mind went to Sharanda. "Before I let you go," I said quickly, "I filed another petition at the same time as Donel's. Do you have any information on Sharanda Purlette Jones?"

"Mr. Clark is the only client of yours I've been assigned. But if Ms. Jones has received clemency, you will be notified today."

"Look out for calls from Washington!" I yelled to Alicia, the legal department's executive assistant, who sat in a cubicle just outside my office. "Donel got clemency! Now we're just waiting on Sharanda's!"

News spread fast through the office and soon everyone was celebrating. Even though I'd been at ORIX for only nine months, they'd all borne witness to the hours I'd committed to this work, and everyone was pulling for my clients. Colleagues came by to congratulate me as I called the prison to share the news with Donel. He had no idea that his nightmare was over.

Finally, I heard Donel's voice on the line. Being summoned out of the blue for an emergency call usually meant bad news—a death in the family, a disaster—and the anxiety in his voice when he spoke was palpable.

"Brittany? What's going on?"

"Donel!" I couldn't contain my excitement. "You have just received clemency from President Obama. You're going home!"

A silence followed. It was so long I almost thought we'd lost the connection. Then I heard the deep exhale of a breath long held. When Donel spoke again it was between tears he couldn't hold back.

"Thank God! Thank you, Brittany! You never gave up. Man, it's been a long time coming. Is this real?"

"Yes, Donel," I said, crying with him. "It's real! You are going home!"

We spoke a few minutes more while the news sank in. Then Donel said, "And Sharanda? What about Sharanda? Is she going home, too?"

His question gave voice to the one thought restraining me from total joy. "We don't know yet!" I said quickly. "But they're still calling folks. Waiting!"

I promised Donel I'd call De-Ann to share the news, and then I hung up to let him contemplate his impending freedom and call his family. It wouldn't be immediate; he wouldn't just walk out that day. Unlike presidents before him, Obama had implemented a four-month waiting period before release, to aid the reentry process, during which Donel would have to spend several weeks in a halfway house before he'd truly be free. But after twenty-two years in the federal penitentiary, Donel was overcome with emotion.

For the rest of the afternoon I sat in my office, taking calls from Donel's friends and family, feeling their joy and relief over the phone, listening to their strong, stoic fronts give way to grateful, relieved sobs as the news took hold. After the initial rush had died down I just sat there, unable to focus on my work. In the quiet of my office, ignoring the buzz of conversations that drifted by the glass walls, I waited for that second call from Washington.

By five o'clock, I knew it wasn't coming. I packed up my stuff and left the office quietly, trying to avoid seeing anyone. I felt guilty at feeling anything other than rapture on this tremendous day. But heavy in my chest was the boulder-weight of failure, the life sentence Sharanda Jones continued to bear.

It wasn't yet seven when I crawled into bed at my apartment. I hadn't eaten. I stared at the ceiling, wrapped myself in disappointment, and drifted off to sleep. A few hours later, I was roused by a ping from my phone on the bedside table, and picked it up to find a familiar notification: a Corrlinks message from Sharanda.

"I saw the list," she wrote. "I'm so happy Donel got clemency! I know I'm next. We share the same lawyer. Smile. I love you."

Not for the last time, it seemed like my clients knew me better than I knew myself.

Chapter 12

STEPPERS KEEP STEPPIN'

Donel Clark was awfully quiet at lunch. Late-July sun shone through the floor-to-ceiling windows that looked out at the park greenery, reflecting beams of light off the restaurant's gleaming steel accents. Donel hadn't taken his eyes off the cypress trees outside since we'd sat down, even when the waiter brought him a steaming plate of fish and chips. We were at Savor gastropub in Dallas's Klyde Warren Park, celebrating his official release from federal custody earlier that day.

"Are you okay, Donel?" I asked. "What are you thinking about?"

He looked at me across the table and smiled. "Look, Brittany. Just look at those kids." I followed his gaze across the emerald lawn. In front of the food trucks lining the square, children of all ages splashed in the park's fountain and chased one another through the trees.

"Can you believe that, Brittany? That's freedom!" He looked back down at his plate, emotion washing across his handsome face. *"That's* freedom."

At six o'clock that morning, wearing a crisp white polo shirt, plaid shorts, and gleaming white sneakers, looking the clean-cut family man he'd always been, Donel had finally signed out of the halfway house where he'd spent three months, sleeping in a bunk bed in a dorm room shared with eighteen other men. The reality of the halfway house had been a shock. When his sister picked him up from the prison in Seagoville, Donel had thought he was stepping into a new life, one in which, after twenty-two years, he'd finally have control over his time and personal space, finally get to hold and see his loved ones. But the rules of the halfway house didn't allow for that. He could leave only to look for a job or go to church. He was subject to random drug tests and was not allowed a smartphone or other Internet access. Visiting hours in the halfway house were severely restricted. And when he went to job interviews or, later, to work, he had to report in every few hours from a landline, the halfway house version of a standing count in prison.

Worse, Donel was forced to cope with the culture shock and adjustment of life on the outside without his daily coping mechanism, running. Even in prison he'd been able to use the makeshift track, running three miles a day without fail, unless the unit was on lockdown. It kept his mind calm and his body healthy, he said, his emotions in check. At the halfway house, they wouldn't even give him permission to run around the block.

Now he was free. "Finally, I can run!" he'd said as we toasted his release with our glasses of iced tea and water. As of today he would no longer be subject to midnight dorm shakedowns and check-in telephone calls, though he still had four more years on supervised release, with restricted travel, random drug tests, and home searches. But at least he could run.

Donel looked out over the park again, a small smile playing at his lips. Regardless of the challenges, there was the pleasant breeze, the green of the leaves, the shouts and giggles of running children. "You know, Brittany," he said, "when I read the president's letter to me, I could hear every word in his voice. Just as clear as if he was standing in front of me."

President Obama had taken the time to personally write letters to clemency recipients. "Remember," he wrote to Donel, "that you have the capacity to make good choices. By doing so, you will affect not only your own life, but those closest to you. You will also influence, through your own example, the possibility that others in your circumstances get their own second chance in the future. I believe in your ability to prove the doubters wrong. So good luck and Godspeed."

Donel took that responsibility seriously, for himself and for those who, in his view, he had left behind.

"I feel horrible about Mike and Wayland," Donel said, struggling with the pepper grinder, shaking instead of grinding. "And Sharanda. I mean, man, at least I had a release date. I think about them all the time."

I reached over and gently showed Donel how to grind the pepper. He laughed in embarrassment. "It's things like this," he said, "that make me think, Does everybody know where I've been? Can they see it? I mean, *man*." He laughed, examining the pepper grinder. "I've never seen one of these in my life."

"I filed a sentence reduction motion for Mike in the courts," I said. "It's been a few months, so I hope we hear something soon. And I'm wrapping up a clemency petition for Wayland."

Donel looked relieved. "Thank God," he said. "It's not right for me to be out here and they're still in there. Mike tried to get me not to do it. 'This ain't for you,' he said, more than once. I begged him to let me come work for him."

Mike's motion had been on my mind a lot. I'd started on a clemency petition for him but had a hard time reaching him to get the details I needed to finish it. It wasn't his fault. Mike was housed at USP Victorville, a high-security federal penitentiary in Southern California notorious for the violence and mayhem that ruled the yard. Mike once told me, "You can lose your life or your sanity in this place any second." Frequently, I would hear nothing from him for weeks at a time when the entire prison went on lockdown after a fresh spate of killings or stabbings.

As that process crawled along, I continued to seek avenues for Mike through the courts. A year before, in July 2014, the U.S. Sentencing Commission voted to once again retroactively modify the federal sentencing guidelines, this time reducing the base offense level used to calculate all drug offenses by two points. It was a modest but, significantly, a *retroactive* change, and every day of freedom recovered mattered. Keyon qualified for another sentence reduction under the amended guidelines, and we chipped away at his sentence a bit more. But even with the new amendment, the drug quantity threshold was still a hurdle in Mike's case since the judge had held him accountable for more than fifty kilograms of crack.

When I dug back into his case files, though, I found inconsistencies that might lean in his favor. His presentence report held him accountable for over fifty kilograms of crack, but at one point during his sentencing hearing, the judge cited "over fifteen kilograms." When the quantity findings are ambiguous, courts typically go with the most conservative number, and based on the smaller quantity, Mike's new sentencing range under the amended guidelines was 292–365 months. I filed a motion arguing for him to be sentenced to the low end of the range, which would be time served. It was worth a shot.

There was also Mike's health to take into consideration. I pointed out in my motion that Mike was suffering the consequences of a severe left-side stroke. Doctor's orders for immediate speech therapy had been ignored for nine months after the stroke occurred in 2011, and as a result, Mike was unable to read, write, or speak with any degree of fluency. He had difficulty making phone calls, as his speech impediment was severe; his stammer worsened with frustration and stress, both fairly inevitable due to the presence of the guards and his difficulty in formulating his thoughts. Other men in prison helped him to write his emails. His prison-appointed speech therapist reported negligible progress. Mike needed an intensive program, as soon as possible, and he wasn't going to get it in prison.

While we waited for a decision from the court, I found myself in much closer contact with Mike's two sons, Mike Junior and Marc. Toddlers when Mike received his sentence, both boys were now in their midtwenties, as tall and handsome as their father. Like Donel, Mike had done everything he could to raise his sons from prison. Though his absence created a painful void in their lives, they still cherished him as a father figure.

One evening Mike's younger son, Marc, texted me and asked if he could come by to talk about the pending motion.

We been let down so many times by lawyers, he texted. *You just different. You bring us a lot of hope.*

A few days later he sat on my couch, all long legs and wide shoulders, eyebrows furrowed on his handsome twenty-five-year-old face. "De-Ann told me your mom was in prison, too."

"She was," I said. "Not nearly as long as your dad. But every day was like a year. I can't imagine what it's been like for you."

"I miss him. He was everything to us. We went from seeing him every single day before prison to once a month right after he went, and then nothing after they moved him to California. I've saved some money, and I'm thinking about going out there soon. I want my girlfriend, Nancy, to meet him. I mean, that's my dad, you know?"

I did. Marc looked at me. Beyond his tough exterior, his lean muscles and tattoos, I saw the child who'd waited at home to play catch with a father who never returned. He was trying hard to be strong. I thought about the burden he had to carry, and how little room there is in this world for young Black men to show any sign of vulnerability. It took courage to reach out and open up to me in this way.

"How long has it been since you've seen him?" I asked.

"Almost seven years," he said. His voice wavered just a little, a tiny crack in his confident demeanor that hinted at depths of grief beneath. "He always told us he was coming home, but as I got older, I just kind of stopped believing it."

"That's a long time," I said softly. "Go visit him, Marc. Your dad would be so happy to see you. And proud."

"It's been so long. It's hard, man. To see him like that, to not be able to take him with me when I leave. Do you think he'll ever get out? Do you really think he has a chance?"

I understood his hesitation, and his fears. In video interviews supplementing their "Living Death" report, the ACLU interviewed family members of those serving life without parole sentences. In one, a mother whose son had served twenty-two years for selling a ten-dollar crack rock looks bravely into the camera. "I know this is hard to say, but sometimes I think it would be easier if he had died. This is like a death sentence. But we don't get to bury him. If he had died, it would be easier."

It seemed to me that something similar was operating for Marc. He wanted desperately to see his dad. But he was afraid that a visit would dredge up the pain of his initial loss, prolong this endless goodbye, the endless mourning. A single visit was no balm for that kind of suffering. I thought suddenly about my drives down to Gatesville with Jazz to see our mom, cracking jokes with false bravado all the way there, our silence on the way home, Jazz driving and staring hard at the highway ahead like she wanted to strangle it, me sitting in the passenger seat with my face turned to the window so she couldn't see my tears. Then the drained exhaustion of the day after, the headaches. Mama was gone for two years. Mike had been away from his sons for twenty-two.

"There's a lawyer who I deeply admire," I said finally, "who has helped a lot of people society said were beyond redemption. Took cases all the way to the Supreme Court in order to change the law. His name is Bryan Stevenson. And what he says is that in order to get people free, you have to believe that you can. You have to believe in things you cannot see, with conviction in your heart."

Marc listened to me intently, searching my face for reassurance, a rekindling of hope. I could only offer my truth.

"He is right," I said. "And I do believe. I truly believe that your dad will be free. And I need you to believe it, too."

When he left my apartment, Marc seemed deep in thought. The next week he sent me a text.

Me and my girl bought plane tickets. I'll tell my dad you said what's up.

Marc and his girlfriend flew out to California to visit Mike in Victorville. Later, he told me the conviction he heard in my voice encouraged him to go. "Your belief helped me to believe," he said. "It gave me the courage to do what I'd been wanting and needing to do for years."

Still, it was a bittersweet visit. Sweet to see his beloved father in the flesh for the first time since he'd been transferred to California seven years earlier, both men hugging and crying, overcome with emotion. Bitter to see the state of his father's health—his speech painfully slow, movement and responses delayed. The last time Marc had seen his dad, Mike seemed unbreakable, could hold all three boys at once, lift them off the ground as they hung from his arms during the end-of-visit goodbye, fit all three in the breadth of his loving embrace. Now his speech was halting, and while his arms were still long like his sons' and his chest broad, he lacked the strength to squeeze Marc as he used to. "That stroke really messed him up, Brittany," Marc told me. "We've got to get him out of that place. He needs physical therapy and speech therapy. They're not even trying to help him in there."

As the reality of their father's health condition set in, so did the weight of the life sentence. With Mike's health in jeopardy, his sons were even more determined to see their father free.

A FEW MONTHS later, on September 16, the judge finally ruled on my motion. The court's order was short and to the point: "The defendant's previously imposed sentence of imprisonment of life is reduced to 365 months." I tried to quickly do the math in my head. Three hundred sixty-five months divided by twelve was a little over thirty years. Mike had already served more than twenty-two years, and now that he no longer had a life sentence, he was eligible for good time credit, which meant he had to serve only about 86 percent of his sentence. Factoring in his time served, Mike would be out in four years.

We'd given back his sentence of death by incarceration. Mike would no longer die behind prison walls. We'd won!

After leaving an urgent message for Mike at the prison, which was once again on lockdown, I called his mother. Now seventy years old, she was still living in South Dallas, serving as the strength and backbone for her grandchildren, silently grieving the separation for over two decades from her only two sons. She hadn't been able to visit Mike since 2008, when he had been transferred halfway across the country. When she heard that he would be coming home, she couldn't contain her emotion. "Thank you, God! Oh Lord, thank you!" she cried. "Brittany, you are an angel on this earth. You just don't know what you've done for this entire family. May God bless you, and abundantly so."

Marc was overjoyed, too. "Four years and he's out?" he repeated. "Are you serious, Brittany?"

"I'm so serious!" I said. "No more life sentence!"

"Man, this don't seem real," Marc said. "It's been so long without him that I just can't believe it." I could hear him holding in his tears and wanted so much to tell him to let it all go. His dad was coming home.

I couldn't wait for Mike to hold the sentence reduction order in his hands, to hear his voice on the phone when I gave him the news. His life sentence had been lifted. Soon he'd be free! Communication with the prison was slow as usual, and I had to leave a couple of messages. Finally, just when I thought I couldn't wait another second to give Mike the good news, he called me.

Instead of the joy I expected to hear, he sounded flat. Deflated. "You mean," he stammered painfully, barely getting the words out, "I'm not getting out?"

"You're getting out!" I said. "It's just four more years. We handed back that life sentence!"

I could hear how disappointed he was, hear the pain in his voice as I explained again that he'd earned the reduction but had still been sentenced to the high end of the guidelines. It became clear that in his mind he had connected a favorable ruling with immediate release. "This is great news, Mike!" I said. "You have a date. You're coming home! It's . . ."

"This is a call from a federal prison . . ."

"Thank you," he said. "Thank you so much." He would never say it, but his voice ached with disappointment. I felt the weight of the twenty-two years he had already served through the line. By the time we got off the phone he could barely summon a word, although he tried again to thank me. He wasn't elated, wasn't overcome with happiness. He was a man who'd already suffered far more than I could imagine, facing four more years of hard time.

After we hung up I sat in my office, slumped in my chair, staring at the phone in my hand. The adrenaline I'd felt when I first heard his voice had drained away. For a moment, I felt frustrated. To get someone off life through the courts was near impossible. This was a victory. Surely Mike could do four more years after what he'd been through.

But the longer I sat with it, the longer I realized how petulant that sounded. Who was I to say what four years meant to someone serving that time? I wasn't in a concrete cage. I wasn't separated from my family by thousands of miles and shackles. I didn't have to stand at four o'clock every afternoon so a guard could count me off like a piece of livestock. I thought again of the pain of my mother's incarceration. I tried to imagine multiplying that feeling by ten. And then adding two. It was an absurd exercise. Just as it had been absurd to imagine that four years in a hellhole like Victorville was something Mike could just "do."

I had no idea what to do next. No one else I asked seemed to have any ideas, either. Then I reached out to MiAngel Cody, a federal defender in Chicago I had met the year before at a FAMM event in D.C. celebrating Obama's first clemency recipients. She was a fellow Black woman lawyer at a conference where we were scarce, and something about her poise, confidence, and manner had drawn me to her in the way that you are drawn to someone who the universe intends for you to meet. MiAngel listened thoughtfully and said, "The only thing I can think of is to file a motion asking the judge to reconsider Mike's reduced sentence. Honestly, though, motions to reconsider are rarely granted— you're basically asking the judge to overturn a decision they just made." MiAngel's advice and encouragement felt like a lifeline. "It's a long shot," she said. "But these are Black lives on the line, sis. You have to try."

She was right. If there was a chance it would work, I had no other choice. I called every criminal defense attorney in Dallas I knew, asking for advice on how to approach a motion to reconsider. No one had any. Lots of people offered me unsolicited advice, though. "Don't do it, Brittany. You'll offend the judge. You don't want to frustrate the court. Think of your other clients that may come before him. Think of your career." I thanked them politely and ignored them. Mike's life hung in the balance. Offending the court was a risk I would have to take.

Just days before I had been congratulating myself on what was a major victory. Now I was back to basically making up a motion that I had no clue how to draft. The memory of Mike's painful efforts to express his gratitude despite his profound disappointment at the thought of four more years in prison propelled me forward. I filed a motion to reconsider, thanking the judge for his merciful consideration in the first reduction but arguing once again that there had been no reason to sentence Mike to the high end of the guidelines. I kept my arguments brief and succinct. After all, the judge had already read and considered the first motion. I stressed Mike's failing health, and the Federal Bureau of Prisons' inability to provide him with the care and therapy he needed. I emphasized that Mike had already served nearly twenty-three years. Finally, I pointed out that De-Ann and Donel had received clemency and that Mike's continued incarceration would create an extreme and unwarranted sentencing disparity among codefendants. I urged the judge to reconsider his decision from just two weeks before and grant time served.

I hoped I wasn't making a huge mistake.

NOBODY DOES A flower arrangement like the Ritz-Carlton. Long-stemmed tulips, all white, arched dramatically from elegant vases in the center table of the grand lobby. Not a terrible location for a professional conference. I had just come out of a lecture on risk allocation delivered by partners from prominent international law firms. It was the University of Texas School of Law's renowned Mergers and Acquisitions Institute, and the lobby of the Ritz was brimming with some of the country's top deal lawyers and investment bankers. As I made my way toward my next session, greeting familiar faces as I went, my phone buzzed with an email alert. I stopped just short of the glossy conference room door. The judge had issued an order on my motion to reconsider.

I took a deep breath. I'd submitted the motion only a couple of weeks before. After waiting months on the first decision, I'd expected a far longer waiting period. Maybe the judge had been so offended by my request to reconsider that he'd wanted it off his desk. Fast.

My heart was beating hard in my chest. *Come on, Brittany, have faith,* I thought. *Believe.*

I opened the order and read.

Before the court is the defendant's motion to reconsider sentence (docket entry 158). For the reasons stated in the motion, the motion is GRANTED, and the defendant's previously imposed sentence of imprisonment is REDUCED from 365 months to 292 months.

SO ORDERED.

Granted! 292 months was time served. *Time served!* I couldn't believe what I was seeing. I backed away from the conference room door, tears welling in my eyes as I scrolled to find Marc's number. I wanted to cry, to shout, but surrounded as I was by lawyers and business executives, I held it together. Barely.

"Granted!" I said without even a greeting when I heard Marc's voice. "The judge granted the motion to reconsider! He's free!"

Marc sounded like he had just rolled out of bed. "What? Brittany, what did you say?"

"Your dad. The judge granted my motion to reconsider. It'll take a little time to process but—your dad is getting out!"

There was silence on the other end of the line, and then Marc broke into wild whoops that echoed what I was feeling inside. When we hung up I raced back to ORIX to get everything moving. The latest deal trends in mergers and acquisitions could wait.

In between calls to Mike's mom, his sons, and De-Ann, I tried in vain to get hold of Mike himself at the prison. His counselor was off that day, and no one I talked to seemed interested in setting up an emergency legal call. Mike's ordeal was over and he didn't even know it.

Running on elation and adrenaline, I made a call to an attorney I knew at the Federal Bureau of Prisons' regional office in Grand Prairie. I read him the order and offered to email it to him. "Given the circumstances," I said, "is there any way we can expedite this order to have his new release date calculated? It should be but a week or so out—his sons sure would like him home."

"I'll send this to the Sentencing Computations Department," my friend said. "But, Brittany, if the order reads the way you said, this is a time served order effective as of today. We cannot keep Mike Wilson in prison another day or it will be considered unlawful confinement. He must be released immediately."

"I don't think I understand what you're saying," I said. "What does this mean for my client?"

"It means that as soon as we can get word to Victorville, your client will be released. Today."

If I hadn't tipped them off, the order would have taken at least a week to get into the system. But now, in fear of lawsuits and liability, the corroded machinery of the prison bureaucracy ground into high gear.

I called Marc and Mike Junior back on three-way and told them that in fact there would be no waiting period. Their dad was coming home today! They were ecstatic. "So do we need to pick him up or what?" Mike Junior said. Silence followed as realization set in. Mike was getting out in a few hours, halfway across the country. And we had no time to make arrangements.

We started to panic. My phone beeped with Mike's mother's number.

"Brittany?" Her voice was hoarse from crying tears of joy, but she sounded worried. "Mike's cellmate just called. They said a guard came and told him to pack out. Told him he was getting out."

"Already?"

"That's what he told me. Said Mike left all his stuff, didn't take anything with him. He's just gone."

When I finally did reach the prison, things got even worse. "He's already been released," the administrator told me. "We took him to the Greyhound station. Mike Wilson is no longer an inmate at this facility. And he's no longer our responsibility." After twenty-two years in a maximum-security penitentiary, every movement monitored and controlled, without the ability to read or write or speak clearly, the Federal Bureau of Prisons had released Mike Wilson onto the streets outside Victorville with nothing more than a bus ticket clutched in his hand.

Our elation turned to desperation. Mike Junior frantically searched the bus routes to determine the best way to drive and try to intercept his dad—if he'd even made it onto the bus. Marc would fly out and see if he could reach him sooner—but fly out to where? Mike's mom started calling every bus station from Victorville to Dallas to determine the exact time buses were expected to arrive. I was livid—the prison's lack of care was sickening. Mike was a liability to them, nothing more. Even after seven years at the same facility, nobody cared enough about him as a human being to even try to help him get home. They didn't even know if he'd gotten on the bus.

"Can you tell me his bus ticket number so that his family and I can track it?" I asked another BOP staff member. "Do you know what time the bus is leaving?"

"We aren't allowed to give out that information."

I had to keep from screaming. "Not even to his lawyer? His mother? Can you confirm his final destination is Dallas?"

"We aren't allowed to give out that information," she repeated.

I made a series of frantic calls to Victorville. Mike's case manager confirmed that because of his whirlwind release, the prison had provided him with only two days' worth of his prescription medication. He had a prepaid debit card, which at least gave him food money for a few days, and a means to call home, but after two decades of incarceration and in his current medical condition, I wasn't sure if he'd be able to figure out how to use it.

We couldn't get anyone at the Victorville bus station to confirm that Mike had gotten onto the bus. Even if he had, the bus ride to Dallas from Victorville was more than twenty-nine hours. To make matters worse, Mike would have to change buses nine times, starting with the first stop in San Bernardino. Marc was beside himself. "At our visit, there was no way he could do something like that! How's he supposed to know what bus to get on? His reading's not back yet. And he can hardly speak, especially when he's stressed out!"

A few hours later Mike's mom answered her phone. "Mama?" A stranger in the San Bernardino bus station had let Mike borrow his cellphone to call home. Speaking slowly and with great difficulty, he was able to explain that he'd been able to contact a friend he knew who lived a few hours from San Bernardino. She was driving up to the bus station and would help Mike get a hotel room. We all breathed a collective sigh of relief. Mike was safe for the night. Now we just needed to get him the rest of the way home.

The next morning we bought him a plane ticket to Dallas, after confirming with the airport that Mike could use his prison ID to board. We got permission for Mike's friend to walk him all the way through security to the gate to make sure he got safely on the plane. On the phone Mike was a jumble of emotions—anxious, excited, overwhelmed with the sights, sounds, and sensations of an outside world he hadn't laid eyes on in twenty-two years. "I just packed out before they could change their minds!" he said, his stammer agitated by the stress and exhaustion of his solitary journey through the night. "I didn't take anything with me!"

At DFW in Dallas a kind stranger guided him through the airport to arrivals. Mike walked off his first plane ride as a free man into the arms of his oldest son, whom he hadn't seen in ten years. The two men clung to each other, root and branch, as the other passengers bustled by.

MIKE JUNIOR CALLED me from the car just outside the airport. "My dad wants to know where you are!" he said. "He says he's gotta see you and give you a hug." In all the years I'd been working on his case, Mike and I had never met face-to-face.

"Tell your dad to take his time," I said. "I'll be here!"

But Mike's mom told me later that he insisted on seeing me that day. They fed him some home cooking, took him shopping for something other than prison-issue gray sweatpants, and then Mike's sons drove him over to my new apartment building in the center of Uptown Dallas, across the street from the Dallas Mavericks' home court.

Mike is a big man with a hundred-watt smile from ear to ear. Stroke or no stroke, the hug he gave me was powerful. Here was a man set to die in prison, squeezing me for all he was worth, his grown sons looking on. There are no words to capture the feeling of a homecoming like that. A powerful Black man, back from the dead. Free at last. Over the past several years our lives had been so intimately connected, and yet this was the first time meeting in person. It didn't feel like it. I knew Mike, and Mike knew me. He was my brother.

"You saved my life," Mike kept saying. "You know I had to come to thank you. You're my angel!" Whenever he paused between words, he seemed to smile even wider.

I shook my head. "I should be thanking you for trusting me with your life, to allow me on such an amazing journey." I meant it. I had been complacent, satisfied with the first reduction, content to let Mike spend four more years in prison. If I hadn't heard the pain in his voice, hadn't been jolted out of my own false sense of satisfaction, Mike would still be in prison that very moment. I wouldn't want to spend four years in prison. Why should anyone else? I was grateful to Mike for reminding me that there was nothing more urgent than freedom.

My apartment was on the twenty-fourth floor, and we stood at the floor-to ceiling windows in the living room, the boys looking at Mike, and Mike gazing out at the skyline of the city he hadn't laid eyes on in over two decades. We were all grinning, still stunned by the events of the past forty-eight hours. Mike's sons couldn't keep their eyes off their dad. They were grown men, tall and athletic, with sleeve tattoos on their muscled brown arms, but their looks of unabashed delight as they took in Mike's presence were full of the innocent adoration of much younger boys. *They love their daddy,* I thought. It didn't matter how grown they were. They loved their daddy the way they did when he first went away.

The sky turned from blue to blush pink to a deeper blue, and the city lights began to wink on—the neon green of the Bank of America Plaza Building, the rotating crystal ball of Reunion Tower.

Mike took a deep breath, still smiling, his eyes shining. "Man, I sure am glad to see my city," he said. "I sure am."

When he spoke in that moment, he barely stuttered at all.

Chapter 13

LOVE, FAITH, HOPE

My corporate career showed no signs of slowing down, and ORIX was exactly where I wanted to be. The mode was aggressive, the energy was huge, and so were the spoils of this new chapter of my professional life. But the stark difference between the luxury perks of my job and the reality of my clients' lives inside was beginning to take a harsher emotional toll. I loved my job, but my heart—and increasingly my head—were elsewhere. Instead of enjoying our lavish company dinners, I thought about the food on the prison tray. When I traveled, diving into the turquoise seas of Turks and Caicos, I took advantage of a sorely needed reprieve from the pace of my work at ORIX. But I also thought of Sharanda, of Wayland. They should be able to marvel at the purity of the Caribbean waters, too. I'd go to a market and think, *Sharanda would love this*—only to be reminded of where she was instead.

Whatever satisfaction was brought by the luxe perks and excitement of corporate law was tempered by the reality that still, six years after our first meeting, Sharanda was laboring under the burden of her life sentence. She was always telling me she was proud of me, reminding me how important it was for Clenesha and other Black girls to see women like themselves in positions of power. "I never had that in Terrell," she said. "You keep your head up, Brittany. Keep doing what you're doing." Her faith in me kept me going. In all the time I knew her she had never complained. Every single day, the women around her lost their minds from the pressure cooker of incarceration, and yet Sharanda remained Sharanda—upbeat, generous, making the most of her present. She had made it through the worst of the crushing grief that followed the death of her mother, but for the first time I was beginning to see signs of wear from the long war of attrition she had so far endured with such grace.

Her body hurt. Sharanda's knee joints had worn away, the pain acute from sixteen years of walking on nothing but concrete. A specialist at John Peter Smith Hospital confirmed that both knees were bone on bone and signed an immediate surgery order, only for the Carswell physician to revoke it, prescribing weight loss instead. Chronic pain added to Sharanda's fatigue. She still counseled the most severely depressed incoming women, was still a positive light in the unit. But I could see that the struggle it took to shine that light was mightier than it had ever been.

One Saturday during a short lull between deals I drove out to see her. Her dreadlocks were almost shoulder length now; she'd begun to grow them after Genice's passing. "This place is dreadful," she said, "so I'm growing dreads. And I'm not cutting them till I'm free." She'd pulled her hair into a half ponytail, and the style made her face look even younger. She still smiled and responded to my questions, but I could sense an emotional distance that I had never felt before.

"Sharanda, what's wrong?" I said. "I know it's something. I can feel it."

"It's nothing," she said, forcing another smile. "I'm good. I just . . . the little things are really starting to get to me." She sighed and looked down at her hands. "They're moving me, Brittany."

"Moving you?" I froze with a Cheeto halfway to my mouth. My heart sank. "What in the hell? To where?"

"Not a prison transfer. I don't mean that. But my cell. I've been there ten years. That's like the one part of this place I've made mine. Ten years. And they're moving me."

"Did you tell them you didn't want to move?"

Sharanda looked at me like I should know better. "You know that won't work," she said. "They don't care what we think or feel. I'll be fine." She tried to smile. "I'm just . . . tired."

When I left the prison that day, storm clouds were gathering, and the heavy gray of the sky dimmed the purple pansies the women tended so carefully and turned the razor wire black. At work we could move billions of dollars with a phone call and transform an international conglomerate seemingly overnight. But within the prison system, I was powerless to help Sharanda hold on to even the tiniest grain of dignity—a steel cot in a concrete room she'd had to accept as home for the last ten years of her life.

WHEN SARI HORWITZ of *The Washington Post* first reached out to me, I was skeptical about journalists. We'd had some bad experiences by then, Sharanda and I, spending hours responding to someone's questions only for a brief write-up that lost the energy or essence of what we thought we had expressed. I was starting to feel that media could hurt our clemency efforts as much as help, and felt disinclined to spend much more time with journalists. I didn't *have* any time, for one thing, and while in some ways Sharanda had nothing but time, it took a toll on her to relive those early days of her sentence, brought emotions to the surface that survival inside required her to contain.

Sari was doing a series on the human devastation from the War on Drugs, and she planned to include a story on a clemency recipient and another on a person seeking clemency. Julie Stewart, the president of FAMM, had let her know that I happened to represent both. Would I be interested in speaking with her?

I wasn't, not really. I'd already typed my polite response to that effect, but something made me Google her. I'm so glad I did. Sari was a three-time Pulitzer Prize–winning journalist who had already done a moving story investigating the costs of incarcerating the elderly and infirm. It was a remarkable story, and the photographs by Nikki Kahn, who would be accompanying Sari in Dallas, captured every nuance of the horrors of incarceration.

I met Nikki and Sari at the Saltgrass Steakhouse next to their hotel in Arlington so that I could give them some background information on the case. From the moment I met them I felt at ease. Sari, a small woman with a sleek dark-haired bob and incredible intellectual energy, had been a top *Washington Post* journalist for thirty years; each sharp question led to the next question. Nikki was calm and quiet, her questions equally probing but reflecting an artist's intuition. I felt inspired, sitting across from these two brilliant women clearly at the top of their game. I had planned on keeping my part brief, presenting the case and our plea for mercy as simply and succinctly as possible to avoid any misinterpretation in the write-up, but as soon as we started talking I opened up. Nikki asked how I got involved with the case. I surprised myself when, as I recounted that moment when I first saw Sharanda in the YouTube video in a prison uniform so reminiscent of my mother's, I began to cry.

"I'm sorry," I said. "I just feel so deeply about this. Sharanda has to get out of prison. She has to."

After our meeting, Sari and Nikki changed their schedules, allowing more time to research Sharanda's case. They tracked down everyone involved. They found Sharanda's former friends, Julie and Baby Jack, who had first turned over her name to the feds. When the couple refused to answer the phone, Sari stood on their porch and knocked on their door. They pursued the prosecutors for comment, and the judge, and scoured the trial transcripts just as I had. Sari even got permission from the Federal Bureau of Prisons for a special two-day midweek visit to Carswell during which she and Nikki would be able to spend time alone with Sharanda and Clenesha in the visiting room. It was the first time in all the years of Sharanda's incarceration that she and Clenesha, who was now twenty-four years old, had a chance to see each other privately outside visiting hours.

After the prison visit, Sari and Nikki asked to interview Clenesha in her home as well. Clenesha is a shy and private person, and at first she struggled with the decision to open her home, and her emotions, to two women she hardly knew. "I don't know, Brittany. They were really nice, but I don't know if I want to be interviewed by myself. This is national news. I mean, *The Washington Post*? I just feel nervous."

"Think about it and trust your intuition. There is absolutely no pressure here, and if you feel forced, don't do it. Sari and Nikki will understand. Do what you feel. You know I'll support you either way."

A few hours later Clenesha called me back. "This is my mom's life. And it's *my* life. People need to know. And me telling my story might help someone else with a parent in prison know they are not alone. I'm going to do it."

I know it took a lot for Clenesha to open her home to Sari and Nikki that day, but they had won her trust, and she shyly showed them her small home; it hardly had furniture yet. They followed her with a video camera as she showed cards Sharanda had made for her and other tender examples of their close relationship. "My whole life is on hold," she confessed.

I was so proud of Clenesha's courage that day. "I want to do more for my mom," she said when I told her so. "It's just so hard for me to talk about it to people I don't know. I hate the attention. But I want to do more now. It's time."

Sari and Nikki's diligence and the promise of the forthcoming story lifted Sharanda's spirits. She hadn't been too happy about moving cells, and I felt for her when I got an email with the subject heading "Moved Today." When I opened it, though, I found a lovely surprise.

Guess what. I moved to my new cell today . . . and it's got a window with a view, trees and everything. I can see them from my bed. Never been able to see trees from my cell before. One step closer to freedom!!!

From her new cell window, Sharanda could see the wide green branches and knotted brown trunks of a cluster of elm trees. At night, with light from the hall peering into her dark cell, the elms' black silhouettes stood starkly against the inky Texas sky. If Sharanda lay just right, she could watch them until she fell asleep. During the daily four o'clock count, their vibrant green leaves called the eye away from the endless prison palette of khaki, beige, gray. Those trees looked like freedom. And they were so close. Sharanda's spirits lifted, and so did mine. Hope eased all of our burdens.

ON JULY 13, 2015, Obama announced forty-six clemencies, his largest number since the launch of the clemency initiative. All of the recipients of the president's mercy that day were people who'd been oversentenced as a result of now outdated drug laws; fourteen of them were serving life.

Sharanda was not on the list.

We weren't the only ones feeling passed over. Obama's announcement fell far short of the expectations raised when the clemency initiative was first announced. The Department of Justice had initially estimated that more than ten thousand might be released. So far, only eighty-nine had made the cut. The process was moving at a snail's pace. Still, despite the crushing disappointment we felt for Sharanda, it was heartening to see Obama speaking directly to the camera, his words giving credence to every line of our clemency petition. "I believe that at its heart, America is a nation of second chances," our president said, his hair graying a little now at the temples, the lines in his handsome face deeper, the conviction and idealism conveyed by the tenor of his voice untempered by the weight of his position. "And I believe these folks deserve their second chance."

"Sharanda fits these criteria," I said to the screen, feeling half foolish and half like Obama might be able to hear me if I willed it hard enough. "Please say her name. Please show her mercy."

President Obama did not say Sharanda's name, but *The Washington Post* did. Two days after the blow of the clemency announcement, Sari and Nikki's amazing work was on the front page. The headline couldn't have been clearer: FROM A FIRST ARREST TO A LIFE SENTENCE: CLEMENCY IS THE ONLY WAY OUT FOR SOME NONVIOLENT DRUG OFFENDERS. Inside the paper, an entire page and a half was devoted to Sharanda's story and Nikki's stunning photographs of mother and daughter. On the front page was a striking close-up of Sharanda, her lips turned up in a small, pensive smile, her dark eyes luminous and thoughtful, full of everything that might have been and everything that might still be.

Both the article and the response were tremendous. Suddenly, after years of fruitless emails and pleading phone calls to journalists, television and radio stations, and other media outlets to please, please pay attention, Sharanda's face was everywhere on social media and my phone was ringing off the hook. Sari had included a photo of me sifting through legal documents in my home "office"—the floor of my living room—and suddenly people knew who I was. Reporters and television stations called about Sharanda and our efforts. Grandmothers and parents, sons and daughters called about family members who were facing a similar plight. Please, could I help?

I tried to talk to everybody, to explain to each person that I was a full-time corporate attorney, that Sharanda and Donel and the others were cases I worked on in my spare time, that I wished I had capacity to help more but I couldn't. I steered family members to FAMM or the ACLU and other organizations who might be able to help raise awareness or point them in the direction of a pro bono lawyer. Sharanda's case had seemed incredible to me when I came across it, but what I had learned in the past six years was that there were tens of thousands of Sharandas whose lives were being wasted in prison as a result of the War on Drugs.

The momentum generated by the *Washington Post* article was tremendous. Because of Sari and Nikki's article, two more phenomenal Washington women reached out to me, Chani Wiggins and Tiffany Moore. They were high-profile political lobbyists, and they volunteered to contact members of Congress to support Sharanda's plea for clemency. By the end of the month, Sharanda had been featured on John Oliver's late-night HBO show, and Larry Wilson of Comedy Central discussed her case in detail. Her Change.org petition garnered 280,000 signatures from supporters as far away as England and South Africa. Incredibly, former U.S. attorney general Eric Holder himself tweeted the article. I knew Eric Holder was behind many of the White House's criminal justice reform initiatives, and to garner this level of support from him meant everything.

After years of media blackout, suddenly we were everywhere. And Sharanda is Sharanda. Her plight, and her tremendous dignity in the face of it, moved everyone who came across her story, as I had always known it would. Now millions of people did come across it, and millions were moved. I had filed her petition before the initiative was announced, and filed a supplement to match the condensed format months before. Surely her petition would surface at the DOJ. There was no way she wasn't going to be on the next list.

Except there was no list.

THE DAY AFTER Sharanda's *Washington Post* article hit the newsstands, President Obama made history yet again by being the first sitting president of the United States to visit a federal prison. As he toured El Reno Federal Correction Institution in Oklahoma, he expressly made the case against mandatory minimum sentences and predatory drug laws, and as he peered into the nine-by-ten cells where three men lived—cells no doubt spruced up for the presidential visit—he lamented overcrowding and other inhumane prison conditions. After meeting with six men in prison for drug offenses, he told reporters, "These are young people who made mistakes that aren't that different from the mistakes I made and the mistakes that a lot of you guys made. There but for the grace of God."

Like the video issued with forty-six sentence commutations earlier that week, President Obama's prison visit telegraphed that here, truly, was a man in whom we could place our hope and our confidence. Here was our Black prince, our savior. Those expectations may have been unfair, but I cannot say that I was immune. Perhaps he had been biding his time, building the bipartisan coalition that was now working on the Sentencing Reform and Corrections Act that would, if passed, overturn many of the system failures of the era of mass incarceration. Those of us on the ground hoped he would start granting commutations monthly, weekly even, in the numbers the Department of Justice had promised.

But he didn't. Weeks stretched to months. Sharanda's media coverage and external support continued to swell, but in regard to clemency, the White House was utterly silent. We tried to celebrate small victories, each time the media highlighted Sharanda's case, and of course the release of those who had received clemency from Obama in July. But in truth, the war of attrition continued to wear away at us. Sometimes it felt as if the walls were closing in.

At least I had the distraction, if you could call it that, of my day job. At the same time, as a result of the network I'd built over the years and the recent rash of publicity, I was becoming more active in the movement to change our nation's sentencing laws. One evening in late October, I was getting ready to speak on a panel addressing the crisis of mass incarceration. Mike and his sons would be in the audience; since his release, Mike always came through to support me whenever he could. I loved seeing his huge smile light up the crowd at these events, and seeing him with both of his sons always lifted my spirits.

My phone rang as I was getting ready, and I figured it was Mike confirming plans for dinner after the panel. But it was Clenesha's number.

"I can't do it, Brittany! I can't." Clenesha sounded terrified.

My heart leapt to my throat. "What's going on? Are you okay?"

"How am I supposed to do this without my mom?"

I had no idea what she was talking about. "Do what? What are you talking about? Clenesha, slow down. Breathe."

"I'm *pregnant*," she said. Then I could hear her crying openly on the other line. I took a deep breath. I had never heard Clenesha break down this way. It was impossible to hear the level of distress in her voice and not feel the same.

"It's okay! Everything is going to be okay. We'll get through this." I wanted to soothe her, to ease her pain, to greet her news with the joy a new life deserved. But like Clenesha, I was also thinking of Sharanda.

"I'm happy for a baby," she said, fighting back sobs. "I want the baby. But I can't do it without my mom. How can they make me do this without my mom?"

For Clenesha, Sharanda's incarceration had been like a sudden death. The night before the guilty verdict, Sharanda had painted polka dots on Clenesha's nails the same color as her own so that they could be "twins." She dropped her off at school as usual, told her she'd pick her up that day after school. And that was the last time Clenesha saw her mother free. They spoke on the phone for ten minutes every single day, but the trauma of her mom's sudden disappearance never left.

Sharanda's spitting image, Clenesha was more introverted than her mother, but she hid her pain just as well. I had been surprised by how open she'd been in the *Washington Post* video. They had filmed her in the living room of her first home, holding a card Sharanda had made for her high school graduation. "It's like everything in my life is on hold," Clenesha had said, looking slightly away from the camera, her feline eyes wet with tears. "If I want to move to Canada or something, I can't leave her. I can't even have a baby if I was in love. I can't go through a birth without my mother. That's crazy to me."

Now, only a few months later, she was facing that very prospect, and her usually stoic exterior crumbled.

"Come by my house tomorrow, okay?" I said. "Let's talk all of this out. I'm always here for you."

"I can't do this, Brittany. I can't. Not by myself. Not without her."

"Everything is going to be all right," I said. "I promise. I'll see you tomorrow, okay? Don't worry."

Hearing Clenesha's voice level out a little was a relief. But not five minutes after I hung up the phone, it rang again. This time it was Sharanda, sounding equally distraught.

"Did Clenesha call you? She's not going to make it without me, Brittany. How's she supposed to know what she's doing? I have to be there. I'm not gonna be there. What are we going to do?" In all my years of knowing her I had never heard Sharanda sound like this.

I made it through the panel that evening, more emotional than usual. I kept my eyes on Mike's encouraging, proud face in the audience to remind myself of hope. He was a walking miracle, anything was possible. But I couldn't shake the image of Sharanda in the very first video I'd seen of her, when I was a student at SMU. "I just can't see my daughter graduating without me there. I just can't see it," Sharanda had said. Almost a decade had passed since that video was made. Sharanda had missed every graduation, every milestone. Somehow, mother and daughter had made it through. But something about Clenesha expecting her first child surfaced the pain and heartbreak, the severe trauma, of their separation.

An unexpected pregnancy always ushers in mixed emotions— joy and panic in equal measure. Clenesha didn't want to stress

Sharanda, and Sharanda didn't want to stress Clenesha. By this time we had formed a little family of three, and in this family crisis I was in the middle, fielding calls from Clenesha in the morning, sometimes within minutes of receiving an email from Sharanda, both women in a desperate panic about the likelihood that Sharanda would still be incarcerated for the birth of her first grandchild. It was as though all the pressure of the past years had come to a breaking point, and that point was the tiny being growing to term in Clenesha's golden-brown belly.

Meanwhile, days passed. Weeks. Months. And still, silence from the White House.

I TRIED HARD to hold fast to my conviction that Sharanda's freedom was imminent. Sometimes, in moments of weakness, I felt afraid. Sharanda had never stopped believing, but lately she seemed to be grappling with the nightmare realization that President Obama might not grant her clemency. She'd always talked about her sentence as something unreal to her. "It just don't fit," she'd say defiantly. "It's not for me. Can't even get the words through my lips! I'm getting out of here!" But lately those bold proclamations had been subsumed by worries for Clenesha and the baby. Genice had died in prison. At the edge of all of our minds, held at bay by constant faith, belief, and prayer, was the unimaginable possibility that Sharanda could, too.

In my own moments of feeling overwhelmed, I sought the comfort of my own mom for solace. I'd meet her after work at Mi Cocina, our favorite Tex-Mex restaurant, and order chips and queso, beef enchiladas for my mom, chicken fajitas for me. I'd be exhausted from corporate finagling, she from guiding people in recovery through their first days of detox. I was always in awe of her willingness to put herself in such close proximity to the perils of addiction. By the time we'd worked our way through the first basket of chips, we'd have laughed away some of the emotion of the day.

One evening, after I'd finished catching her up about Clenesha being pregnant and my new strategy to generate direct appeals to Obama from as many people as I could, she set down her glass of water and looked at me, serious for a minute.

"Britt, I can see you're tired," Mama began, her voice softening. I opened my mouth to protest, but she gave me that look I knew well—the one that meant *I'm your mama and I can see straight through you, so hush.* "I know your work is wearing on you," she said. "And I don't mean at ORIX. I mean your *real* work. Your heart work."

I felt her words penetrate all my defenses as only a mother can. *I can't afford to be tired, Mama,* I wanted to say. *There's too much work to do.* But I knew if I spoke, the tears I felt pressing at the back of my eyes would get out. And with them the questions I could not bear to ask myself. *What if she doesn't get out? What if I've failed?*

"What Sharanda and Clenesha are going through with the baby—that's a lot of pain," Mama said. "When I missed your master's graduation, I didn't know what to do. I was just in my cell, on the bed, curled up in a fetal position. Couldn't get up for almost two days, and then only because I had to work. I let my baby down. I let myself down. Your proudest moment to that point, and I couldn't be there. It broke my heart. If you had been pregnant?" Mama looked down for a minute, shaking her head. When she looked up, her eyes were filled with tears. "I don't know if I could have stood the anguish. Sharanda is a brave woman."

"You were there in spirit, Mama," I said. "You've always been there."

"But not in the flesh, Britt. And as a mother, it's an unbearable feeling. But I am here now." She reached for my hand. "You are going to get through this. You and Sharanda and Clenesha. I know that for sure. But what I want you to know is this—I am proud of you, Brittany K. I am so very proud. And it has nothing to do with your rising career in corporate law. All of that is just icing on the cake. I'm proud of *you*. Of who you are. Of the work you are doing. Of how you just won't quit. Sharanda's getting out, Britt.

Just like Mike, just like Donel. Because you won't quit until she's free. And not giving up? That's what it's all about."

Evelyn Fulbright was a straight shooter. If she said it, she meant it. We had been through so much together. But we'd made it. My mom was a fighter, and one of the most courageous women I'd ever known. At her words, I felt flooded with a deep joy, the kind of love that readies you to move mountains.

I grabbed a chip and smiled at her playfully. "I guess I got it from my mama."

"You better know it!" Mama said, and dug into her enchiladas.

I hadn't even known how much the stress of the last months had affected me until my mom lifted me with her words that night. In the weeks to come, I hung on to her faith in me even when my own wavered.

THE WEATHER HAD turned a bitter cold. Christmas was approaching, a festive time for free Americans, not so for incarcerated people and their loved ones. The holidays are a dark time, a difficult time. We all strained to appear in the holiday spirit, to make the most of what we did have, and that effort took its toll. One Saturday I drove up for a visit with Sharanda, the same visit I'd been making now for over six years. For whatever reason, traffic was heavy, and it took twice as long as usual to make my way to Carswell. Traffic and work stress had me on edge, but I knew I had little to complain about. Many people weren't able to make the trip to their loved ones for the holidays at all. Anyone who could, did. Family members risked their jobs or lost a full day of pay to get to the prison, some driving hundreds of miles. I thought of Sharanda, anticipating my visit, and wove through the traffic as deftly as possible.

I pulled into the designated parking area and sat in my car for a minute to collect myself. The air was biting. I could see the women in the low-security camp across the street huddled in groups in the yard, their breath visible in short white bursts, the collars of their army-green coats pulled up over their ears. I pulled my own coat close and took out the clear makeup bag I used for prison visits, with twenty dollars in quarters and ten in ones. I got out my ID and locked my purse in the trunk. I took one more deep breath and watched my exhale dissipate into the air. Then I headed toward the administration building.

There were more visitors than usual. A young Black boy walked quickly past me, his hands deep in his pockets. I'd seen him when I was putting my purse in the trunk of my car, hurrying to a blue Camry and tossing something into the backseat. He'd left something in his pocket, probably. He had no coat and his thin shoulders were hunched forward, his hands in his armpits. He mumbled "Excuse me" and then took a shortcut through the grass to get to his family, rushing to get processed and through to visitation. I was about to follow him when a guard pulled up in a white Jeep and started screaming at the kid, berating him for walking on the grass, threatening to revoke his visitation. He was only ten or eleven, but she yelled at him as if he were a monster, not a human being. The kid stopped in his tracks, scared, and when he passed me again to get back to the concrete I could see that he was trying hard not to cry.

There was no reason for her to yell at him like that, to add that humiliation to the stress of the day. I was so frustrated my hands were shaking as I answered the same eighteen questions I answered every time: Did I have any explosives? No. Did I have any narcotics? No. Name. Car make and model. License plate number. I took my shoes off and went through the metal detector. In front of me, the boy was hurriedly putting his sneakers back on. An older woman waited for him while the rest of the family went ahead. I teared up as she pressed her hand to his cheek, said something softly that made him smile. She reminded me of Mama Lena, of all our grandmothers—always ready with a reassuring hand, despite not knowing what her grandson had endured outside.

Sharanda was already waiting for me in the visitation area,

dressed in her khaki uniform. It had taken me so long to get through the security line that they'd already called her. She smiled and hugged me as always, but there was something in her face I'd never seen before. When we sat down I asked her how she was doing. "Fine!" she said brightly. And then, for the first time in all of our years together, Sharanda's shoulders dropped in resignation and she began to cry.

Even when her mom died, Sharanda had contained her grief at our visits, breaking down in the company of other incarcerated women and in her own cell but holding her emotions at bay in the visiting room. Now, as tears silently fell from her eyes, I could feel her pain pierce my soul. "Brittany," she said, "I'm tired." I put my hand over hers. I didn't care if a guard yelled at us or not.

"It'll be over soon," I said. "It has to be over soon." But at that moment, my conviction felt weak. Sharanda looked up, locking my eyes with her own.

"This time is causing me pain in my core. All the way down. To my *core*."

I'd never heard Sharanda talk like this. I don't think she ever had, not since the day she was thrown in the Dallas County Jail, her purse waiting in the car, cornbread batter waiting at the restaurant. Sharanda looked down and wiped her tears. When she looked up again her eyes were wet, but she wasn't crying anymore.

"Okay," she said. "I'll take the cheddar jalapeño Cheetos today. You want to share peanut M&M's?"

Following her lead, I switched gears and got in line for the vending machines. "You know I really want Cheez-Its," I said. "Let's share a Snickers, too. I've been craving one ever since you told me about that Snickers banana pudding you made last month."

"These women *still* trying to find out my secret for that puddin'!"

I stayed with Sharanda all day. We ate our Cheez-Its and cheddar jalapeño Cheetos and candy and talked about anything and everything in our usual way. Sharanda's mood lightened, clearly through heroic effort, and she even spoke excitedly about the baby.

"The baby is due in May, just five months away. We're thinking of names," she said.

"I love it," I said. "And just wait until you hold that baby!" We had no more tears after the first minute of my visit, but that minute never left my mind.

When I left it was pouring rain outside, torrential rain, cold and gray and ugly. I had to cover my head with my coat to run to the car but got drenched anyway. I was glad. The minute I felt the rain on my skin I let out the pain I had been holding in since I felt Sharanda's. I cried in the car, glad for the water streaming down the windows, shielding me from people in the parking lot. I hadn't sobbed like that in the car since the first prison visit with my mom. I was drained, exhausted. I was angry at the guard who yelled at the kid on the grass. I was hurt by Sharanda's tears, by Clenesha's stress, by my own questions. It had been two long years since we'd filed the clemency petition. Was Sharanda really going to get out? Even to ask the question seemed a betrayal of our efforts, a failure to believe. But I understood Clenesha's desperation. For sixteen years Sharanda had taken every day as it came, embracing her present, serving as a light in the darkness to all who crossed her path. Sixteen years. How much more of this could we endure? How much could Sharanda?

Before I left the parking lot, I pulled out my phone. I pulled up a screenshot of an old tweet that I kept for times when I felt I could hardly go on. When I was studying for the bar in 2011 and was scared I wouldn't pass, I'd tweeted Bishop TD Jakes and asked him to keep me in his prayers. I'd never expected him to respond. But he had. "The last mile is always the hardest. You will win if you don't quit."

I kept the phone on my lap all the way home and kept looking at that tweet. "You will win if you don't quit."

On that hard day, hope seemed distant. Not quitting was all we had.

"MAMA, WILL YOU look in my purse and get my phone?"

"What the hell you got in here, a brick?" she said, pretending to struggle mightily to lift it.

It was around noon on Friday, December 18, 2015, and Mama and I were driving all over Dallas, running last-minute errands for our third annual GEM Christmas party the next day. As usual, my mom was making fun of me for packing my purse with an iPad and other necessities for on-the-go work. I was grateful for her jokes that morning. I'd taken the day off from ORIX. We had a million things to do to get ready for the party—making sure all the girls had gifts to open, and that we'd purchased the right size shoes and clothes for all the girls and their brothers. It was the last Friday before Christmas and traffic was terrible; it seemed all of Dallas had taken the day off to do their last-minute shopping. But I wasn't on edge because of bad drivers.

"The Obamas are leaving for Hawaii tonight," I said. My mom looked over at me. She always knew my heart.

"So today's the last day for it, huh?"

"Yep."

We were quiet for a little while. We didn't need to speak. Both of us knew the stakes. The last round of clemencies had been in July, five months prior. There had been rumors for weeks that another round was coming—after all, holiday clemencies were a tradition even before the Clemency Initiative. Monday, Tuesday, Wednesday, Thursday had crept by, with me checking my phone a hundred times regardless of how tense the negotiations were at work. Nothing. If Obama didn't announce today, there would be no Christmas clemencies at all.

Mama reached into my purse again. She pulled out a picture she knew I carried with me, of me and Sharanda in front of the Carswell Christmas tree the previous Christmas.

"We're just gonna put this right here," she said, and placed the picture on the dashboard. We kept driving, not talking, which was unusual for the two of us. It was a good silence, full of shared understanding of the weight of the next few hours. I was glad my mama was with me. I was glad Sharanda was, too, even if she was only on the dashboard.

It wasn't but five minutes later that my phone rang with a 202 area code. Washington.

I gripped the steering wheel so hard as I answered that I'm surprised it didn't break off. On speaker, a woman's voice echoed through the car. "This is Kira Horstmeyer from the U.S. Pardon Attorney's Office calling for attorney Brittany K. Barnett."

"This is Brittany," I said, my voice as even as I could muster. I pulled into the next parking lot and stopped the car. I could hear my own heartbeat. Mama put her hand over her mouth to keep from screaming.

"I'm calling to inform you that President Barack Obama has granted clemency to your client, Sharanda Purlette Jones. Her sentence will expire on April 16, 2016. Please take a pen and paper to note the exact time we've arranged for you to have a call with Ms. Jones."

My mom was crying, I was crying. We scrambled for a piece of paper, a pen, settled for the back of an envelope. After all these years of believing, I couldn't believe what was happening. The moment was entirely surreal. If my mom hadn't been sitting right there next to me, I would have thought I was dreaming. It was like there were two Brittanys in action at that moment, the one on the phone, listening carefully and writing down the information she gave me, and the real me, standing on the roof of the car with my arms flung out, so many thoughts and feelings rushing through me that my body could barely contain them. *Sharanda Jones will not die in prison. Sharanda Jones is free.*

"Ms. Barnett," the woman said after she'd finished the formal part of her call, "this makes two for you, doesn't it?"

It took me a moment to register her name: Kira Horstmeyer. She was the same attorney who'd called me when Donel got clemency. "Yes," I said. "Yes, it is. We've been waiting for this one. We've been waiting a long time."

I almost lost it then. We had knocked on so many doors, in so many ways. We had knocked and knocked and knocked. And on December 18, 2015, President Barack Obama, the very first Black president of these United States, answered. Everything we had hoped for, planned for, believed in since the day we met had just taken place in real life. Through an incredible act of mercy, the president had finally brought justice. My mother and I sat in silence after the call, just breathing, soaking it all in.

"Sharanda doesn't even know," I said to my mom, her tear-streaked face a reflection of my own. "She's free. She's really free. *Free!*"

SHARANDA TOLD ME later that she'd been sitting on her metal cot in Carswell Medical Center. Outside the small window above her cell, she could see the bare gray branches of the tree she'd grown to love. Women kept coming to check on her. "You feeling all right?" they'd say. "Why haven't you gone out to the yard?" She'd been sitting there all morning, which was unusual for Sharanda.

"I'm fine," she'd answer. "Just feel like sitting in here today."

The last week, everyone had been a little worried. She'd started giving away her things, her cooking supplies, her carefully hoarded items from the commissary.

"She's been in here too long," she'd heard someone say. "She's touched."

But that wasn't it. All week, Sharanda told me, she'd had a feeling. That day it was especially strong. In the morning she'd woken from a dream, an image lingering in her mind of a gold seal. Still, when her counselor called for her about a phone call, she didn't know it was me calling.

The moment it took for Sharanda to pick up seemed an eternity. I almost felt nervous. I think there was still a part of me that thought I might wake up from this, that I might open my eyes to find the day had not yet started, the call that had changed all of our lives never received. But when I heard Sharanda's voice on the line—cautious, guarded, ready for the bad news that unexpected calls often brought—all I felt was tremendous joy.

"Hello?"

"You're comin' home!" I almost sang the words. I wasn't going to spin this out one millisecond longer. "I got the call today!"

I heard a sharp intake of breath. I'd been on two of these calls by now, with Donel and Mike, and was used to the moments of almost nonresponse as the news sank into my clients' consciousness. For the psyche to survive prison, a protective shell forms. Even good news has to penetrate the fortress of emotional defenses. Even liberation news.

There was silence, almost as if Sharanda had dropped the phone. "She's here," her counselor shouted from the background. "She's just crying."

Sharanda came back to the phone, still sobbing. "Thank you, Jesus, thank you, thank you, Brittany. It's just been so long. So long."

"I'm so happy," I said, between sobs myself. "I'm so happy for you!" I took a deep breath. I wanted her to know everything, to never not be in full control of the details of her life ever again. And I wanted to bury my face in my mama's shoulder and just let it all go. All of it. All of the fears and frustrations, all of my helplessness in the face of Sharanda's daily ordeal on the inside. For years I had stood so proximate to Sharanda's suffering that I could feel it even in my stillest moments. There were times when her words kept me fighting. And times when mine kept her encouraged. Those moments created a cadence between us. Now, I felt so close to her joy and freedom that I treasured it as my own.

"Your release date is April the sixteenth." At that, any semblance of Sharanda's guarded tone lifted entirely. Her voice broke with feeling.

"I'll make it for the baby! I'm going to be home for my grandbaby!"

"Yeah, you will!"

We talked over each other, each saying the same thing. I could hear the counselor sniffling in the background, too.

"Where your mama at?" Sharanda asked.

"Right here," I said, and my mama said, "Hallelujah."

"I knew it!" Sharanda let out a beautiful laugh. "Thank you, Brittany."

"Sharanda, I love you so much."

"I love *you* so much. You worked so hard for this. I'll be home for the baby." She kept repeating it. "I'll be home for the baby!"

When we ended the call, I sat in the car with my mom. We didn't have to say anything. We were both thinking of Sharanda standing in that office, the realization of what had just transpired slowly sinking in. Her life was saved with a stroke of Obama's pen. Her sixteen-year nightmare was finally over. And yes, Sharanda Jones would be home for the birth of her granddaughter.

When Sharanda walked back to the unit, the women of Carswell stood still along the hallway and clapped as she passed. It had been a long, long time, but Sharanda Jones was coming home.

Part Three

DAWN

The weary traveler by midnight who asks for bread is really seeking the dawn. Our eternal message of hope is that dawn will come.

—DR. MARTIN LUTHER KING, JR.

Chapter 14

XVI

Black people hold church, or, as we say in the South, "chuch." And we hold it anywhere. It had nourished me at Mama Lena's dining table where food was like spiritual healing. I'd seen it in the Hole, our sacred space of hoodfests and classic cars, where a dap could be an ecumenical experience. I knew how to deliver a wave and well-pitched "Ayyyyeee" at the gas station to hit your soul like a Negro spiritual. It was a Southern preacher's sermon that summoned within me the great courage to leave Red and strut forward on faith and grit. Looking back, it was all church.

The 1990s New York hip-hop scene was no different. Saturday nights were a temple of call-and-response MC battles, lyricists competing for next week's superlatives, Black hips winding to bone-deep beats, and the fashion show of it all. The sacred was unfolding in an eight-count rhyme.

If you were lucky enough to be at the Palladium in NYC's East Village on July 23, 1993, you would've had the chance to see both Tupac Shakur and—the real attraction for Brooklynites—Biggie Smalls. Fresh off the drop of his debut single, the instant classic

"Party and Bullshit," Biggie was the borough's fastest-rising star, the hottest MC on the streets. You might have been too mesmerized by the lineup of rap superstars in front of you—not just Pac and Biggie, but also Redman, Nas, Chuck D, and multiple members of the Wu-Tang Clan—to take much notice of the man standing beside Biggie. Baby-faced, with a light caramel complexion, sporting the vibrant fashion that personified early nineties swag, he would have blended right in.

But Corey "Buck" Jacobs was there. Just as he'd been right there the month before, nodding his head to the beat on the set of Biggie's on-screen debut. Just as he'd been there working the streets for the months in advance, promoting Big's first single, ensuring it was on everybody's playlist, popping bottles in the clubs to make sure the place was hyped when the song came on. Just as he'd been at rehearsals, the sound check, behind the wheel of the car driving Pac, Big, and his best friend Puff Daddy to the show that night.

Standing onstage that night, arm around Biggie as the big man worked the crowd into a frenzy with his Fulton street flow, all his hard work seemed to be paying off. Corey could see it, feel it, taste it. Biggie was destined for greatness. And so were Puff, Bad Boy, and Corey's own management and promotional group, Butt Naked Ent. They were on the cusp of the impossible—power and influence on a global scale.

They were young, Black, and gifted, creating trends and changing the culture. The world—as Nas would rap a year later—was theirs.

Until it wasn't.

He had long been out of the game, but one month after that iconic show at the Palladium, twenty-three-year-old Corey Jacobs was indicted by a federal grand jury in the Eastern District of Virginia on twenty-nine charges related to conspiracy to distribute crack cocaine.

I didn't know any of this the first time I agreed to a call with Corey. In fact, I almost didn't call him at all.

———

"WHAT YOU DOING over there?" Sharanda's friend Vickie asked on speakerphone.

"Just cooking," said Sharanda, her voice full of the pleasure she got from her kitchen, her hands a blur as she seasoned the meat, chopped the greens, stirred the macaroni. I was laid out on her couch in the living room, eyes closed, relaxing into the smell of the food, the sound of Sharanda's voice.

"You making your mac and cheese?" Vickie asked. "What you put in yours?"

"Cheese," Sharanda said.

I had to laugh. She would defend her recipe secrets to the death. Vickie laughed, too. "Who's that over there with you?"

"That's just Brittany, my lawyer."

"Oh, you got business. Let me let you go."

"Oh no," Sharanda said. "She's just over here halfway asleep. Like usual." She smiled over at me.

Sharanda was right. It seemed like whenever I was off work I was on her couch, dozing in and out, listening to her move around the kitchen while she tinkered with her recipes. I could finally let my guard down and succumb to the exhaustion that had been building these many, many months.

"Come on, Brittany." I opened my eyes to Sharanda setting three gorgeous-looking turkey burgers in a line in front of me. "Time to taste-test. Which one do you like best?"

I sat up, stretching. Before biting into the first turkey burger I checked my messages. There was another message from Karen Morrison.

I sighed. "She wants to know if I'm gonna take the case."

Sharanda already knew who I was talking about. We'd been discussing Karen and her request for weeks. "Well?" Sharanda asked. "You gonna do it? Another lifer?"

I wasn't sure. Instead of answering, I took a big bite of the best turkey burger I'd ever tasted.

When Karen messaged me repeatedly last April about a potential new client, Corey Jacobs, I had been adamant in refusing. Donel had just been freed, but Mike was still in prison, and in any case there was no way I was taking another client until Sharanda was free. Plus Corey already had a lawyer, a renowned one, so what would I even be doing? My answer was no. I didn't hear from Karen, who had found me on Facebook after the *Washington Post* article, again until the very same morning I got the call from the Pardon Attorney's Office about Sharanda's clemency. She couldn't have known—the public announcement hadn't been made yet. Still, there she was again, advocating for her old friend. A week later, she'd called again.

I sighed deeply and settled into the depths of the couch cushions, basking in the delicious smells of caramelized onions and simmering candied yams. There was something wonderfully comforting about chilling on Sharanda's sofa while she cooked her heart out in her own kitchen.

"Well," said Sharanda, "it wouldn't hurt to talk to him, would it?"

I didn't know. The emotional toll of the battle for Sharanda had drained my internal resources. And while her freedom had empowered and invigorated me, I had been hoping to refocus that energy into my corporate law career. My role at ORIX was growing by the day, but with all the pro bono work on criminal cases, I hadn't had the time to immerse myself the way I wanted to in the business side of things. I'd been told from the beginning of my career that I was uniquely positioned for advancement because of my accounting background. Understanding both the legal and business sides of transactions gave me an edge. I wanted to use my free time now to enhance and sharpen my skills, to continue to climb the corporate ladder.

"Sometimes I just wish there were more of me," I said through a mouthful of turkey burger.

"You've been talking about this a lot, though. Whenever you

say you're not taking any more cases I'm like *yeah, right.* If you ask me, I think you miss it."

"It's just getting hard to manage my corporate career with casework."

"Oh, I know how hard you go! But I also know how Corey feels right now. Even if you can't take the case in the end, just the fact that you took the time to talk and listen will help him. Believe me. Just have the call."

What could it hurt? I thought. At the very least, I could tell him myself that I couldn't take him on as a client. He deserved that much.

WHEN I CALLED Corey Jacobs at Terre Haute United States Penitentiary in Indiana, where he was sixteen years into a life sentence, I explained that I wasn't some big-time criminal defense lawyer. I'd had some luck, but I wasn't like the high-profile lawyer he had already. I was corporate, I said, doing all this pro bono.

But Corey was undeterred. He didn't take no for an answer, and he wouldn't let me sell myself short, either. In contrast to the laid-back Southerners on the Wilson case, Corey had that New York hustle, an intensity you could feel all the way through the phone line, conveyed through a thick Bronx accent. He was forty-six now, his voice rich and smooth, and he spoke fast, with passion, punctuating his sentences with *Know what I'm sayin'?*

"Brittany," he said. "You're a fighter. You believe in your clients. I know you're the one. Look, I got that lawyer because she's supposed to be the best. She's had success with clemencies. My friend agreed to help me, to pay her top dollar. But I've had this lawyer for over a year and nothing is happening."

Corey told me that when his lawyer had finally visited him, the visit was totally demoralizing. "I looked in her eyes and saw—nothing. I was nothing to her. She even had the facts of my case wrong."

I could detect deep hurt in his voice. He told me he'd gone back to his cell feeling tired and low. He had laid low for a while, until his neighbor in the next cell brought him a newspaper from the library, telling him to read the cover article.

"I'll be real, Brittany, I wasn't feeling it that day," Corey said. "I almost threw it out without looking at it. I just didn't feel like reading, know what I'm saying? But I did. Beginning to end. It was you and Sharanda in *The Washington Post*. And I said *that's* what I need. Someone from the culture. A believer, a fighter. Someone who will look at me and *see* me. I thought, with her in my corner, I *know* I'm getting out."

I was touched, I told him. But I was at capacity, I tried to explain, with my responsibilities to my existing clients and to—

"Look, Brittany," Corey cut me off. "I know you're probably tired. And God knows you deserve rest. After all those years of fighting, I'm right here on your bumper, asking you to take *my* case now. I know it's a big ask. But I'm fighting for my freedom. For my life. And you're the one. You are the *one*."

He took a deep breath—his first, it seemed, since we'd started talking. "I would greatly appreciate it if you took me on as your client."

His eloquence, his enthusiasm, and his desperation deeply moved me. I could tell that Corey Jacobs was not a man who enjoyed asking for things. Before prison, he probably never had to. He was a proud man, with a powerful charisma I didn't even have to be in his physical presence to feel.

Later that night, as I was getting ready to head home from work, I couldn't stop thinking of Corey's contagious enthusiasm, despite sixteen years in prison. I heard his voice—positive, hearty, upbeat—in my head. I remembered the way he'd paused before asking me to take his case. The way his boisterous voice got quiet, tentative, like this was his very last shot. And I thought about how I had felt talking to him. Awake and invigorated, maybe for the first time since the elation of Sharanda's release. Inspired. Corey

Jacobs was a *force*. An extraordinary, intelligent Black man, locked away from all the world for the prime of his life.

What was I agonizing over this for? I knew what I had to do. I pulled out my phone and texted Sharanda.

I'm taking the case.

A few seconds later I had her reply.

Well, I guess he's getting out, then.

JUSTICE IS BLIND—she's also slow. There was nothing I could do to make the wheels of justice turn faster, or sometimes at all. And for my clients and all of the desperate individuals who'd been buried alive by the draconian drug laws of the eighties and nineties, time was running out. President Obama had less than a year remaining in office. As some critics of the clemency process had already pointed out, he would have to grant the total number of clemencies from his first seven years in office every single week to get even close to the numbers the Clemency Initiative had originally promised. And Corey was going to be a tougher case than most. He didn't have just one life sentence. He had sixteen.

From the beginning I was struck by how similar Corey's case was to Sharanda's. Like Sharanda, the feds had no physical evidence against him—no drugs of any kind, no evidence of buys, no assets or large sums of money to seize. The entire case was based on the testimony of codefendants who received vastly lesser sentences than Corey in exchange for their testimony. And Corey had received the exact same eight points in sentencing enhancements as Sharanda: a four-point leadership enhancement for his alleged role in the conspiracy, a two-point gun enhancement for a gun codefendants said he used to carry, though no allegations of violence were made, and a two-point enhancement for "committing perjury" while testifying on the stand in his own defense. No matter how many times I came across the issue, the fact that enhancements in federal cases could be based upon the uncorroborated word of a snitch continued to blow my mind. Learning about Corey's case was like watching the same horror movie over and over again.

Corey may have been sentenced like the ruthless leader of an international drug cartel, but in fact he was far from it. Born in the Bronx, he had been raised by his grandparents. After graduating from Mount St. Michael Academy in the Bronx, he'd enrolled as an engineering student at Norfolk State University in Virginia when some friends from home approached him about getting into the game. They had the hookup in New York and could really make some money in Virginia, they said. Corey made a choice he'd regret for the rest of his life.

"For real, Brittany?" he told me on one of our many subsequent phone calls. "I was immature. Paying for college was a struggle, but it wasn't only that. We were trendsetters, know what I'm saying? Taste makers. I wanted to be the flyest kid out there. And I was what, nineteen? I stuck my toe in the game for a minute. Then bam. Quicksand."

His childhood friend Sean "Puffy" Combs, who was like a brother to Corey and with whom he'd promoted parties and shows for years, was interning at Uptown Records. Whenever they were together, Puff used all his powers of persuasion to get Corey out of the game. "Leave that shit alone, fam," he told Corey. "I'm telling you, the music industry is where it's at. Being in the pocket. Hittin' that beat. And I need you. It's time to get all the way out of that game and all the way into this one."

Corey knew Puff was right. He left Virginia and moved back to New York.

Where culture, music, and commerce met, that's where you'd find Corey. A creative visionary, he seized the moment, applying all the entrepreneurial insight he'd learned from dealing to legitimate businesses. He silk-screened tees and jackets with hip-hop slogans, cutting his costs by working with an artist who taught silk-screening to kids in Harlem. He secured a traveling booth at the Black Expo for his wares. He cofounded a basketball program for underserved youth. He also threw parties and managed rap artists—he had an incredible gift for spotting talent. One of his biggest producing credits was the classic Lost Boyz album *Legal Drug Money*.

When the feds arrested Corey, he hadn't sold drugs for years. But their case against him dated back to his college days. And at the turn of the century, they were hanging Black men in Virginia for federal drug cases.

On May 22, 2000, the courtroom was somber. Judge Henry Coke Morgan, Jr., addressed Corey at sentencing: "Do you understand that you are facing a mandatory life sentence in prison? There is not a great deal of flexibility as far as sentencing is concerned." The judge's hands were tied by the mandatory sentencing laws. Despite this being his first criminal conviction, Corey was given sixteen life sentences, one for each substantive crack cocaine charge.

To CREATE A compelling narrative and give Corey a real shot at clemency, I needed to get to know him as a person, and fast. I emailed him a questionnaire of lighthearted get-to-know-you questions: how he liked his eggs, his favorite color, whether he preferred sunrise or sunset. I needed to capture the man behind the sentence for the petition, and for myself. Corey's responses were engaging, full of the enthusiasm and joy that were clearly hallmarks of his being. He liked his eggs fried hard, missed the flaky, buttery taste (*My God,* he wrote) of a freshly baked croissant, preferred sunrises to sunsets and the ocean to lakes. He loved the color blue and the book *The Count of Monte Cristo*. But my more serious questions received carefully considered, thoughtful answers, which hinted at the daily struggle of incarceration in a maximum-security prison.

What scares you the most?

Losing myself, Corey wrote. *Being forced to do something in here to survive that is contrary to my very being. My whole life I've been about bringing pleasure to people, especially to our people. Whether it was in the form of fashion, or a great artist, or a party to dance their pains away—I'm a lover, not a fighter. I'm for Black excellence, Black joy. So that's my biggest fear: having to do something to survive that'll kill me in the end—if not my body, then my soul.*

During his stint at Pollock USP in Louisiana, overcrowding had led to a hideous rise in violence. Corey had been stabbed in the back while writing an email, suffered a collapsed lung, and almost died. After that, afraid for his life, he'd had to defend himself from attack twice. To live in the face of that kind of violence is terrifying. Other than those two incidents of self-defense, Corey had one of the most exceptional programming records during his incarceration that I had ever seen. He completed three major residential programs and earned more than a hundred certificates in courses to substantially enhance his education and personal development. He wrote an antibullying children's book series called *The Good Bully* and a book on domestic violence called *Unmasking Mr. Wrong.* He also designed a prototype for Square Up Now, a reentry program he wanted to launch that was tailored to provide assistance to men and women transitioning back into society from prison.

Despite Corey clearly exceeding the Clemency Initiative's criteria for an exceptional record through his rehabilitation efforts, any record of misconduct in prison—almost impossible to avoid—can jeopardize clemency. We would have to account for the self-defense incidents at Pollock. Given how volatile the environment, that wouldn't be hard to mitigate. I filed a request under the Freedom of Information Act and received extensive data on the excessive incidences of violence at Pollock. A further complication was the high quantity of ghost dope arbitrarily attributed to him at trial—over 850 kilograms of crack. These were the main reasons his current attorney gave him for not applying for clemency.

Corey's attorney worried me. A well-respected clemency expert with three decades of experience, she wasn't likely to welcome direction from a pro bono corporate lawyer, no matter how successful. And I understood that. I certainly wouldn't have liked it if one of my clients had brought in another attorney after I'd spent months working my butt off on their case.

But the more I spoke with Corey, the more it seemed his lawyer had barely been working at all. I was shocked to learn that after negotiating a top pay rate for taking his case, with Corey's friends pitching in to help cover costs, Corey's clemency attorney had essentially handed the bulk of the work back to Corey himself, telling him to write his own narrative explaining why he should receive a commutation. When Corey asked for guidance or feedback, he said, she was dismissive. When he eventually submitted his work to her, she took weeks to respond. And when she finally replied, all she told him was that he should not apply for clemency—at least not now. Despondent, Corey asked to meet with her in person. Reluctantly, she agreed.

Corey had a list of questions about his written narrative that he wanted to discuss with her, as well as several ideas about how to garner more support for his petition. But when he got to the meeting, his lawyer spent the first twenty minutes reeling off legal issues that seemed confusing to Corey. When she mentioned a prosecutor from a district court in North Carolina, he realized why.

"Hold up," Corey said. "That's not me. That's not my case."

"Oh, my mistake!" she said, laughing. "Of course it's not! I must be jet-lagged. Let me start over."

Corey's heart sank. This fancy lawyer wasn't even familiar enough with his case to discuss it. When he sat back in his chair, he had a single thought in his head: *I'm gonna die in here.* Struggling to maintain his optimism, he pressed on.

"I heard the judge in my case wrote a letter supporting Clinton Matthews's clemency petition," he said. "He's serving life for drugs like me. I think we should ask the judge to do it for my case, too."

"What makes you think that just because Judge Morgan did that for Clinton, he'll do it for you?" she said dismissively. "That's not an avenue worth pursuing."

"That's why I knew you were my last hope," Corey told me. "That whole time after we talked and you weren't sure whether you were going to take my case? I couldn't sleep. I mean, I had torn out your article and put it in my vision board folder. I believed in my heart it would manifest. But maybe you'd say you couldn't do it. And that would be it. That would be it for me."

The more I thought about it, the more frustrated Corey's attorney made me. Her behavior wasn't just negligent—it was exploitative. After making a few phone calls to people I trusted, I told Corey I wouldn't be able to continue unless she was off his case altogether. He moved swiftly to make that happen.

That Monday, I sent a letter to Corey's original sentencing judge, the honorable Henry Coke Morgan, Jr., detailing Corey's case and significant accomplishments while incarcerated, and asked him to write a letter in support of Corey's clemency petition. His old lawyer had been skeptical that Judge Morgan would do for Corey what he had done for others, but it took only two days for the judge to reply to me:

> In reviewing my comments at the sentencing, I am certain that I would not have imposed a life sentence had Fourth Circuit jurisprudence, at the time, not virtually mandated it. . . . I also agree that under the present sentencing jurisprudence I would not have imposed a life sentence on Mr. Jacobs and therefore support your request for clemency on his behalf.
>
> Mr. Jacobs's behavior while in prison reinforces the merits of his clemency request. I hope that you are successful in this endeavor.
>
> Sincerely yours,
> Henry Coke Morgan, Jr.

I was ecstatic. A letter of support from the sentencing judge was a huge deal. We'd hit the ground running. Which was good, because Corey's case was complicated and the clock was ticking. This time, I didn't have a year to meticulously prepare the petition, or fret and fuss over every aspect the way I had with Sharanda's and Donel's. President Obama would be out of office within the year, and I knew too well how much time it took for the Pardon Attorney and Department of Justice to review and consider petitions.

I gave myself one month.

AT THE SAME time I tackled Corey's clemency head-on, more than half my life was consumed by ORIX's current deal to a acquire a Brazilian financial services firm. It was intense, detail-oriented work on which millions of dollars could turn on a single mistake. It wasn't just that the ORIX work was hard or around-the-clock. It was that it was still consistently pushing me, challenging me, testing the limits of my confidence, forcing me to step up. I was often the only woman at the table and the only Black person anywhere in sight, and I took great pride in completing each new task with an excellence my foremothers would have been proud to witness.

I would work at the office until around ten and then come home to work on Corey's petition until the early-morning hours. Knowing how important public support had been for Sharanda and Donel, I was building him a website, too. His friend Karen helped me gather personal photos, old case files, and support letters from Corey's many, many friends and supporters. He and Karen had known each other since high school in the Bronx, and she was a terrific help in bringing Corey to life on the website. I knew that the clemency process—in fact, the entire effort to transform the criminal justice system—required people who were otherwise detached from the issue to have real empathy for those behind bars. To do that, they had to be able to see them as human beings. Sixteen life sentences would make Corey seem like a monster on paper. Making sure everyone got to see all sides of him was absolutely essential.

Corey quickly became more than a client. By virtue of his experience, and his boundless energy, he became a mentor and friend, talking me through difficult moments at work, sharing his own strategies for mental focus. We emailed through Corrlinks almost daily, discussing things we'd read and were thinking about. We talked about his latest chess match, our childhoods, and our grandmothers, who'd played such a central role in our young lives. We started studying books together, beginning with *The Short and Tragic Life of Robert Peace,* about a brilliant young microbiology student struggling to fit in at Yale while maintaining his roots and home life in poverty-stricken Newark, New Jersey.

"How are you doin', Britt? Tell me about your world," Corey asked during one of our early conversations.

I babbled on about a difficult problem at work, getting so technical and in the weeds I was sure I had lost him. But no. Corey was right there, with insightful guidance on how to work with strong personalities and creative solutions for issues that had seemed to reach a dead end. His business sense was intuitive, gifted. Not for the first time, I wondered what entrepreneurial heights he might have surpassed if he hadn't spent the last sixteen years locked in a metal cage.

When we had only five minutes left on our allotted fifteen-minute call, he switched gears. "So okay, Britt, that's work. But what about you? What are you doing to keep your mind right? You exercising? Do you meditate?"

I laughed it off, made some joke about running on autopilot, the weeks it would take to quiet my racing thoughts. But in reality I had never thought about it.

"Britt, your mind might be a lethal machine, but even machines need oil. I've seen way too much genius just burn down to empty. You need a plan to take care of you. Meditation is the key. I'm gonna send you some articles on it tomorrow. You gotta put yourself first."

As we hung up the phone, I thought about how my clients took care of me in all the best ways. How Mike showed up for all my speaking engagements, his kind face giving me hope when it was thin on the ground. The hours I spent laid out at Sharanda's house, listening to her counsel, letting her fuss over me. And now Corey, dropping Yodaesque knowledge from maximum security, reminding me to seek mental sanctuary so I could replenish. My clients were forever thanking me for my role in their lives, but it paled in comparison to the role they played in mine.

On February 19, right as dawn was breaking, I put the finishing touches on Corey's petition, both a two-hundred-page full-length version and the condensed petition required by the Clemency Initiative. I had met my one-month deadline. Now all we could do was file it and wait.

In the next weeks, I studied more books to discuss with Corey, and I threw myself back into my work at ORIX. I started to shadow the business guys, and at night I dug into books from pioneers in the private equity and venture capital worlds, determined to perfect my craft. But something was off. Instead of the rush of focus and adrenaline I had anticipated, I felt unfulfilled. My work at ORIX was still thrilling, everything that I thought I wanted. But I found myself missing the daily sprint of Corey's last-minute clemency appeal. My mind wandered. I'd start watching a CEO's YouTube lecture and find myself checking Bryan Stevenson's Equal Justice Initiative website instead, or returning to a heavily marked-up section of *The New Jim Crow*. I even asked for more petitions from the Clemency Project to screen, unable to ignore that the clemency window was closing for thousands of incarcerated people still buried alive. Nor could I ignore what these new feelings told me about myself: Increasingly, it was the social justice work I did in the silent midnight hours that fed my heart and soul.

In March 2016, the White House hosted an event to welcome home recent clemency recipients. Sharanda and I were thrilled to be invited. Sharanda was barely out of her prison cell and already an advocate for those she'd left behind. Normally it takes about two months to process the paperwork to get a clemency recipient out of prison and into the halfway house. But there was something about Sharanda. Even though it had been Christmas, the staff at Carswell worked overtime and came in on their days off to get Sharanda Jones home. Everybody knew she shouldn't be there. And everybody who knew her, loved her. Sharanda walked out of prison and into Clenesha's arms a mere two weeks after our clemency call. And now, three months later, we would be attending an event at the actual White House. "From the penitentiary to Pennsylvania Avenue," I said as we reached the airport. "Here we go!"

Sharanda hadn't been on a trip as a free woman in almost seventeen years, but if she was feeling anxious, she didn't let on. If you'd seen her walking through DFW Airport, you would have thought she flew every day. She walked briskly, with purpose, rolling her small suitcase behind her to stand in line at the Starbucks as if it were the most natural thing in the world.

Still, a lot had changed since her incarceration, and while Sharanda always tried to take everything in stride, I knew that her readjustment to the outside could be exhausting. I tried to be sensitive to it, but sometimes I was too late. After we checked in to our hotel in D.C., I told Sharanda I'd see her at dinner, and it wasn't until I was in my room that I realized she'd probably never used a keycard to open a hotel room door. When I took the elevator down to her room, I found Sharanda sitting on her bed, shaking her head and laughing. "Thank God a housekeeper came by!" she said. "You should have seen me out there trying to slide the card all over the door!" We laughed, but little incidents like this only reinforced for me the extreme isolation incarcerated people endure in prison.

When we arrived at the White House the next day, President Obama wasn't present, but just knowing that he and his beautiful Black family lived there, at 1600 Pennsylvania Avenue—in a house built by slaves—was extraordinarily moving to both of us. I have a picture on my desk of a photo Sharanda took that day with Valerie

Jarrett, Obama's senior adviser. In it, Jarrett is gazing at Sharanda as though she can't believe this vibrant, smiling woman had ever served any time in prison, let alone sixteen years and nine months of a life sentence. Many people from the Obama administration who met the clemency recipients that day had the same expression. It was easy to see what it meant: *This is a former prisoner? This is who we're locking up?*

I could understand their confusion. For most of its history, our country has worked so hard to demonize incarcerated people that we forget that they are our mothers and fathers, daughters and sons. Everyday people, all. Human beings who are not bad people, just made poor choices. I believe in the power of proximity, and at the White House that day, I was glad to see those so close to the highest office of the land rubbing shoulders with those who had for decades dwelled in our lowliest dungeons. Once those in power broke bread with those for whom mercy and justice had finally met, surely they would cease to see the thousands of waiting applications as anything other than human beings. Or so I hoped.

Seeing Sharanda embracing other recipients of clemency at the White House was incredibly moving. It was also an acute reminder that if Corey was ever going to have the chance to do the same, we had a lot of work to do.

The next morning, Sharanda and I waited nervously in a sleek white conference room just a few blocks east of the White House, in the Tenth Street offices of Covington & Burling, where Eric Holder was a partner. Sari Horwitz had surprised us by arranging a meeting with the former attorney general, the visionary behind the Clemency Initiative, at his law office. I was about to meet the first Black attorney general of the United States, a man I deeply admired and respected. I sat up straight, hands folded in front of me, full of nervous anticipation. But when Eric Holder walked in, relaxed, no tie, smiling at us so warmly it was as though he already knew us, I felt immediately at ease. He thanked us for the meeting and asked many questions, listening intently to each of our answers. Toward the end of the meeting, I asked him the question that had been weighing heavily on my mind since I submitted Corey's petition.

"I'm a corporate attorney," I said, "and I love that work. But my passion is criminal justice reform. I feel that mass incarceration is the most pressing civil rights issue of our time, and if I'm not doing everything I can to get people like Sharanda free, what am I really doing about it? I'm feeling conflicted about my career. I have other clients awaiting clemency and we're nearing the end of this historic push, and Obama's presidency. I feel like I have to do everything I can now, like there isn't time for anything else. Do you have any advice?"

Mr. Holder didn't hesitate. "Follow your passion," he said. "Do what you love. I know exactly what you're talking about. In fact— wait. My brother just sent me a wonderful quote about this today! Let me find it."

He scrolled through his text messages. His frank response— not tempered with any caveats, any implied judgment that leaving such a career path might be rash—had surprised me. Mr. Holder looked up from his phone.

"Here it is," he said. "'Where does my greatest joy intersect with the world's greatest need? Let me go there.' It sounds to me, young lady, like you know the answer to that already."

A FEW WEEKS later, I flew to Indiana to see Corey at Terre Haute USP. It was the first time we were meeting in person.

The day was so colorless the sky and buildings melted into each other. Razor wire unspooled in place of the pink and purple flowers I'd grown used to during my visits to Sharanda. I missed them now. Even those small splashes of color would have done something to mitigate the bleak, muted despair cloaking the formidable gray buildings of Terre Haute. There were no men in the yard, or on the barren concrete that stretched around the old gray buildings, crisscrossed with chain-link fences and more barbed wire.

The farther into the depths of a men's maximum-security

prison you go, the louder the clanging, echoing noise. The closer the air. The tighter the constriction in your chest. I tried to breathe through my mouth. Prison corridors smell like sweat and metal, iron and chains. Like the sharp edge of fear and the blunt edge of misery. But I'm glad I followed the guard through the concrete labyrinth to the attorney-client meeting room that day. Because soon after I sat down, in stepped the indomitable Corey Jacobs— larger than life, full of energy and purpose.

Corey's confident swagger made his soul appear to tilt on its axis, so much so that his walk seemed to defy gravity. But Corey's spine was straight, just like his words. He had a piercing gaze and a disarming smile. He opened his arms and enveloped me in a big hug.

"Man, it's good to see you, Britt! Here you are right in front of me! God is the greatest."

We spoke about his petition only briefly. By this point Corey felt fully like family. His refusal to be defeated inspires me to this day. Faced with a slow death sentence that few would be able to endure, Corey stayed true to himself. He had so much charisma, but the strongest feeling in his presence was a sense of profound calm. It makes a certain pragmatic sense: To survive in the nightmare of prison this long, his optimism and groundedness had to be persistent enough to drown out the nihilism surrounding him.

It was certainly loud that day in our meeting. The door to the meeting room was open throughout our visit, and I was jarred by the constant clanging of the keys, the sudden, hollow bangs of steel locks unlatched and metal doors banging open and closed. After a hectic workweek, every grating noise made my jaw clench, the knots in my neck and shoulders tighten. But Corey was unbothered, leaning forward and talking over and through it. It was so good to see him in person. His wire-rimmed glasses gave his timeless baby face a professorial air. Some of the youthful slimness from those early-'93 photos had given way to a larger, more muscular build—but his expressive brows and quick smile remained the same. When I flinched at a particularly loud bang, Corey smiled at me.

"You been meditating, Britt?" he asked. "How's that going? Getting your mind right?"

"I read all the articles you sent," I said, "but I've been so busy with work I just haven't had time."

"You start short, and then build up," he said. "It's a practice. I do about sixteen minutes a day—you could start with half that. We should set a time, meditate together every day. It really focuses your mind, keeps you sharp. Let's do it right now. Come on."

"Right here? Now?"

I couldn't think of anywhere less relaxing than this boxlike room in maximum security. Just as I thought it, I caught myself. This was probably the most peaceful room in the prison.

"Just breathe," Corey said. "Close your eyes. Feel your body in the chair. Picture the ocean in front of you—I know you love the ocean. Just watch the waves and breathe."

I took a deep breath and closed my eyes. And with Corey guiding me, I did my very first formal meditation right there at Terre Haute USP. He was right. As I breathed across the table from Corey and focused on the rolling surf in my mind's eye, I *did* feel the horrors of the facility fade into the background. And it wasn't only the prison that faded. Tension I'd held in my body all week seemed to melt and lift. It wasn't easy to let my thoughts go, but once I did, a feeling of well-being hummed.

"Thank you," I told him. "That felt good."

"You should do it every day!" Corey said. "Somewhere under the trees, in nature. I just read this crazy article about the way being in nature affects your well-being. It actually rewires our brain in some way. My own practice is pretty advanced at this point, but reading that, I thought, *damn,* I meditate every morning but I can't try the nature part until Obama comes through for us. There are no trees here. Matter of fact, I haven't seen a single tree in *years*. Can you believe that?"

Corey kept talking, but I didn't hear much of what he said after that. Just being able to see trees out her cell window had lifted Sharanda's spirits when they were lowest, had given her the strength and the glimpse of hope she needed. But Corey hadn't seen a tree in years. *A tree.* The high gates around the prison prevented men from seeing any even when in the yard. Imagine never laying eyes on something so simple as a tree. No elm, nor oak. No cypress. No blooming magnolia. No palm tree or cedar tree or lemon tree or pine. In their place, razor wire and concrete, bare dirt and tarmac. Steel.

When I left Terre Haute that day, all I could think about was Corey's wish to see a tree. The moment I left the gates I began taking in the textured trunks or young branches of each one I passed with renewed attention. Corey's incredible energy, his refusal to be defeated by the inhumane punishment of sixteen life sentences, was all the evidence I needed of a simple truth: A system that did everything in its power to dehumanize and still failed was a vulnerable system. And a vulnerable system can be transformed.

I left my visit with Corey in a new state of consciousness. I no longer wanted to be just a lawyer. I wanted to use my platform to promote the greater good. In the new American age of mass incarceration, the need for freedom was far too urgent.

Chapter 15

MIDNIGHT

After my visit to Corey, we began regularly meditating together, at 8:16 every morning. We worked our way up to sixteen minutes. Sixteen because it was a number of great significance
to Corey—he had a whole philosophy built around it. My own
math mind soon got on board, and the significance of the number
sixteen in our lives seemed endless: Sixteen life sentences. Sixteen
letters in each of our names. Sharanda had served sixteen years.
Mike's first sentence reduction, September 16. His second, October 16. Sixteen was a spiritually charged number, and 8:16 was the
perfect time for us. It was amazing how clear-minded I felt, how
energized.

And after every session, I felt closer to making a momentous
personal decision that just months before I would never even have
considered. As the sand slipped through the Clemency Initiative
hourglass, I found myself continuing to struggle mightily with the
question: Should I leave ORIX?

I had worked so hard to get where I was. The main reason I
went to law school in the first place was to leverage my accounting

degree in corporate law, and ORIX was the best place for it. I loved the hectic pursuit of the deal, the pulse of global power surging through the offices on the cusp of a major acquisition. The absolute conviction that anything was possible if you put the best minds to it. And there was the security of a six-figure paycheck. I couldn't live on goodwill and symbolic stipends, and I didn't want to. I was still knocking down student loans. And I liked having nice things, traveling, helping my mom and Jazz without worrying about it.

I was also often the only Black woman in the boardroom with C-level executives during deal negotiations. I felt I had a responsibility to keep walking into those rooms and show that Black women deserved to be at the table. To forge a path that others could follow, the way Christa and others had done for me.

But time was running out on Obama's second term, and there was no telling what the next president's approach to clemency would be. If we didn't get Corey free in the next eight months, there was a strong chance he wouldn't get out at all. Ever. We all knew the stakes. And with a man's life on the line, spending ten hours a day ironing out IPOs and closing private equity deals for multibillion-dollar corporations held little meaning. I searched deep within myself.

Our 8:16 meditation sessions helped. But sometimes you need your dad. I went to visit him in his new home in Rockwall, which had its own five acres and a pond, just like Daddy Sudie's. We sat together on the back of his truck and watched the sunset. I told him all my concerns, all the factors I'd been weighing over and over, losing nights of sleep.

"At ORIX, I know just what I'm doing, where I'm going. Every day is different, but there's still a routine to it. I mean, without a firm, what will I even do all day? How will I make money?"

My dad listened attentively all the way through. "Stop thinking about the challenges," he said. "Imagine the possibilities instead."

The sun melted, turning the sky orange. The pine trees around the property were backlit by the vibrant sky. We sat together, watching. Since my first job with Chase Bank at seventeen, I had been on this career track. My concerns about flying from the corporate nest were sensible, and real. But so was Corey. So was my passion for justice. What new realities might I create if I just walked through my fear? As I sat shoulder to shoulder with my dad in the waning Texas light, the answer suddenly seemed very clear.

As if he had heard my thoughts, my dad spoke again.

"Take the leap, BK," he said. "Follow your heart."

I waited until May so that I could collect my year-end bonus, which was enough to cover my cost of living for twelve months. And then I took the leap. The moment I did, I felt so much peace. And full of energy. I was going to get Corey free. Period. And I was going to devote every minute of my time pursuing justice for all those suffering under draconian drug-sentencing laws.

IMMEDIATELY, I STARTED to pound the pavement for Corey. I wasn't just working full-time to secure his freedom, I was working overtime. It's astounding how much you can get done in a ten-hour workday when you're not tied to a desk or the minutiae of corporate law. Mike's brother, Wayland, had received clemency on May 5, 2016, boosting the wind in my sails as I got going. That spring, I flew all over the country, searching out people and initiatives that could help get Corey out of prison. I racked up airline miles, collected countless business cards. I fell asleep at my computer in hotel rooms in multiple states.

Obama's Clemency Initiative, once and still a beacon of hope for so many, had turned from being a potential tool for mass liberation to a bureaucratic nightmare. The previous spring, U.S. Pardon Attorney Deborah Leff had resigned in frustration, citing a lack of resources and staff to process the flood of petitions her office was receiving. The DOJ was reversing her recommendations, she said, and an increasing number of clemencies her office believed should be granted never made it to the White House. There were simply too many levels of review before the thousands of clemency petitions even made it to the president's desk. And the reviewers were federal prosecutors, the very people who had pushed for harsh sentences in the first place. Between a lack of capacity, red tape, and bureaucratic inertia, there was the very real threat that thousands of people who met the criteria would miss out entirely on the opportunity for relief.

When I interned for a federal judge in Houston, I'd watched mass incarceration operate with rubber-stamp efficiency. It was like witnessing a factory dismantle car parts rather than human lives and families. But the clemency process, intended to undo some of the worst instances of oversentencing, seemed unable to process the sheer numbers of those affected. The system was experiencing a circuit overload. So much so that in the spring of 2016, Deputy Attorney General Sally Yates sent out an urgent message for lawyers to submit petitions by mid-May in order to give the DOJ time to review any new petitions before Obama left office. Her announcement jolted the clemency work to a fever pitch.

I amped up my commitment with the Clemency Project, which was facing problems of its own. The same massive swell of hopeful clemency petitioners that had overwhelmed the Pardon Attorney's office had maxed out our capacity. Despite being the largest pro bono effort in history, even four thousand lawyers were not enough to handle the thirty-six thousand people who ultimately applied. Hopeful petitioners had been waiting months just to be assigned a lawyer.

I was still volunteering on the project's screening committee, still supervising and training lawyers to get petitions completed and submitted, when they asked me if I could help recruit and train more lawyers. But where to find them? I had been a student when I'd first won reductions for Keyon and started fighting for Sharanda; what I lacked in experience I made up in dogged deter-

mination and the passion and energy only the young and unfettered possess. Maybe I could tap into that same energy among the
students at my alma mater, SMU.

I reached out to Jennifer Collins, the dean of the law school,
and proposed a pop-up clinic. I would teach a class of law students
everything I could about the executive clemency process. Instead
of reading case law, teams of students would draft actual clemency petitions under my supervision, to be submitted to the White
House. Forty students signed up. Instead of the one or two cases
we were urging lawyers to take on through the Clemency Project,
we were able to take on twenty.

Knowing that the window for clemency was rapidly closing, I
also took on three new clients of my own, Darryl "Lil D" Reed,
Charles "Duke" Tanner, and Trenton Copeland. Barely out of his
teens, Darryl was arrested at the age of twenty in Oakland, California, and had served twenty-eight years in prison by the time I
took on his case. His presence in the Bay Area was legendary. Even
from behind bars he mentored Bay Area rap legends MC Hammer, E40, and Too Short, and worked to empower inner-city
youth. Duke Tanner was a former professional boxing star, swept
off the mean streets of Gary, Indiana—one of the poorest cities in
the Midwest—in his youth by wealthy investors to train. Boxing
was his way out of poverty and he eventually compiled a 19-0 record as a pro. He supported many in the old neighborhood, paying
for youth gyms, rent, childcare, school supplies; whatever people
needed, Duke tried to provide. But when an injury disrupted his
rise to stardom and both his parents were diagnosed with a terminal illness, he got into the game. Set up with a fake buy that never
took place, Duke was arrested at the age of twenty-four and sentenced to life without parole, despite an outpouring of support
from trainers, sponsors, and the community. Trenton was my
exact same age, and from Pensacola, Florida. He'd received a life
sentence for drugs at the age of twenty-seven and was entering his
sixth year in prison. He reminded me so much of the guys I'd
grown up with in Commerce.

Each case struck a personal chord for me. Each man was an individual, with his own essential story. And each man was a victim of the disastrous policies stemming from the War on Drugs. Our inhuman drug laws had stolen the prime of their lives. I worked to file petitions for all three, and when another lawyer dropped the ball on a case, I took on the case of Burnett Shackleford as well.

IN JULY, I traveled to Philadelphia for the Democratic National Convention. I wasn't on any panels, didn't have a speaking engagement lined up. But I had made a targeted list of attendees that included members of Congress, influencers, and advocates. I was determined to make a personal appeal to anyone in a position to help Corey and my new clients.

In a gathering that large, and in an atmosphere as charged as the 2016 election season, it was hard to get anyone's attention. I didn't quite know where to start. But I was there. I networked as though my life depended on it. After all, my clients' lives did. In the bustling confines of the Wells Fargo Center, I talked up senators and congressional aides. I told Corey's story to anyone on my list who would listen. I got business cards and email addresses, phone numbers and names of other people who might be able to help. I handed out one-pagers, sent emails, made plans for conference calls.

But the most impactful moment of that trip came when I attended an art for social justice installation featuring a panel called Truth to Power, focused on criminal justice reform. Before the panel, I was sitting in a chair, scrolling through my phone, looking to see if any of the morning's contacts had emailed me back, when an energetic white guy with a shaved head approached me.

"You're Brittany Barnett, aren't you? I think I met you and your client Sharanda at the White House," he said, shaking my hand. "I'm Michael Skolnik."

I knew who he was. At the time, he was Russell Simmons's

political consultant. I knew him for his work connecting social justice causes with celebrities and pop culture. He'd been the guy to get "I Can't Breathe" shirts to LeBron James and other NBA stars following Eric Garner's death, and to help plan President Obama's screening of the Vice Media film about criminal justice reform, *Fixing the System*.

"It's great to see you again! Do you have anything prepared for this panel?" he asked. "Like, you want me to cue you up for anything?"

I gave him a blank look before I understood. I was just there to watch, I told him. To learn.

"Are you kidding me?" he said. "You shouldn't be in the audience. You should be *on* this panel."

Which is how I found myself, ten minutes later, onstage at a DNC-related event in a FREE COREY JACOBS T-shirt and ripped jeans, participating in a panel on how to fix our criminal justice system. It seemed everyone on the panel was familiar with my work on Sharanda's case. I had been so focused on getting my clients free, I hadn't really thought about how my work and the amplification of her story moved others. I shared my clients' stories that day, but I also talked about the systemic nature of the problem. There were thousands of Coreys and Sharandas buried alive in America's prisons.

Watching the panel that day was attorney Jessica Jackson, who, along with the political commentator, author, and activist Van Jones, had cofounded #cut50, a national bipartisan organization dedicated to cutting the prison population by fifty percent in ten years. The next day, we had a phone call to discuss my work with Corey. Sitting in my hotel room, my aching feet elevated on a hotel pillow, I told Jessica that I'd recently quit my corporate job to work on clemency cases like Corey's full-time. I was halfway through making another appeal for Corey, when she cut me off.

"Can I call you back in like twenty minutes?" she said.

Sure, I told her.

I leaned back in the chair, trying to catch a quick nap before strapping my shoes back on and marching down to attend another event. Virginia Congressman Bobby Scott would be there, and a letter from him would be very helpful. I let my mind wander. I must have fallen asleep, because before it seemed like any time had passed, my phone was ringing again.

"Brittany," Jessica said, "I just got off the phone with Van. We're starting a campaign called #ClemencyNOW, and we've been looking for someone to lead it. Are you interested?"

"Seriously?"

In twenty minutes, things had gone from zero to a hundred. I'd thought that I was talking to Jessica about raising awareness for Corey—but it turned out that unbeknownst to me, I'd been in a job interview. Van had already talked to her about my work, Jessica said. They believed I was the person they needed to lead their new initiative.

Over the next hour or so, Jessica explained the initiative to me. Essentially, the goal was to put public pressure on President Obama to grant more clemencies in the final months of his term in office. As of July 2016, he'd granted clemency to only 562 people, even though thousands more met his criteria. #Cut50 was asking the president to triple the resources dedicated to the process, and to eliminate a lot of the bureaucratic red tape that slowed it down.

I was intrigued but skeptical. I had no experience as the leader of a large-scale justice campaign. I wasn't even quite sure what a campaign of this order would look like. On the other hand, I had resigned from ORIX not only to free Corey but also to take advantage of this window for clemency, in any way possible, for thousands of others. Jessica's offer would provide me with a national platform. I knew I had been effective with my individual clients, but I'd never built a campaign before, or taken on any kind of movement role. Would I be effective?

A few hours later, Van Jones called me himself. I'd met Van once before, also at the White House with Sharanda. But most of what I knew about him I knew from his television appearances, on CNN and elsewhere: that he was a bold leader in the social justice space and dedicated to the fight.

"Brittany, you were able to achieve more victories in half the time, working as an individual than I've seen whole organizations manage to accomplish," he said when he called me. "We need you. The people need you."

"I just don't know if I'm qualified to do this," I said. "This is not where my experience lies."

"It's where your experience is *going* to lie," Van said, emphatic, his voice rising to the pitch I knew from television. "You're a brilliant young lawyer, committed to the cause. Our prison system is a five-alarm fire, Brittany. You know this. And you're the firefighter we need."

I thought of all the clients I'd worked with up to then. It had been my personal attention that had been so meaningful for them, and that same attention had helped move the wheels of justice. But what if I could take that attention and attach it to a national organization? What if I could make everyone see the deep and senseless cruelty at the heart of our nation's prisons? What if I could take these people and their families directly to the doors of the White House and make sure that the president himself saw them?

"Okay," I told Van. "I'm in."

ONE THING YOU should know if you're ever contemplating calling the former attorney general of the United States: He doesn't usually pick up. But the day I called, using the card he'd given me that day in his office with Sharanda, Eric Holder happened to be waiting for a call from someone else. His call was scheduled for 4:30, and I called at 4:20. Divine.

Also divine? Mr. Holder was drafting a *New York Times* op-ed that day, focused on oversentencing and mass incarceration. He was looking for an example, a person whose story could humanize his argument for criminal justice reform. Someone whose plight exemplified the huge cost of our current unjust policies. And I was calling to discuss just such a case.

Attorney General Holder was delighted to hear that I had followed my passion and was pursuing justice full-time. He was also deeply moved by Corey's story, and disgusted by his life sentence. And he was impressed by the fact that a federal judge was writing in support of his clemency. More than that, he identified with Corey.

"We're both New York kids at heart," he said. "A Queens kid and a Bronx kid. And he's been behind bars as long as I've held any kind of office."

There was a pause.

"Do you think he'd mind if I used his story in my op-ed?" the attorney general asked me.

"Mind?" I answered. "He'd be honored."

Eric Holder's op-ed, "We Can Have Shorter Sentences and Less Crime," appeared in the August 11, 2016, edition of *The New York Times*. The morning I saw it, I stood on my doorstep in Dallas and cried, thinking of Corey, and Sharanda, and all the other people trapped behind bars. I wanted to get them all out, and it seemed like the political machine might finally be moving in that direction.

But it wasn't moving fast enough. Energized by Holder's op-ed, and in an effort to share the national platform of #ClemencyNOW with the families and advocates who needed it, I began to plan and organize my first multiday, nationwide social justice event—#ClemencyNOW's Hope for the Holidays. As director of the campaign, I would gather more than seventy-five family members of clemency seekers to converge on Washington in November, along with activists and attorneys. During our first D.C. visit, deputy attorney general Sally Yates had told the clemency recipients and their guests that the administration viewed every clemency petition as a heartbeat. I wanted them to experience each petition as *multiple* heartbeats. I wanted the administration to know and feel, as I did, the ripple effect of each unjust sentence—

268 - BRITTANY K. BARNETT

the sons and daughters, wives, mothers, grandmothers, and husbands, who suffered alongside their incarcerated loved ones.

Putting together an event of this magnitude would require a massive effort, and as September turned to October, my days and nights were taken up with quarterbacking an incredible team in everything from nuts-and-bolts logistics to invitations to program design. Jon Perri of Change.org came through again, and Nkechi Taifa and Amy Povah helped us fundraise. Michael Skolnik's team helped us with production and secured D.C. permits. Phone2Action created a text campaign and my friend Breon Wells got Congressman Hakeem Jeffries to agree to speak. Corey's friend Karen worked with Mindy, GEM's program director, to coordinate travel for dozens of families and organize the hotels, food, and charter buses for everyone who we confirmed could attend.

Most important to me was making sure that the people in prison could in some way be present and have their voices heard. I set up legal calls with eight men and women in federal prison and recorded heartfelt messages to their loved ones and direct pleas to President Obama. I taught myself how to use the program Audacity in order to overlay the audio over a picture of each person to create a video that would help it seem as if they were actually in the room with us. And I had T-shirts made with the slogan I'd used since my first campaign for Sharanda: THERE IS NOTHING MORE URGENT THAN FREEDOM. Our efforts swiftly gained momentum, trumped only by the increasing pressure and anxiety we all felt.

The clemency process is maddeningly opaque. After all, there is no exact formula for mercy. Essentially, you send a petition to the president and then you wait. And then you wait some more. For months, we'd operated on edge, never knowing when Obama would order more people free, never knowing when we might get a single call from the Pardon Attorney's Office that we'd been among the lucky ones. Now, with weeks to go before the election and just a few months until Obama would leave office, I was afraid to put down my phone even for a second. I was afraid I'd miss the call and they wouldn't call back. My clients suffered even more, calling me every day to hear if there was any news, any inkling that they would be next. Sadly, there didn't seem to be any rhyme or reason for who got clemency and who didn't.

Then, less than two weeks before we would bring the families of incarcerated people to D.C. for an action directly in front of the White House, Donald Trump was elected president.

The idea that a candidate who had run on a far-right, law-and-order, nationalist platform—a man who had, in the nineties, taken out a full-page ad in *The New York Times* calling for the *execution* of the Central Park Five—was about to become the president of the United States was deeply upsetting to anyone involved in prison reform. In our minds—and probably his—Trump was the antithesis of Barack Obama, a compassionate, evenhanded man who wanted to fix a system he saw as deeply flawed. Obama wanted to put *fewer* people in prison, not more. Trump, if his speeches were to be believed, wanted the opposite.

The day after Hillary Clinton conceded, I fielded calls from concerned family members, some of them in tears, asking if our event was still on. How could we possibly free people when a man like that was president? *Of course it's still on,* I said. *They're still in prison, aren't they? That means we still have to get them out.*

In retrospect, I think a part of me was just numb that November. Trump's election wasn't really a surprise to me the way it was for a lot of Americans. I was deeply saddened, of course. And ashamed. But in the short term, the election didn't really change things. If anything, the prospect that one of our most enlightened presidents was going to be followed by potentially one of its most oppressive only heightened our resolve to push on through the end of Obama's term. Those few months had been important before. But now we knew they might be our last hope.

While the election had put much of America into a shocked stupor, it jolted urgency into the clemency movement. Obama would be leaving office in just eight short weeks, and with the clock ticking, we had to save as many lives as we could. And there were so, so many still buried alive.

That is why on November 14, 2016, as the final moments of Obama's presidency ticked down, I stood shoulder to shoulder with those families, advocates, and formerly incarcerated men and women, a megaphone in my hand and Sharanda by my side. Every person there represented a person locked in prison.

I'd planned #ClemencyNOW to be a two-day event. On opening night, major news outlets had covered us in front of the White House; a daughter would be giving a *Vice News* interview about her father's life sentence while a mother was interviewing with NBC imploring the president to free her son. Waiting for a loved one serving a virtual life sentence "is like waiting for someone in a coma," said Angela Warren, whose husband and father had been locked away for over a decade. "You know the person is breathing, but will they ever return?"

We'd also held a panel discussion at Google's headquarters called "Life After Life," where Sharanda and five other clemency recipients shared their stories in the hope that it would ease the passage to freedom for those who still awaited presidential mercy. Everyone on the panel had been freed from a life sentence. I even arranged for Alice to Skype in from prison to share her story in her own eloquent and powerful words. When Alice's round, smiling face appeared on the screen, Sharanda's eyes filled with tears. Despite her prison khakis, Alice looked regal as ever, her hair pinned in a forward-combed natural slant, reminiscent of Nefertiti's crown. Calm and poised regardless of whatever indignities she'd been put through at the prison to make it to the computer screen, she beamed out at all of us.

"My greatest pain," she said after sharing her remorse for her involvement as a telephone mule in a conspiracy, "is having been separated from my children for over two decades, and now missing out on my grandchildren."

"Ms. Alice," I said, my own voice quavering, "I've known you since I was a baby attorney, as you all used to call me, a law student trying to help a woman facing the same fate as you are now. Tell me, what is the mood among the women where you are?"

"Very somber," Alice said. "Because they know that President Obama is committed to granting clemencies. And time is truly running out. However, I felt a shift in the atmosphere. Hope is in the air, because it has spread like wildfire in the compound that this event is taking place in. Thank you all."

By the morning of November 15, the Washington power structure had gotten wind that a major clemency event was unfolding. That's when we took our rallying cry right to the front steps of the Department of Justice, where we would deliver two million signatures to the DOJ. Moments after we'd reached the steps, passing cars began to honk in support, media cameras flashed. A twelve-year-old girl tearfully clutched a sign emblazoned with the image of a father she knew only through fifteen-minute phone calls. A forty-five-year-old woman held the photograph of her four children's grandmother, twenty years in prison. Fathers, daughters, wives, grandparents—the families of the incarcerated stood strong as we rooted ourselves into the concrete steps of the Department of Justice, the very picture of dignified determination mixed with pain.

I called my sister MiAngel Cody to the microphone, the federal defense lawyer who had pushed me to file Mike's motion to reconsider. MiAngel was such a force, hazel eyes flashing from a face of flawless brown skin. She spoke with knowledge and power about the very issues about which I sometimes felt I was shouting into the void. Her passion lit the crowd as she called the names of those still waiting for mercy. Ferrell Scott. Alice Johnson. Corey Jacobs. Eric Wilson. William Underwood.

My client Darryl "Lil D" Reed stood next to me, his survivorship propping me up. On August 30, Corey's forty-eighth birthday, Obama had granted 111 more clemencies, with Lil D's among them, just two months after I'd submitted his petition. Darryl is small in stature but gigantic in charisma, intelligence, and personality. A California man, he stood shivering in the D.C. cold, no doubt still in the throes of disbelief at his recent release. Only two weeks after walking out of the prison gates, he stood in front of the DOJ with the rest of us, determined to leave no one behind.

Jason Hernandez took the mic next. Sentenced to life in his early twenties, Jason studied the law and wrote his own clemency petition from a federal prison cell. He'd been one of the "Obama Eight," the first people President Obama had ordered freed. He had since become a tireless advocate for those he left behind, still incarcerated, a breathing reminder of the possibility of redemption. "I'll be honest," Jason said, his breath visible in the frigid November air. "With the passing of the guard, the passing of the torch from President Obama to Trump, I feel that I'm at a funeral. And that the death is going to be clemency. I feel that urgency, and I'm pretty sure the president feels it as well.

"Now, I love the president like a father," Jason continued, his voice rising and cracking with emotion, "and I can't thank him enough for what he's done for me and what he's done for my family. But dammit, Mr. President, you got to do more."

A young man raised his fist and kept it in the air, no matter the bitter cold. Serrell and Skyler Scott, the son and daughter of Ferrell Scott, who was serving a life sentence for a marijuana conviction, leaned on each other. I saw my client Trenton Copeland's mother turn and bury her face in another mother's shoulder. Ebony Underwood, whose father, William Underwood, had been incarcerated for twenty-nine years, stood with her face turned to the sky, tears spilling down her cheeks. Not in despair, but with the relief that comes when an unbearable burden is lifted by a sharing of pain. It was as though each time someone stepped to the mic, we all breathed a sigh of relief. We were not alone. And with voices this loud and a message this pure, how could those in power fail to hear us?

The next day, families would leave at dawn to drive back down South or catch flights to the Midwest or California. Attorneys and activists would return to our grind, exerting pressure in any and every way we could to those in power. That night, we walked back toward our separate hotel rooms, hoping beyond hope that the bright light of the supermoon was a sign of things to come. We had delivered two million signatures to the Department of Justice that day. Two million people who supported the successful resolution of all of our clemency petitions. Two million people who prayed for justice to be served. We were drained, but empowered. Our gathering had been one final, impassioned plea to the White House: Please, do not pass us by.

ON NOVEMBER 29, just over two weeks later, the federal government answered our call. It was not the answer we were looking for. Instead of a list of clemencies, the Department of Justice released six hundred names of incarcerated people whose clemency petitions had been denied. Denial was a devastation. There was no appeals process for clemency, and there was no telling whether Trump had any interest in granting clemency for drug offenses. Without retroactive sentencing laws, this was it. Back in Dallas, I desperately scrolled down the list of names on the Department of Justice website with single-minded focus, dreading what I would find. *Please don't let Corey's name be on the list*, I kept repeating to myself. Finally I reached the last name. It wasn't his. The fist in my chest unclenched. If Corey wasn't denied, he still had a chance. I went frantically back to the top just to make sure. But this time, I started to see names I knew. And the pain I had steeled myself against the first time began to hit.

Ferrell Scott: Clemency denied. William Underwood: Clemency denied. Lashanda Hall: Clemency denied. Roderick Reed: Clemency denied.

I experienced each familiar name as a punch in the gut. For these women and men—some of whose family members I had just held in my arms in D.C.—the slim light of hope offered by the Clemency Initiative had just gone completely out. Worse, if that was even possible, there had been no forewarning of this announcement, no time for attorneys or family members to gently inform those waiting in prison. I got an urgent text from Diddy, who had heard about the list of names published without preamble on the DOJ website and was worried for Corey.

What if he doesn't make it? Is this the last one for Obama?

I felt Diddy's panic and tried to reassure him, even in my own moment of darkness. Even for a man as powerful as Sean Combs, the criminal justice system seemed impossible to take on. But it was hard to stay hopeful when for so many, the light had just gone out for good.

I spent the day reaching out to the families whose loved ones had just lost their one chance at freedom. They were terrible calls. Serrell Scott, Ferrell's daughter, was crying so hard she could barely speak. "I couldn't even get the words out to tell my dad," she said. "What is he going to do now? What am I going to do?" I'd grown very close to his children, Serrell and her brother Skyler, in the lead-up to Hope for the Holidays. Skyler wasn't answering his phone, and I was worried about him. All these kids wanted was to be with their dad. What sense did this make?

By evening, I was exhausted, empty. It was devastating to hear the anguish in the voices of those who only two weeks before had stood on the White House lawn with hope in their hearts. I sat on the couch in my Dallas apartment, staring despondently out at the lights of the city.

And then I got one more call.

"Sherene, how are you? Thanks for calling me back. I'm so, so sorry about your dad." Sherene's father had been on the denial list. I had been trying to reach her all day.

When she answered, though, it wasn't just grief that I heard in her voice. She sounded cold, hard. "Look, Brittany. I know you have connections. I know you know someone in Washington. You have to help us!"

"Sherene, I don't know anyone," I said. "If I did, everyone would be free. Everyone." I slipped farther down off the couch. I was so drained from sharing in everyone's grief. I couldn't believe the conversation I was having.

"How'd you get Darryl out, then? Everyone's always telling us they can't help our dad because of his case. But they called Darryl a kingpin! How'd he get out? We know you know somebody. Why you holding out on us? It's not right."

Her accusations hurt. I hadn't slept in weeks. I was doing everything I knew how to do and then some. And this family thought I was holding out on them? Her dad wasn't even my client. I wanted to weep.

"Who do you think I know?" I said. "I don't know anybody. I know who you know."

"Don't lie, Brittany. Eric Holder is like some kind of mentor to you. That's why all your clients get out."

"He doesn't know me like that. Sherene, believe me, if I had any say, your dad would be free. I promise you."

After the phone call I left the couch and lay on the cold floor. I'd never felt lower in my life. All these people, buried alive. I'd thought if only those in power could hear us, more would be freed. The denials were cruel. And now their families were doubting me? My intentions, my integrity? It hurt. But I couldn't judge Sherene. What kind of pain would I feel if it were my dad?

My cheek pressed to the cold, hard floor, I checked my email on my phone, hoping for a message from Skyler. He'd sent one saying he was okay. And I had a new message from Corey:

Listen to this, Britt. Get some nourishment. You gotta stay up.

I scrolled down to find the text of "A Knock at Midnight," a sermon by Dr. Martin Luther King, Jr., with a note from Corey telling me to find the audio online so I could be nourished by King himself.

I plugged in my headphones. In the sermon, King uses the parable of the neighbor who knocks upon his friend's door at midnight, seeking three loaves to feed a hungry traveler. The man's need is great, King reminds us, because the loaves of bread he seeks are spiritual loaves. The bread of faith, the bread of hope, the bread of love. The man's friend refuses him. "Do not bother me; the door is now shut," his friend says, "and my children are with me in bed, I cannot get up and give you anything." In his tremendous tenor, his voice rolling with the calm power and depth of the sea, King explains that the man continues to persistently knock; he will not be denied. He urges us to embrace the hope, faith, and love necessary to continue our struggle for justice in midnight's darkest hour. With faith in his friend's generosity, and out of a deep need to provide loaves to his visitor, the man knocks. "Midnight is a confusing hour when it is difficult to be faithful." His voice sonorous, King intones, "The weary traveler by midnight who asks for bread is really seeking the dawn. Our eternal message of hope is that dawn will come."

Listening to King's voice ringing out from the pulpit, I felt warmth begin to flow where only a wrung-out feeling had been. King's tenor lifted me from within. His words were a balm for my wounds and his message soothed my soul. Dawn will come, the sermon promised. Even after the darkest night, dawn will come.

I listened to that recording on repeat the whole night through.

It was hard to know how to thank Corey Jacobs for everything he did for me. That night was so difficult—to have pushed so much over the last year, only to see thousands of people's hopes dashed in an instant. My pain could not have equaled that of those whose last fire of hope for freedom had been extinguished. And I was just one part of a vast and growing movement; no doubt many of my fellow freedom fighters were feeling lost that night, also struggling to find the strength to go forward. But Corey would not let me fall into the depths of despair, would not let me relinquish hope. It was his enduring gift to me, to be there when I needed it, to help me see that midnight through to the dawn. To help me keep knocking when at first I had been refused.

Three weeks later, on December 19, the Department of Justice released a list of 231 people granted clemency by President Barack Obama. Corey Jacobs was one of them.

Chapter 16

Genius Behind Bars

The night sky alone in the mountains outside Tucson, Arizona, is enough to heal what ails you. The universe arches over you in a navy dome, every constellation as vivid and architectural as in an astronomy textbook. After seven years of nonstop hustle and work, it was time to rest, recuperate, and reflect. I had checked myself into a hotel and spa, and as I stood on my patio and looked up at the stars I inhaled the clean air and the quiet. I felt transported back to the Bogata of my childhood.

Anyone used to constant forward motion can tell you that it's not always easy slowing down. You allow yourself to feel things you've held at bay until this point. Those things wash over you like waves. You can try to keep your feet rooted firmly in the sand, try not to be sucked in by the undertow. But the ocean is stronger than you and the waves will come.

There was still so much work to be done. But sometimes the task seemed so enormous, it was difficult to know where to begin. True, there had been successes. I had pursued sentence reductions for Duke Tanner and Robert Carter, and won. Duke's reduction relieved him of a life sentence. Along with Corey, two more of the clients I had taken on in the last push of the initiative had received clemency, Trenton Copeland and Burnett Shackleford. Their calls had come from the pardon attorney himself, bringing my total to seven. I was tremendously proud and humbled to have experienced this part of the legacy of America's first Black president, and of course I was elated for them. But as always, the successes made the road ahead seem that much harder. Corey's clemency was a "term" commutation, which meant he'd have to spend two more years in prison before going to a halfway house. And of course, for every one of my clients who'd made it out, there were tens of thousands of people just as worthy still suffering behind bars.

In taking a break, I was seeking more than stillness. I was seeking clarity. The truth was I was scared. I'd slipped the golden handcuffs at ORIX to throw myself into a battle that had a clear end date. But now Obama was gone. Clemency was gone. The battle was over, but the war wasn't. I didn't know if there was a place for me in the battles ahead. I didn't know if I had it in me.

At the Arizona resort, I signed up for private meditation sessions, hikes, massages, even equine therapy. I tried to live in the moment. To look out at the mountains without feeling that I should be on the phone, at my desk, on my laptop, looking for more legal loopholes. Just to breathe. There was so much work to be done. No wonder my breath felt ragged in my throat sometimes. No wonder it was so hard to be still.

Self-care for Black women is a radical act, made even more difficult now that the concept has been co-opted from its radical roots into a mode of escapism. I mean self-care in that early sense: to *replenish* in order to more fully engage with community and justice work, as when the poet Audre Lorde stated, "Caring for myself is not self-indulgence, it is self-preservation, and that is an act of political warfare." Like any radical behavior, it must be learned. And practiced. And learned again. It is one thing to know that consciously, and quite another to do it—to make oneself one's sacred duty.

Out in the Arizona mountains might have been the first time in my life I had ever really done it. It felt incredible. And it felt hard. Teachers, lawyers, social workers, activists—anyone who works with the directly impacted, anyone who confronts the system day in and day out—will tell you that residual trauma is real. This is especially true for Black women, who for generations have carried the weight of the world on our broad and capable shoulders, wedging our bodies in doorways in order for our brothers and sisters of all races to walk through. Human beings are built for empathy—built to absorb and experience the pain of others. Adrenaline, urgency, the forward momentum of the work, all of those things can propel you when you're in the thick of it. But when that stops and the world stills, it matters not how great the victory. You feel the losses sustained along the way. And the exhaustion.

A FEW DAYS later, I left Arizona rested and grateful but still in a complete fog as far as what my future held. I returned to Dallas and binge-watched too many Netflix documentaries to name. I watched one on the Black Panther Party, and then started it over again. I watched Ava DuVernay's *13th* and *I Am Not Your Negro*, about James Baldwin, and they only reinforced what had become so crystal clear through this clemency journey: that the current crisis of mass incarceration was only the latest incarnation of the long, violent history of the oppression of Black people in this country. That every single human being left behind by President Obama's Clemency Initiative was buried alive by laws and social norms that had a direct link to our nation's sordid foundation: genocidal colonization of native peoples and the chattel enslavement of Africans. That my own journey was inextricably bound to this history. And my own liberation was tied to that of every single person unjustly chained in America's prisons.

I felt inspired. But to do what? I still had no idea, and no energy with which to do it. I may have been a little depressed. I walked around my house in a daze in sweats and a T-shirt, barely eating. I stayed on the couch under a blanket. I couldn't muster the energy to leave the house. All my life I had been so certain of my path, so driven toward my next goal. Now I had no idea what lay ahead.

My lack of clarity made me emotionally raw and vulnerable in a way I had never let myself be before. Sharanda fussed over me, cooking my favorite foods in the evenings after she got off work, and Palyn, her one-year-old granddaughter, made me smile. Corey coached me in emails from prison. I spoke on the phone frequently to all of my clients, listening as they related the challenges and the triumphs of reentering a society they'd been away from for so long. I filed motions to get Sharanda, Mike, Wayland, Terry, and Donel off supervised release early and advocated for Corey's early release to a halfway house. I lay on the couch and waited for some kind of sign to tell me what the hell I should do with the rest of my life.

Just as I was getting ready to restart the Panthers documentary for the third time, I got an email from Taylor Dolven, a journalist from *Vice News,* who'd done great work covering the #ClemencyNOW campaign. "A while ago I did an article on a man named Chris Young, who is serving life without parole for drugs," she wrote.

> Now the federal judge in his case has resigned in protest of mandatory minimum sentences, and is talking about Chris's case in the media as an example of why he did so. It's pretty extraordinary. Chris was wondering if this might open the avenue for clemency for him—or for something. He asked me to reach out to you and see if you'd have a conversation with him, just for advice.

A federal judge resigning in protest of drug sentencing laws—that was big news. A federal judgeship is a lifetime appointment, an honor that many judges yearn for. And this judge had resigned? I had to check it out for myself.

Taylor had attached three items to her email: her original *Vice* piece on Chris Young, a recent interview from *The Tennessean* with former federal judge Kevin Sharp, and Chris's sentencing transcript. The first line of *The Tennessean* article read: "Kevin H. Sharp sent Chris Young to prison for life and he thought it was wrong." I sat up a little and kept reading.

There had been many Chrises in the six years Judge Sharp had served as a lifetime Obama appointee on the bench, but Chris Young's case was the one he recalled in his interview with *The Tennessean*—the one that, according to the reporter, made Sharp choke up and brought tears to his eyes. I got a familiar feeling in my chest; after what felt like weeks of dormancy, it felt good to have that feeling again. Intrigued, I opened the court transcripts. What I read there over the next few hours was extraordinary. Yes, I told Taylor, I'd have a call with Chris.

One phone call later, my grand confusion was dispelled. Chris's incarceration story was a by now familiar travesty of the justice system, but his life story was remarkable. It exposed the flaws not only in criminal justice but in all the oppressive systems that underpinned inequality in America.

There was no longer any hesitation on my part. The answer for what to do with myself was right in front of me. Only this time, there would be no Clemency Initiative to provide a ray of light. We would have to do everything through the courts.

Chris Young's life depended on it.

CLARKSVILLE, TENNESSEE, IS about forty-five minutes northwest of Nashville, on the border with Kentucky, built along the river and divided by the two-lane highway and nearly defunct railroad tracks. Populated by military families connected to Fort Campbell Air Force Base on the north side and pockets of concentrated generational poverty on the south, the town has an average income of $21,395 a year. This is where Chris Young was born, in 1988. Like me, Chris was part of the second generation of the crack epidemic.

But Chris grew up with a suffocating level of poverty I'd never known. And unlike me, he didn't escape the epidemic's legacy.

Through emails and phone calls, Chris filled in the intriguing sketch Taylor had presented in *Vice*. Chris's story exemplifies the role that extreme poverty, intergenerational trauma, and societal neglect play in both the War on Drugs and the mass incarceration crisis. We talk a lot in the United States about the right to a second chance—"We are a nation of second chances," Obama reminded us. But every time Chris and I talked or wrote, I was left with the same overwhelming feeling: Freedom from his life sentence wouldn't be a second chance at life for Chris. In so many ways, it would be a first.

Chris's first memory was of a little shotgun house on a dead-end corner in the epicenter of an area ravaged by unemployment, drug infestation, and gang violence. His very earliest memories, like mine, are joyful ones: running wild with his older brother, Robert, and their dogs, riding around town in his grandfather's spectacular limousine. Chris's grandfather owned the local funeral home, and Chris remembered its shiny floors, its funny smell—flowers, formaldehyde, air freshener, death. He never knew his father. His mother was young, single, and poor; he remembered the grip of her hand when they went to the local Mapco station on the corner in order to use the payphone, how she admonished him to watch where he stepped to avoid the crack pipes and used condoms littering the pavement. For a time they stayed with his mom's boyfriend, Mickey, in a house across town, and were happy.

By the time Chris was seven his mother's relationship with Mickey was unraveling. He and Robert spent hours at the house of their cousins Cudas and Ree, soaking up knowledge from Cudas, whom they idolized. For both boys, Cudas served as a role model. He had a nice car with shiny chrome wheels, the dopest outfits, beautiful girlfriends. Only sixteen himself, Cudas guided his younger cousins through boyhood. He looked out for them, bought them shoes for school, notebooks for class. Like many young Black boys with few role models, Robert and Chris turned to the hood's own version of success to emulate. Cudas was a symbol, for both boys, of what successful young adulthood should look like. He was also a drug dealer.

Cudas introduced Chris to the music of the hip-hop artists he dreamed of emulating—Tupac, Master P, UGK. Chris sat in Cudas's room whenever he could, listening to the thump of his cousin's fifteens, memorizing the lyrics to every song. Whenever no one was around, Chris slipped Cudas's gold herringbone chain around his neck and rapped into the mirror, imagining himself a star. Cudas was the "flyest, toughest, most charismatic guy" they knew, Chris said, and they were so delighted to be in his presence that at first they didn't mind when their mom started leaving them with him for longer stretches, sometimes days at a time. Cudas's house, where they went when she needed to "unwind," was around the corner from the dope spot.

Eventually, Mickey put their mom out after another brutal fight, and for a time they moved in with their grandfather, then into another tiny house in the hood. Chris's mom's addiction worsened. Around the same time, when Chris was seven, he began experiencing his first sickle cell crises. The pain attacks came without warning and lasted for days. His mom and Robert traded off sitting with him as he screamed and writhed. Sometimes he landed in the hospital, and there was an African American sickle cell specialist in Nashville that his grandfather took him to when the pain grew intolerable.

By this time Chris's mom didn't bother to hide her habit from her sons anymore. Chris got to where he could tell whether she'd been smoking out of a can or from a plastic rose stem holder by the sting in his nostrils when he got home from school. The family had been on food stamps for a while, but that didn't pay for electricity or water. The neighborhood matriarch, Big Mama, who was Robert's paternal grandmother, let the boys take baths at her house when they asked, and she fed them when she could. Sometimes they stayed with her. But for the most part, the boys were on their own.

Concentrated poverty never tells the whole story, and it doesn't define a person. Neither does having an addicted or incarcerated parent. Chris was very, very bright, and despite the absence of social support and programs to alleviate the economic stress of his home life, he continued to achieve in school. He was analytical, questioning, and intellectually curious, with a tremendous aptitude for math. He had an incredible gift for memorization, but he also understood what he memorized on a conceptual level, or sought more information until he did. He constantly got in trouble in math class for failing to show his work, although his computations were always a hundred percent correct. "I can do it in my head," he told his teacher. "What I got to write it down for?"

Chris was ten years old and in the fifth grade, walking home from school, when his grandfather's girlfriend pulled up next to him and shouted at him to get in the car. She took them three blocks away where a crowd had gathered and an ambulance waited, lights flashing. Chris jumped out of the car and pushed through the crowd just in time to see first responders lift Cudas's lifeless body onto a stretcher. He had been shot in the head. In the red lights of the ambulance as they followed it to the hospital, the red lights of the traffic signals, the red flowers in the waiting room, Chris saw only his cousin's blood, pooled and puddling on the sidewalk.

Cudas's murder was a turning point for both Chris and his brother. Robert was three years older than Chris and considered Cudas his mentor, father figure, and best friend. A few months after the murder, at age fourteen, Robert was arrested for the first time, for selling fake drugs; Chris remembers that half his brother's face was scraped raw from where the police ground it into the gravel. In the aftermath of the trauma sustained from seeing his cousin bleed out on the pavement, Chris's own grades dropped dramatically. The boys' mother had entered a series of abusive relationships, and they witnessed the worst of it. Robert would throw himself in front of their mother every time, trying to fight grown men to protect her. Chris woke up at night in a cold sweat, dreaming of Cudas. He started acting out in ways typical of schoolchildren who have witnessed extreme violence—struggling with anger management, challenging authority, fighting.

A school principal who'd noted Chris's potential attempted to intervene by knocking on Big Mama's door; she was the backbone of the community and the woman to turn to in a crisis. The principal asked her to take Chris in for a time, to offer him some stability and keep him out of the hands of child welfare. She agreed, and by the end of sixth grade, Chris had brought his grades up again. He had Big Mama's affection, electricity, a warm meal every evening. He loved Big Mama, and he told me on the phone that he owed his life to her; his greatest fear was not getting out in time to tell her so as a free man. But Big Mama cared for a lot of kids, and her resources stretched only so far. There were no more trips for Chris to the sickle cell specialist; she had no means to get him to Nashville and no way to pay for the sessions if she had. During Chris's pain crises, which happened with more frequency in his early adolescence, he writhed alone on the bed, sheets a soaking wet tangle.

Though he improved in school, his isolation and trauma continued to manifest in his behavior. He fought a lot, acted out with teachers whose classes seemed so dumbed-down he could have taught them himself. A new seventh-grade teacher, Ms. Groves, noted Chris's exceptional intelligence from the beginning. When a local paper featured her classroom, she chose Chris to be in the photos taken to accompany the article, and he was pictured on the front page, working diligently through a set of advanced math problems as Ms. Groves looked on proudly. He'd always been good at math, really good. Now people would know. It felt good, Chris told me. He felt seen. Like he was somebody. For a time, he thrived under Ms. Groves's watchful eye. She broke up fights before they happened, encouraged his voracious reading habit, made sure he had lunch, even bought him a Christmas present—a series of Harry Potter books that he consumed over the holiday in a binge of nonstop reading. But when a scrap with some neighborhood kids prompted Big Mama to put him out again, he found himself back in his mother's house, in as dire straits as ever.

His mother's addiction was worse and she was no longer working. Chris wanted more for himself, a different life and a future, but didn't know how to get it. Meanwhile, he needed to eat, but no one would employ a fourteen-year-old for the number of hours he needed to help his brother buy food for the household and pay the bills. Chris wasn't looking for spending money. He needed to put food on the table. Trying to stay away from drugs—disgusted by the filth they sowed around him, and the chaos—he asked his grandfather if he could work in the funeral home. Chris's grandfather had distanced himself from his daughter as her addiction spiraled out of control, and as a result from the boys, too. But he relented, putting Chris to work mopping floors and cleaning up after the embalming procedures, sometimes pointing out some interesting feature of anatomy as he worked on the bodies. Chris liked being away from the streets, back in what had felt like such cavernous, echoing rooms in his youth, which now felt much smaller. But his paycheck was only two hundred dollars every few weeks. His brother and friends made that in a day. Almost all the young men Chris knew in the Main Street hood swapped drugs for dollars. Most did it just to get by. Main Street was a dilapidated area under the yoke of suffocating poverty. The pull of the streets began for most as economic necessity.

Working in the funeral home exacerbated Chris's sense of isolation. His brother had been less open with him—in part because he'd started to use himself, though Chris didn't know it at the time. Alienated in his youth due to sickle cell—his pain crises struck without warning, causing him to miss school functions and social events—Chris acutely felt the distance between the funeral home and the streets where his friends hung out. He doubled down on his rap game, expressing himself through introspective lyrics that eased his stress through creative release. As for many Black boys in the hood, rap beckoned as a way out, a road to success that didn't depend on peddling poison. But Chris was self-aware enough to know he wasn't particularly talented. The bottom line was simple: To get money in the hood, you had to sell dope—the same poison that had ruined his mother and put him in this predicament in the first place. It was a sick cycle, one he was astute enough to be aware of but not worldly enough to break. He started selling weed, a few dime rocks, continued to work sporadically at the funeral home, relied on his big brother. He stayed on and off at Big Mama's house, but lived mostly at his mom's in conditions below the poverty line. They ate what he and his brother could provide. At the end of his junior year, after missing weeks due to a sickle cell crisis and exhausted from late nights on the grind, he dropped out of school to hustle full-time.

Chris stopped by his mother's house one night to pick up some clothes and found his brother there, high. They argued, and when Chris left the house things were still heated. Robert texted him, something about Chris looking after his daughter when he was gone. Robert had been struggling with stress and depression for the past few years; Chris knew he'd shake out of it eventually. He didn't respond to his brother's text. When Chris returned to the house a few hours later, Robert lay splayed out on the sofa. The blood pooled thickly around the outline of his body, just as it had with their cousin Cudas. Robert had shot himself in the head.

Devastated, Chris felt he'd lost the only person in the world who knew and understood him. He was eighteen; Robert had been twenty-one. His brother had sat by his side during every sickle cell crisis of his childhood, begging him to stop screaming. "I wish I could take the pain from you, lil bro. You gotta be strong." They'd fought side by side all their lives, scrapping hard whenever someone insulted them for having bedsheets over their windows instead of curtains, holes in their shoes, that unwashed smell in their hair. As boys, Robert had scraped together change from around the house and on the street so they could eat, splitting the cheeseburger into two perfect halves. He'd even taken the heat for Chris's first drug stash so Chris wouldn't have to go to juvie. He had taken care of his little brother all of his life, and the weight of their final argument was a heavy burden for any man to carry. Now Robert was gone, leaving Chris with a hole in his chest and his brother's beautiful baby daughter to look after. He did what he could.

Less than a year later, Chris got pulled over at a traffic light and charged with possession and intent to sell six grams of crack— about the weight of a newly sharpened pencil. He pleaded guilty and got community corrections. A year later he was arrested once more, again at a traffic light, this time with possession of less than half a gram of crack—half the weight of a mini paperclip. Just as before, the charge wasn't major enough to warrant jail time, and he was given community corrections. The combined weight of the drugs from both charges was less than that of three pennies.

Now barely nineteen and struggling to get a job with two felony drug convictions, Chris continued doing what he knew best to survive: selling crack. In 2010, the feds were moving in on a drug conspiracy centered in Clarksville. On the night they moved on the gas station to arrest Robert Porter, the alleged leader of the conspiracy, Chris was standing at the car talking to Porter and was arrested. When they searched Chris's car, they found the trunk packed with Christmas gifts for his niece. Chris was not one of the more than twenty-five people on the original indictment. In all probability, he would never have caught the case but for his presence at the gas station that night. At the time of the arrest, he was twenty-two years old.

Sunny Koshy, an assistant United States attorney in Nashville, was notorious for piling on enhancements and deploying aggressive, bullying tactics to ensure a plea deal, or, failing that, the longest sentence possible. Initially, Koshy offered Chris a fourteen-year plea deal. To Chris, fourteen years seemed a lifetime. Yes, he sold drugs, but he was adamant that he was not part of a larger conspiracy. He refused the fourteen years, thinking his lawyer could negotiate the prosecutor down to something he could live with. By the time Koshy came back to him with a new deal, it was for twenty-two years—and only if Chris snitched. At this point, most members of the conspiracy had pleaded guilty and received sentences ranging from three to twenty-five years—including those in leadership, with indisputable wiretap and other evidence against them. Chris could see no logical reason why his plea deal should equal the harshest punishment of the whole indictment. And he was no snitch.

Chris opted to utilize his constitutional right to go to trial. In retaliation, nearly two years after Chris's initial arrest, Koshy filed notice of an 851 enhancement. Now Chris wasn't going to court to avoid a fourteen-year sentence, or even twenty-two. He was on trial for his life. And he had almost zero chance of winning.

The 851 enhancement has been described by more than one federal judge as the federal court's "dirty little secret." It's a sentencing enhancement that can apply if the defendant has prior felony drug convictions no matter how old or minor, driving up the length of the mandatory minimum sentence for the current offense based on past offenses. But—and this is key—an 851 goes into effect only if the prosecutor *in his or her sole discretion* files "notice" of the prior felonies in the courts. If they do, regardless of the seriousness of the prior offense, mandatory minimums rise dramatically. Whether or not to file the 851 is entirely up to the prosecutor. The defense has no say in the matter, and neither does the judge or jury. And once it's filed, sentencing is set in stone. With two prior drug felonies, the defendant's mandatory minimum of ten years becomes a mandatory minimum of life. So when Koshy filed "notice" of Chris's two priors—both committed when he was a teenager, for drug amounts less, it bears repeating, *than the weight of three pennies,* barely enough for a single high—he triggered an automatic living death sentence for Chris Young.

In 2013, Human Rights Watch issued a report warning against the practice of filing 851s, arguing that threat of the enhancement essentially created a "trial tax" for those who exercised their constitutional right. Prosecutors wield the threat of enhancement as a weapon to coerce guilty pleas and snitching. That more than 97 percent of all federal drug cases never go to trial, the report argued, is evidence not of guilt, but of prosecutorial abuse of the enhancement. Attorney General Eric Holder agreed. Six days into Chris's trial, on August 12, 2013, Holder issued a memorandum to prosecutors instructing them not to file 851 enhancements in order to induce guilty pleas, and to abstain from its use at all unless "the defendant is involved in conduct that makes the case appropriate for severe sanctions."

Many prosecutors disregarded the directive. Sunny Koshy was one of them. He didn't have to file the enhancement. And he could have withdrawn it at any time up until the date of sentencing— particularly under orders from the attorney general, orders that Holder followed up a few months later with an even more strongly worded directive. But Koshy, like many prosecutors, flouted Holder's instruction. And under the current system of unfettered prosecutorial power, there is no check on the vindictive egos of those who wish to punish defendants for insisting upon their constitutional right to trial.

Chris spent the next four years of his young life in county jail awaiting trial and sentencing. That fact alone should seem impossible, unconstitutional, a human rights violation. But the notion that one is innocent until proven guilty is long gone from the American criminal justice system. Across the nation, the majority of people in jail—in some states more than eighty percent—have, like Chris, not been convicted of any crime. By the time the accused get to trial, they've already served years of their lives behind bars.

In jail, Chris did what he could to reclaim his time. There was a decent library in Warren County Jail, and he took full advantage of it. He read and studied and studied and read. "I took it like college," he said to me later. "Pretended my cell was a dorm room. We had books, and I had all kinds of time on my hands. Jail was hard, but my escape was learning. I studied *everything*." More than a year before his trial date with Judge Sharp, already fully aware of the inevitable outcome of an 851 enhancement, he began to prepare the statement he planned to deliver before sentencing. He composed and he revised, all in his head, never writing down a word. Every day, in the shower, Chris practiced his statement. Over and over and over again. He spoke the words in rhythm, and spoke them again. By the time he stood before Judge Sharp on the cusp of his twenty-sixth birthday, he was more than ready to deliver.

Chris walked with a limp due to avascular necrosis in his hip caused by his sickle cell; he minimized its effect by adopting something akin to an old-school gangster lean, one shoulder lowered, all the swag. Koshy, the prosecutor, would point out his walk as a sign of disrespect to the courts in his closing, but anyone paying attention could see that one of Chris's legs was essentially shorter than the other, due to a lack of oxygen getting to the bone during pain crises. He stood tall as he could before the bench, shoulders squared, and greeted the court.

"First and foremost, I'd like to say thank you, Your Honorable Judge Sharp, and to the courts for letting me speak today," he began. "I hope everyone here has been having a good morning."

Then Chris launched into the speech he'd been practicing for months, speaking at a rapid-fire, rhythmic pace.

"Before I was found guilty at trial I had planned on coming here impressing you, Judge Sharp, leaving you disposed to me, showing you that these four years I've been incarcerated I've been studious with my time, taking copious notes. To accomplish this I was going to speak on a variety of topics, one of which being American history. I'm familiar that William Penn purchased Pennsylvania from the Delaware Native Americans, how Washington disbanded the troops in 1783, how on March 16, 1783, Washington delivered the speech that made the troops avert their plans—"

Gently, Judge Sharp intervened. "I don't want to interrupt you, but can I stop you for a second and slow you down a little bit so that I can catch what you're saying? I want to listen to you, and, also, the court reporter has to take it down."

"Yes, sir."

"You may have a speed that you have to do this in," Judge Sharp said. "But if you can slow down, it would help me because I want to hear what you have to say."

"Thank you for listening," Chris said. And he picked up where he'd left off: "—how Pass and Stow recast the Liberty Bell the first time it was cracked, how Frederic Bartholdi designed the Statue of Liberty, how John Adams and Thomas Jefferson both died on the fiftieth anniversary of the Declaration of Independence, July 4, 1826, how Constantino Brumidi consummated the fresco of George Washington that's at the Capitol in 1865, how at the beginning of the twentieth century the whole world was in civil and political uproar leading to the assassination of a few political figures, including our own twenty-fifth president, McKinley, how in 1913 the Federal Reserve system was established, how in 1934 the SEC was established. I'm familiar with President Nixon and the Watergate scandal, how 1960 to 1970 was the greatest economical decade in our country's history, the GNP doubling and nearly tripling. I'm familiar with Margaret Thatcher and Ronald Reagan's theory on the government's role in society, the 1987 Wall Street crash . . ."

When I first read Chris's opening in the transcripts, I noticed his sentences had a perfect rhythm, no doubt a part of his memorization. When my surprise abated I began to sink into the content—a list, but a fascinatingly coherent and thematically linked list, of scholars, inventors, and historical figures and their accomplishments. His speech lasted for twenty-five transcript pages—forty-five minutes at the podium—and was truly extraordinary. In it, Chris spoke of Nero, Van Gogh, Cromwell, Descartes. He described the amazement he'd felt when he'd learned in prison that the CEOs of McDonald's, Carnival Cruise Lines, and American Express were all Black men, and the impact that discovery had on his vision for his own future. He shared stories from his childhood, rife with poverty and trauma: constant pain from sickle cell anemia, weekly baths at the neighbors' when the water got turned off, his mother's crack addiction and abuse at the hands of her boyfriend, his discovery of Robert's suicide. He recounted the extreme lack of financial resources and social pressures that led to selling drugs at a young age, and his goals and dreams if given the chance.

In all the transcripts I'd scoured, I had never seen a defendant stake his claim in this way. Not to plead his innocence, or to ask for relief. Simply to state, in his own words, how he came to be in this place, and what he might accomplish if he got out "in a reasonable amount of time." To say "I'm here. If the point of jail is rehabilitation, in my four years in county I have accomplished this. I am Chris Young. Know me."

At the end of his speech, Judge Sharp thanked him, and he recommended a few books Chris might like to read based on some of the people he'd mentioned in his speech.

"Thank you," Chris said, "for treating me like a man and looking at me like a man. Some people naturally look at us like we're something else just because we've made mistakes and we've ended up on the other side of the law."

Judge Sharp nodded. Then came the inevitable. He sentenced Chris to life in prison without the possibility of parole.

WHEN I FLEW to Nashville to meet with Judge Sharp, four years after Chris's trial, he still vividly remembered that speech. I had been fascinated by Judge Sharp from the moment I read Taylor's *Vice* article. In all of my other cases, I'd appealed to judges to write letters on behalf of my clients with fingers crossed, practically begging. Here was a federal judge speaking out of his own accord on excessive sentencing in the federal courts. A man who had left the prestige of a lifetime appointment in protest. This was a man I knew I needed to meet. I found his email on his firm's website and reached out, telling him I was representing Chris Young and would love to arrange a meeting with him. He responded within the hour and invited me to Nashville.

Judge Sharp had been a working-class kid from Memphis before he signed up for the military and started going to the library.

"I saw myself in him," he said of Chris. "I used to read all this history, Greek and Roman stuff, and I sounded those names out in my head as they were written, just as he did. *So-crates*. He was entirely self-taught. It was just remarkable. The difference was, the GI bill gave me the opportunity to go further than that library. And Chris—encountering this knowledge for the first time, sucking it up like a sponge—had just as much potential as I did. The difference was, he was locked up in a jail."

Judge Sharp was a tall man with a silver head of hair and mustache and attentive, green eyes behind his glasses. He took me on a tour of the construction site that was his future office and spoke with emotion and conviction about Chris and his case. He'd been hesitant to interrupt Chris once he started, he said. "I didn't want to mess him up, but I wanted to hear what he had to say. And, in truth, I wanted to prolong the inevitable"—having to sentence Chris to life in prison.

Over the years he'd thought incessantly about Chris. He told me the story of an American soldier who'd been captured in the Vietnam War and held in a camp. "The man memorized the name of hundreds of POWs who came through the camp for more than two years," the judge recalled. "When he was finally rescued, he recited the names from memory for the officers. He did it to the tune of 'Old MacDonald Had a Farm.' When they tried to get him to stop and simply recite the names, he couldn't do it. Chris's speech, the way he rattled it off from memory, the rhythm he had to attain to do so, reminded me of that POW."

That made total sense to me. "In a way, Chris is a prisoner of war, too," I said. "A prisoner of the War on Drugs. The damage this war has inflicted—there is no overstating it. In Chris's case, it's like he's being punished for surviving."

Judge Sharp shook his head. "At some point I cleared the courtroom except for the defense attorney. 'Give me something,' I told her. 'Give me something so I don't have to sit here and do this.' She had nothing. None of us had anything. I was a federal judge with a lifetime appointment and I was completely powerless." Sunny

Koshy's sole discretion to levy the 851 enhancement had essentially bound Judge Sharp's hands. His next words were emphatic, spoken with utter conviction: "There was no justice in that courtroom that day," he said. "As long as these laws are on the books, there never will be."

I took this moment to press the question that had fascinated me ever since Taylor Dolven pointed me back to the article she'd written about Chris. "But you resigned your judgeship," I said. "Walked away from a lifetime appointment. Was it really because of Chris?"

Judge Sharp paused, as if he were weighing his words carefully. Then he took a deep breath and looked directly at me. "The three least culpable guys in that conspiracy charge—of which Chris was one—went to trial. They thought, and rightfully so, that more than ten years for their low-level involvement was absurd. But they're the ones with life sentences. All three of them. I don't know how to fix that. Looking at Chris, I thought, here was someone who was obviously intelligent, had so clearly been denied opportunity to make anything of himself, would so clearly have gone in a different direction were there one available. There was no justice present in the courtroom that day. The only way to explain that sentence was as an act of revenge. And I wasn't in the business of revenge. Or at least, I did not want to be. So I left the bench."

He looked down at his hands. "It was just so foolish, so unnecessary," he said. "A waste of human life. If there's anything I can do to help get that young man out," he said, looking up at me, "I'll do it."

I left Nashville moved that a middle-aged white man with a lifetime federal appointment would give that up to seek true justice for a young Black man like Chris. I knew that it didn't matter who was in power. Chris was in prison—a hundred thousand Chrises are in prison. Come hell or high water, we had to get them free.

Chapter 17

DAWN WILL COME

I leaned forward from the backseat of a sleek black Escalade as my driver approached a three-story red brick building. You could've mistaken the place for a college dormitory were it not for the razor wire and noticeable absence of windows. We parked in front, and I took a long look at the Fort Dix Federal Correctional Institution in New Jersey. It was the day before Thanksgiving, and there was a lot to be thankful for. Corey Jacobs would be walking out of that prison at any moment.

Those first steps of freedom are a sacred moment that I'd always reserved for my clients and their families. So when Corey asked me to be there for his, I was honored but also a little nervous. Staring at the front door of the prison so as not to miss a single moment, I ran through scenarios in my mind and how I would respond to each. "What if the guards delay his release because we are parked too close to the front door? Can I hug him when he walks out? What are the rules? Do I have all my files?"

Diddy was determined to make Corey's release special, and he was texting me the whole time, wanting the play-by-play.

LET'S GO!!!!!! This is crazy. I can't believe this. I gotta speak to him right away.

Moments later, Corey walked out of the prison in a gray prison-issue sweat suit, smiling wide, his swagger getting stronger with every step he took away from that building.

"He's *baaa*-ack," I called, joy in every syllable.

"I don't even know how to feel right now!" he called back. He was walking faster as he got nearer to the car, but his stride was smooth, confident, like he'd never been locked up at all.

"You should feel amazing!" I said. "Look at you!"

"So that's what a Caddy truck looks like, huh?" Corey said, taking in the Escalade. In his voice was almost a childlike sense of wonder. This would be the first car ride he'd taken in nearly eighteen years.

"Hey, Corey," I said. He was only a few steps away now.

"What's up, Brittany, the best lawyer eva!" Corey said, and hugged me so tight I almost lost my breath. He raised his hands in the air. "We back! We back, baby!" Corey's contagious ardor for life had survived sixteen life sentences.

The Federal Bureau of Prisons gave me limited time to transport Corey from New Jersey to the halfway house in Los Angeles where he'd start his new life. At the airport, Corey navigated a sea of people, bright lights, and terminal signs. I watched carefully as he handed the TSA agent his prison-issued identification to ensure the agent did nothing to offend Corey's dignity. In these first moments of freedom, tenderness and grace are of utmost importance, and I was ready to intervene if anyone dared to disturb Corey's first steps as a free man.

Diddy spared no expense for his best friend's homecoming. There was a silver Range Rover awaiting our arrival at LAX, equipped with a driver with strict instructions to deliver Corey to the halfway house. Corey was thrilled, but as we got close he didn't want to be seen pulling up in a luxury SUV. I understood why. It was important to him to finish his journey on his own terms and with humility. We had the driver park a block away, and Corey and

I walked together through a cool L.A. evening to the front doors of the halfway house.

A halfway house is just that—a place of suspended animation somewhere between dehumanizing prison conditions and a semblance of freedom. Corey touched my arm and we paused a moment outside. I could see him steel himself for the indignities he had just left behind, the institutional mind games, the power trips. Once inside, there was familiar prison processing, forms to fill out, regulations to follow. Corey was again reduced to his prisoner number, 17061-112, a stark reminder that he was still in federal custody and would be for almost an entire year.

But he was no longer in prison.

After lots of questions and background checks, the halfway house relented and gave Corey a twenty-four-hour pass to visit his best friend, and so we had a feast at Diddy's house the day after Thanksgiving. Diddy was like every loved one I'd ever seen welcome one of my clients home. After years of pain, held breath, and disappointment, Diddy was like a kid at Christmas. He'd planned this day with unbounded excitement. He called me several times beforehand to make sure of the foods Corey wanted for his first meal home, the music he wanted to hear. "Britt, which do you think Corey would like better for the ride over?" he asked anxiously. "A black Maybach or silver?"

"Always bet on black," I said.

So Corey and I rode to Diddy's house in the back of an elegant black Maybach, sitting on butter-soft seats and taking it all in. The L.A. sunset splashed over the entire sky, and palm trees lined the road.

Corey turned to me. He had shown no emotion but elation and joy all day, but now there was something else. "Britt, I want to thank you from the bottom of my heart. I know the sacrifice you made, even if nobody else does. Another minute in there would have killed me. Then you came along. We are connected forever. Forever. I owe you my life. There are great things to come. Believe that."

When he finished talking, he lifted his glasses to pinch the bridge of his nose, eyes closed a moment, overwhelmed with emotion. Then he leaned forward to the driver.

"Would you play 'You're Next in Line for a Miracle,' please?"

As Shirley Caesar's soaring voice hit every soul-stirring note, I looked over at Corey and saw with crystal clarity what mattered to him, what kept him going, and just how strong he was to have survived eighteen years in prison. I had literally just watched this man walk out of prison with what I thought was nothing. But I was wrong. It turned out Corey left prison with something profoundly valuable: a treasure chest of survivorship.

The gates to Diddy's place opened and the Maybach slid down the driveway toward a white mansion. Real pillar candles lined the drive, each one carefully lit. Just in front of the mansion stood Diddy, arms outstretched, welcoming his friend home. Corey leapt out of the car, and the two men hugged so tight that I am sure both of their feet left the ground. Two brothers, reunited after twenty years. It was like watching a mirrored reflection of the same person. My heart filled to see such a giddy display of Black brotherhood. They had the same laugh, the same swagger. "We back! We back, baby!" It was glorious. In that moment, I knew Corey Jacobs would be okay.

A WEEK LATER I was in a different car, heading in a different direction. Rolling, luxuriant fields of blue grass stretched out on either side of the highway along the way to the Federal Medical Center in Lexington, Kentucky. The emerald expanse of Kentucky's famous Thoroughbred farms ringed the landscape, complete with picturesque herds of glistening mares swinging over the hills, their foals by their sides. Statuesque old oak and blue ash trees lined the roads and peppered the fields on the way to the prison.

I was on my way to visit Chris for the first time. I planned to spend the day there, hanging out with him the way that I used to with Sharanda. More than anything, I wanted to hug him. Chris hadn't had a visit from anyone since he'd left the jailhouse three years before, and those visits were always from behind glass. He had mentioned in passing how he hadn't had a hug in seven years. He maintained a brave face. I could not imagine going without the healing power of a hug for so long.

Chris kept himself busy working in the law library, tutoring other men in prison for the math portion of their GED test, scouring the magazine subscriptions—*MIT Tech Review* and *CNET Magazine*—that Corey had sent to him as a "welcome to the family" gift. He emailed me nearly every day about the articles he read, posing questions and making unique and often profound observations. Chris's intelligence was undiminished since his youth; if anything, his years of study in prison had allowed the flourishing of a brilliance that never failed to remind me of the power of human resilience. I had a notebook on the driver's seat beside me, a notebook I considered my "Chris book." Whenever I talked to Chris, I kept this vocabulary and idea journal with me. After our conversations, I furiously recorded the topics we'd discussed, and the ideas Chris had shared, lest they be lost.

I discovered very quickly in our calls and emails that Chris was an eternal dreamer with an endless imagination. One call he'd be thrilled with some AI invention, imagining its possibilities, worrying over its limitations and the potential problems it might create. The next he'd be crowing over venture capitalist Ben Horowitz's blog in which Horowitz used rap lyrics as a lens to break down business and managerial principles. He followed Horowitz and Marc Andreessen's private equity group a16z, mulling everything from their branding to their business model. "Tell Corey there's that sixteen again!" he said.

Chris's greatest passion was tech. Women and men incarcerated in federal prison can email using Corrlinks, but they don't have access to the Internet. Nonetheless, using books only, Chris taught himself how to code. He was versed in Python, an advanced coding language. When I connected him to a friend of mine in the forefront of tech innovation, the two became pen pals, engaged in a lively exchange about the latest in coding, encrypting, and physics. Chris's cell might be small, but his dreams were huge. Lately he'd been sharing new ideas he'd had about using psycholinguistics and social media algorithms to help people who were suicidal. "If only I could have gotten to Robert in time," he'd said. "This is for him."

I made my way to the front of the prison and parked. While all my other clients had exhausted their appeals and other legal remedies by the time they got to me, Chris had one more bite at the apple. We had ten months to file a motion of habeas relief. I planned to argue ineffective assistance of counsel, and I'd asked Chris to document everything he remembered about every conversation he'd ever had with his attorneys. I was hoping the details he provided today would be just what my argument needed. And I couldn't wait to finally meet him in person and hear more about his suicide prevention idea, which I thought had tremendous potential.

A few minutes later, Chris came through the door, a huge, open smile on his handsome face, standing proudly at his full six feet two, a whole inch regained since the surgery corrected the length disparity in his hips. Like Corey, he projected an inner calm, and his observant, steady gaze was that of a man not easily ruffled. He had worked out hard in the six weeks since his surgery, off crutches before expected. There he stood tall and strong, without any support, his grin belying the struggle it had been to get there.

"I told you I'd be walkin'!" he said.

I stood up to meet him, my arms wide open. He walked right into them, and as I hugged him I could feel his body start to relax, the weight of his own arms become heavier as the tension in them eased. Seven years without a hug. Seven. My arms tight around him, I remembered what it felt like to hug my mama for the first time in prison, to push through the miserable plastic glass that separated us. The salt and pine scent of her skin, the strength of her arms around me. I remembered, and I hung on.

———

Hope is fuel. It was time to get back to work.

I had given up my corporate job to pursue my passion, and now I'd had a crash course in what it was like to take part in a movement and organize on a national level. The end of President Obama's Clemency Initiative also meant the formal end to the Clemency Project and #ClemencyNow, both of which had been keyed toward maximizing the number of people we could free with Obama in office. I was a woman motivated, but without an organization or resources. And with a new president in office thought to be hostile to our efforts, I needed to find a new vehicle with which to get people to freedom.

Many organizations were shifting their attention away from the federal level to more local and state issues. A renewed state focus was certainly important: The vast majority of incarcerated people are chained to the state system. Still, the relentless on-slaught of the War on Drugs had resulted in exponential growth in federal incarceration rates. There was certainly no shortage of worthy candidates. President Barack Obama had granted commu-tations to 1,716 people, more than any other sitting president, yet more than thirty thousand men and women in federal prison had applied. Thousands of people were still laboring in prison under the dark cloud of outdated drug laws. Of the nearly 185,000 peo-ple in federal prison in 2018, 46.2 percent were there for drug of-fenses. Almost half of the people in federal prison serving life without parole had been convicted of a drug crime, and 80 percent of them were people of color. Through Obama's Clemency Initia-tive, I had come into contact with many of these individuals and heard their pleas not to have to die in prison. I couldn't leave them there now.

Neither could my clients. Both Sharanda's and Corey's concern for those they'd left behind began almost the moment they got the clemency call. Sharanda had begun campaigning for Alice and others as soon as she stepped off prison grounds. I knew from my work with all of my clients and from the teachings of Bryan Stevenson and others that the best solutions come from those closest to the problem, those directly impacted. As I was planning my next move, it occurred to me that my best possible partners were the people right in front of me, the people I loved. Sharanda, Corey, and I set to work, and between the three of us, the Buried Alive Project was born.

Ultimately, we decided to focus the project on the area of the system in which the three of us had the most proximity and experience: the sentence of life without parole for federal drug offenses. There was something exceptionally unjust and cruel about a life sentence—different from a lengthy sentence in kind and degree. Short of execution, it was the most severe penalty permitted by law in America. It screamed that a person was beyond hope, beyond redemption. It suffocated mass potential as it buried people alive. It took a particular kind of grace and dignity to survive such a sentence; I knew because I'd seen it in my clients and friends. The scourge of mass incarceration would not be resolved by solving the issue of federal drug sentencing alone—we knew that. But it was our niche, and a niche gives you a handhold and the potential to make real systemic change in that area—in order to expand to others.

The Buried Alive Project's mission would focus on freeing people serving life sentences today under yesterday's drug laws. As lawyers we are often forced to work within the bounds of laws that are outside the bounds of moral consciousness. Progressive lawyering is a cornerstone of transformative justice. I wanted to build a team of lawyers to free everyone we could, even if we had to do it one by one. We wanted to salute the audacity and courage it takes to wake up every single day in the face of a life sentence. I had always worked in partnership with my clients on their freedom, and we wanted each person in prison represented by the Buried Alive Project to feel that they were a part of their own liberation strategy.

Equally important, though, was making the suffering and unfairness visited on those inside a much higher-profile issue. The irony of being buried alive is not just that we are dooming people to die, but that the problem itself is buried. When I spoke about my clients and their sentences, people were floored. They had no idea this was happening in America. As we launched the project, we aimed to merge statistics and stories in order to amplify the human element that was so often overlooked. Stories like Alice's, like Chris's—invisible to the public eye, yet so necessary to drive change. SMU law students had worked hard during my pop-up clinic to file clemency petitions under Obama's initiative, and I saw the potential not just to harness their tremendous energy and dedication, but to begin early to influence their perception of those whose lives would soon be in their hands, and their own power to make change.

We began in the fall to organize at the newly launched Deason Criminal Justice Reform Center at my alma mater, SMU Dedman School of Law. Sharanda read and responded to hundreds of letters we received from people serving life sentences. Corey designed our logo and website. I worked to train pro bono lawyers to take on cases, and threw myself into more cases. The Deason Center served as a research partner and training operation, teaching advocacy skills to law students to help the Buried Alive Project maximize its work.

In the first four months of the project alone, a team of forty-five SMU law students devoted more than five hundred volunteer hours to helping us identify and research cases of hundreds of people serving life without parole sentences handed down under federal drug laws. SMU statistics students helped to analyze thirty years of data from the United States Sentencing Commission. English students with a focus on creative writing wrote powerful profile stories to humanize the narrative of those serving life without parole sentences. Both Chris and Alice, Sharanda's dear friend from Carswell, were among the very first stories we featured on our website, and both were equal partners in making sure their stories were told in the way they wanted. Soon Alice's story would move the world.

I HADN'T EATEN all day. I sat in a New York City hotel room in the summer of 2018, feeling both elation and complete exhaustion. My navy blue suit was still hanging in the closet. I never got the chance to put it on. I was in New York for a full day of meetings to raise awareness about the Buried Alive Project, but I had canceled all of them. Alice Johnson was getting out of prison.

Our website's photo of Alice showed her smiling with such grace that it was hard to believe she'd taken the picture in a prison uniform, from a federal penitentiary, while serving a mandatory life sentence. She'd been that way since the very first day I met her in person at Carswell: graceful and determined. Over the years, Alice had lost every appeal in court, and in January 2017, President Obama denied her clemency petition. I wasn't Alice's lawyer then, but I was always looking for ways to advocate for her freedom and to lift up the story of a woman who'd uplifted so many other incarcerated women. And I wasn't alone; many criminal justice reform organizations had helped keep her name alive. Jennifer Turner, the lawyer who wrote the groundbreaking report for the ACLU featuring Sharanda and Mike, had remained in constant contact, searching for avenues for her freedom. We spent long hours on the phone strategizing, sending emails back and forth, reading case law and articles. "What about that Sentencing Commission's drugs minus two amendment from 2014?" Jennifer would ask. "We can try to find a way to be creative with the amendment—let's research how we can expand its reach to apply to Alice!" I'd say. We researched for months; ultimately, we kept hitting dead ends.

Everything changed in October 2017 when Alice, who understood the power of storytelling and the arts, took her fate into her own hands. She recorded a mic.com interview, telling viewers about her journey to prison for her first-ever conviction, the joy of being a grandmother, and her passion for prison mentorship. Alice is an incredible orator, and the response to the video was immediate and viral. It picked up traction on social media, shared by celebrities like Common and Jesse Williams.

Eventually, Kim Kardashian West saw Alice's video on Twitter and was moved to both tears and action. She formed a legal team consisting of her personal attorney, Shawn Holley, Jennifer Turner, and Mike Scholl, a highly regarded attorney from Memphis, where Alice had been convicted. Alice asked me to join the team, and we immediately began to work together to formulate fresh ideas. With Kim on board, we had an exponentially larger platform to raise awareness and fight for Alice's freedom. As I got to know Kim in meetings and phone calls, I was impressed by her genuine dedication, not just to use the power of her millions of fans and social media followers, but to dive deep into understanding the unfair laws that allowed for Alice to be sentenced to life. It was Kim's idea to reach out to Ivanka Trump to try to secure a meeting with the president. Jennifer and I drew on our previous clemency experience under Obama to come up with a strategic plan and draft a compelling clemency petition. The entire process took months of late-night strategy sessions, lawyering, and intensive behind-the-scenes negotiations. On Alice's sixty-third birthday, Kim Kardashian West met with Donald Trump to make an impassioned plea for Alice's life and request that he grant clemency. One week later, on June 6, 2018, he did.

Her first day of freedom was a dizzying flurry of work. Suddenly, my small New York City hotel room became a mobile command center of one. After twenty-one years in prison, Alice Marie Johnson was coming home. Even before the news broke publicly, I had already called prison officials in Washington, D.C., to ensure that Alice's release would be smooth and quick. I'd already spoken to her family to prepare them for the important logistics and the crush of media. Jennifer Turner and I had already cried tears of true joy, trying to wrap our minds around the tremendous effort we'd just been a part of. Most important of all, Kim and the legal team had called Alice to tell her President Trump had granted her clemency. As she cried and praised God at the news, I thought of the moment I met her at Carswell. I remembered her determined face marshaling women around at their rehearsal, using the arts to keep their hopes up. I remembered her despair when Genice died, as though a piece of herself had died, too. She had been so much for so many. And by the afternoon of June 6, 2018, she was running into her family's arms, leaving her life sentence at the prison gates.

Sharanda and I cried on the phone that night. We shared a special kinship and pride over Alice's release. Sharanda told me that when she saw the news footage of Alice running toward her family, she yelled at the screen, "Run, Ms. Alice, run! Before they change they damn minds!" We laughed with joy until our sides hurt.

AFTER THE OVERWHELMING success of her campaign for Alice, Kim wanted to continue pushing to use her platform for justice. She took up Chris's case, again seeking in-depth understanding of his situation. She secured another meeting with President Trump in order to advocate for Chris, and the media responded. For a week, Chris's story was front-page news. His release seemed imminent. Eagerly, we waited. And waited. In the prison TV room, Chris watched his story splashed out over the screen, his photo side by side with Kim Kardashian's. CNN, NBC, CBS, every entertainment show and network sported similar headlines: Who is Chris Young? Chris endured harassment from some of the guards, resentful of the media attention he was receiving. He tried to keep as low a profile as he could, although there was really no such thing anymore. But on the phone with me, he was exuberant. "Brittany, I'm gonna move to Austin. That's like the third top tech hub in the nation, which means it will be the first soon! I've been working on my app and if I can just talk to some guys on the ground, I bet I can be ready to launch within six months for real."

On the day of Kim's meeting with Trump, Big Mama, Chris's surrogate grandmother and protector, was honored at her funeral in Clarksville. She had passed away that very week. I spoke to Chris every day during that time, urging him to hang on.

Though in his typical stoic way Chris downplayed his own trauma, the wait amounted to psychological torture. To endure a life sentence, hope and optimism are as essential as breath. Chris believed, like the rest of us, that he would be released any minute. But the minutes dragged on to months without relief. To give up belief that he might wake to freedom was not an option, but each day that passed led to crushing disappointment. Chris was trapped. And the loss of Big Mama, who he hadn't seen since being transferred to federal prison, was a terrible blow. The mental fortitude he displayed in those few cruel months cannot be overstated.

Ultimately, it became clear that there would never be another Alice Johnson. After weeks of hearing nothing, our hopes for clemency faded. All three branches of Chris's government—legislative, judicial, and executive—had failed him. But we pressed on, continuing to knock. I assembled a larger legal team, including two outstanding litigation attorneys, Jillian Harris and Drew Warth, both from top law firms, to help me seek relief through the courts.

Some hopeful progress was made on December 21, 2018, when President Trump signed the First Step Act into law. The bill was called the most significant federal criminal justice reform legislation in decades and garnered overwhelming support from people across the political spectrum. Aimed at reducing recidivism and easing harsh penalties related to federal drug offenses, the bill included four modest sentencing reform provisions. It made retroactive the reforms enacted by the Fair Sentencing Act of 2010, which reduced the disparity between crack cocaine and powder cocaine sentences at the federal level. It also eased the three-strikes law so people like Chris Young automatically received a mandatory twenty-five years instead of life. But in an outrageous irony, the law's scope did not reach Chris and others like him. In one of many compromises made by progressive reform advocates to secure conservative support, the three-strikes revision and several other provisions of the bill were not made retroactive.

The First Step Act was just what its name indicated—a much-needed first step that provided long-awaited freedom and reunited families, but there was much more work to do. And nothing was more urgent. So many more Chrises, Coreys, and Sharandas were waiting.

I WAS LATE. I'd driven to Rockwall earlier that afternoon to pick up the brisket my dad had spent all night smoking on the grill. Briskets in Texas are a big deal, and my dad makes the best, with just the right combination of smoke, heat, and time. Foil-wrapped to seal in the juice and big enough to feed sixteen, its aroma taunted me from the backseat. I hadn't eaten all day. When Sharanda put on a dinner, I knew to save room. Tonight was a truly special occasion.

Two days before, Alice had arrived in Dallas for a visit, and Sharanda was throwing her a feast. Donel, Terry, Wayland, and Mike would all be there. Jazz was coming over, too. "Is Sharanda making those greens?" she'd said. "Let me get my Tupperware together now!" Even De-Ann had driven in from East Texas. I couldn't wait to see everyone.

Every time I pulled into the parking lot of Sharanda's apartment building, I was struck by a vivid reminder of our journey. There, just kitty-corner from her new complex, in a perfect location for the diner it now was, was Sharanda's former soul food restaurant, Cooking on Lamar. Painted black now and nondescript, its presence might have haunted someone less optimistic. But not Sharanda.

"I've been over there," she'd told me. "The lady's real nice, but she's having trouble with the menu. I told her *soul food*! You got to drive all the way over to South Dallas to get some good candied yams in this town. If I wasn't so focused on my food truck, I'd help her out!"

Halfway down the hallway to Sharanda's door, the heavy brisket in my arms, I could smell exactly what she was talking about. She and Alice had been cooking for two days. "We haven't slept!" said Sharanda. "Laughing all night like kids. I know you're going to like the food, though. We did it real big."

Before I could knock, Alice swung open the door. "Hurry in here before the neighbors start asking for food!" she said. "Someone already stopped Sharanda today and asked her to cater a lunch! Everybody wants a plate!" She helped me set the brisket down and gave me a huge hug. "I'm so glad to see you, Britt. So glad."

Twelve months out of prison now, Alice looked radiant. I was always surprised that I was taller than her—something about her regal presence made her seem much taller than she was. She'd been traveling all over on her book tour, she said, tired but happy. "I cannot rest," she said. "All those women I left behind? I have a responsibility to them." Sharanda was the same way. Survivor's remorse haunts every formerly incarcerated person I ever met, that heavy sense that every moment of their newfound freedom is a moment someone else spends in prison.

The next few hours were a flurry of joy and warmth. The guys and De-Ann arrived soon after and filled their plates to overflowing with melt-in-your-mouth ribs, cornbread, mac and cheese, candied yams, greens, black-eyed peas, Alice's peach cobbler— you name it, those two had prepared it. With the addition of the brisket, there was enough food to feed a village. Sitting around the table with Alice leading us in a moving blessing, I felt soul-rich with family. Mama Lena's Sunday dinners and Sharanda's abundant table were both squares on the same quilt. Wrapped in love and belonging, I listened to my clients laugh and joke with one another, their humor a balm for shared memories that no one should have to endure. As always, I was moved by their tremendous grace.

Across the room, Wayland proudly showed De-Ann and Jazz pictures of the house he and Mike had flipped—their first. They'd done all the construction work themselves and had turned their first flip over for profit in less than two months. Wayland's trucking business was doing well, too, though whenever she saw his trucks, Sharanda would joke, "You sure you actually do any work? Those trucks are too clean!" Now that they'd been reunited, the brothers did everything together, even lived together in a house across the street from their mom's. Wayland was revising two novels he wrote while in prison and considering penning a third. He was such a good jailhouse lawyer that I thought he might pursue the law as a free man, but he joked that if he never in his life saw another court document again it would be too soon. I could understand that. Watching Wayland laugh about something with Jazz until tears came out of his eyes, I tried to imagine being separated from my sister for even half the time he and Mike had spent apart. I couldn't. Donel had his own trucking business, too, and true to form, he had spent the first part of the evening asking me to check over some paperwork for a new contract, worrying over getting every detail exactly right.

In the kitchen, Mike leaned against the wall, listening attentively as Sharanda talked about her vision for her food truck. "I want to hire all men and women from the halfway house," she said. "Remember how terrible those first few weeks were? Trying to get a job, the way people would look at you when they found out you had a record, with disgust almost? I want people to feel welcomed. Give them a real chance."

"I know that's right," Alice said, helping herself to more peach cobbler. "I'm working on a new play and would love to hire a production team coming out of prison."

Sharanda cooking in her food truck instead of her cell, Alice staging her plays on Broadway instead of in the prison chapel—imagining all the possibilities of their freedom brought me so much joy. Both had been set to never breathe air as free women for the rest of their time on this earth. Their presence was nothing short of a miracle. Yet here they were, in Sharanda's own kitchen, breaking bread together and laughing. And I got to be with them.

The joy was great, sweetened by the pain underlying it. The laughing, loving, brilliant people in this room, clearly no threat to anyone, had spent a collective one hundred thirty-three years in prison as a result of the disastrous policies of the so-called War on Drugs.

My phone rang. Corey had said he'd FaceTime, and now here he was, larger than life, calling in to Sharanda's dinner from a yacht on the Riviera.

"Corey, look where you are!" I exclaimed as he panned the turquoise sea with his phone.

"Life after life!" he said.

"Is that Corey? Let me say hi," Sharanda said, and I passed her the phone.

After almost twenty years locked in a concrete and steel cage, Corey had hit the ground running. As senior adviser to Diddy at Combs Enterprises, he was counseling Diddy on strategic business decisions. He would frequently send me "Coreygrams," videos of him enjoying freedom's small pleasures: Eating fresh lettuce. Dipping his foot in the sea. Biting into a fresh croissant. Each "gram" was punctuated with a joyful "Life After Life!" His energy and light empowered me every day.

WORDS CANNOT BEGIN to touch the exhilaration of seeing my clients free and living their best lives.

Even Keyon, my very first client, was free—released in 2018 after thirteen years, just in time to attend his daughter's high school graduation. And he was doing well, too, promoted to sales manager at his job at a car dealership after only eight months. Now thirty-six years old, with the support of his loving family, Keyon's life was beginning anew.

As I lay in bed that night, sated not only with food but with true kinship, I thought of the long journey we'd all taken together. My clients were family. They taught me that freedom meant much more than an opening of prison gates, and even more than an end to draconian sentencing laws. It meant economic liberation and independence to determine one's own destiny. The beast was not just a failed criminal justice system but a culture deeply rooted in economic oppression and history.

Through my criminal justice work, I have encountered some of the most brilliant minds humanity has to offer. We must not only free them from prison, we must act to unchain their creative and entrepreneurial powers to better the world.

A man I deeply admire, businessman and philanthropist Robert F. Smith, encourages us all to be thoughtful and conscious about our highest and best use. In the wake of my clients' freedom, I started to ponder just those questions. How might I combine my corporate experience and love for the art of the deal with my passion for people directly impacted by the criminal justice system? I want to change the narrative, to shift the paradigm. I want to highlight and celebrate the world-changing impact that formerly incarcerated people can have when they are placed in environments where their energies can be used not merely to survive but to thrive.

There must be a fundamental shift in the core of what we believe about justice. There is no doubt that laws need to change. Unduly harsh sentencing laws have caused untold misery at great expense. But systemic change does not all have to come from Congress or state legislators who move with no sense of urgency even when human lives are at stake. Systemic change can also come from directly impacted people when they are out of survival mode and have access to opportunity. With every freedom secured, my clients are pushing forward a movement of power and human potential that this country has been locking away for decades. The ripple effect of their liberation and the positive impact they will have on their communities and all those they encounter will help to create systemic change.

This life has taken me on a remarkable journey—one that continues to transform my understanding of justice and the very definition of freedom itself. Every day I celebrate the lives of the many people who have given me the privilege of representing them. In so many ways, they have freed me, too.

A FEW DAYS after the dinner, I answered my doorbell to find a postal worker holding a large, heavy box. It was a package from Chris. He was being transferred from Lexington back to a high-security U. S. penitentiary—a decision we had fought and lost—and had given me a heads-up he would be sending me some of his books.

When I slit open the white box covered in dozens of stamps, a handwritten note fell out:

Please take care of these for me, Brittany. I don't want them messed up in the move. They're all I've got!

Inside the package were some of Chris's favorite books. The topics ranged from quantum physics to philosophy to history to computer programming. Chris's margin notes covered almost every page, containing the brilliant seeds of projects and ideas, both intellectual and practical, from the pen of a young man with little formal education.

Seeing Chris's writing in the margins of the coding book, his meticulous notes signifying unflinching determination, I thought about what our creative minds could be doing if we weren't always fighting oppressive systems. I thought of a fifteen-year-old Chris standing on the block during the midnight hour, selling crack to survive, knowing he had so much more to offer the world. Long before steel dug into the skin of his wrists, Chris was handcuffed by a suffocating socioeconomic environment that offered no access to channels of opportunity.

As I continued to leaf through the pages, reading Chris's lines of inquiry, noting how carefully he interrogated his own initial conclusions, I felt a surge of outrage. But that was soon followed by an overwhelming sense of hope. Here was an extraordinary American mind. Here was human intelligence in all of its beauty. Here was Chris's gift to the world—one that, once unchained, would benefit us all. Within the walls of America's prisons lies genius.

Let us free it.

The Buried Alive Project works to dismantle life without parole sentences handed down under outdated and inhuman federal drug laws through transformative litigation, legislation, and humanization. For more information, please visit:

buriedaliveproject.org
Twitter: @buriedaliveproj
Instagram: @buriedaliveproject

GIRLS EMBRACING MOTHERS empowers girls with mothers in prison to break the cycle of incarceration and lead successful lives with vision and purpose. For more information, please visit:

girlsembracingmothers.org
Twitter: @GEM_AmplifyHER
Instagram: @girlsembracingmothers

Acknowledgments

This memoir would not have been possible without the love and support of many people.

My mom, Evelyn Fulbright, you molded our minds to be fierce and spirits brave. Thank you, Mama, for your transparency and for allowing me to tell our story in all its detail. Your unconditional love empowers me. I am so deeply proud of you.

Jazz, my life would be so boring without you. Your carefree spirit gives me permission to live life without layers. And Likeya, your love is always understood. Thank you for supporting me.

My dad, Leland K. Barnett, you are the gentle wind that carries me. I adore and admire you to no end. Thank you for holding my hand through this thing called life and for knowing when to let go so I can fly. I know you are always there to catch me. May every day be "just another day in paradise."

There are heroes in this world that go unsung, yet they touch so many lives along their way. Billy Scales, my bonus dad, thank you for your love and instilling hard work and down-South values in us.

I don't know where I would be without my grandparents. Your wisdom and prayers put my mind at ease. Knowing I had your prayers interceding on my behalf helped me to fight harder.

There is absolutely no way I could have completed this book without Sarah Fuchs, an incredibly gifted and remarkable woman. During our two years together on this unforgettable journey, you dedicated your life to making this book all the brighter. Thank you for your collaboration and commitment.

My editor, Kevin Doughten, your thoughtful edits and honest feedback helped shape this book into what it is. This book is so much stronger because of you. I am so very grateful for you and the entire Crown team: David Drake, Annsley Rosner, Gillian Blake, Dyana Messina, Ellen Folan, Julie Cepler, Emily Hotaling, Rachel Aldrich, Ted Allen, Lydia Morgan, Carisa Hays, and Kaley Baron.

I would like to thank my book agent, Gail Ross, who believed in me from the very beginning. I am truly blessed to have you by my side.

To Van Jones, you have been a mentor, connector, and friend. You are an accelerator for people, organizations, and causes. Without you, there is no telling when this book would have been written.

Jesse Ihde, I am thankful for your selfless guidance and dedication to helping me create the foundation to begin this book. Your help was crucial for this project.

My co-counsel and friend, MiAngel Cody, I can't thank you enough for poring over early drafts of my memoir. I marvel at your foresight and encouragement throughout this journey. You challenge me to probe deeper, for greater truth. I am forever grateful.

Thank you, Breon Wells, Avery Cunningham, and Jordan Jacks for reading and rereading drafts. Your contribution was invaluable.

I would like to thank the following SMU Dedman School of Law graduates whose important research contributed to this book: Aaron Diggins, Emily Heger, Faith Castillo, and Emily Nash. Your willingness as law students to work to help transform our nation's criminal justice system is truly admirable.

I could not have completed this book without the loving embrace of all of my friends and family, far too many people than I can name here, who were a constant source of encouragement during this process. You all motivated me more than you could possibly know.

The Girls Embracing Mothers team, I knew writing my first book would be a time-consuming effort, and I'm so thankful that I had you all with me every step of the way, carrying GEM to new heights. Thank you for your dedication to empowering women and girls impacted by maternal incarceration.

To President Barack Obama. Thank you for your gracious, life-saving mercy and historical clemency legacy. The dignity, intelligence, and courage you showed throughout your eight years in office are an inspiration for everyone.

A very special thank-you to my clients for trusting me with your lives. I have so much love for all of you. We are forever bound. Each of you have left your fingerprints on my soul. My heart is forever altered.

About the Author

Brittany K. Barnett is an award-winning attorney and entrepreneur focused on social impact investing. She is dedicated to transforming the criminal justice system and has won freedom for numerous clients serving life sentences for federal drug offenses—seven of whom received executive clemency from President Barack Obama. Brittany has founded several nonprofits and social enterprises, among them the Buried Alive Project, Girls Embracing Mothers, XVI Capital Partners, and Milena Reign LLC. She has earned many honors, including being named one of America's most Outstanding Young Lawyers by the American Bar Association.

Twitter: @MsBKB
Instagram: @msbkb

This book was set in Dante, a typeface designed by Giovanni Mardersteig (1892–1977). Conceived as a private type for the Officina Bodoni in Verona, Italy, Dante was originally cut only for hand composition by Charles Malin, the famous Parisian punch cutter, between 1946 and 1952. Its first use was in an edition of Boccaccio's *Trattatello in laude di Dante* that appeared in 1954. The Monotype Corporation's version of Dante followed in 1957. Though modeled on the Aldine type used for Pietro Cardinal Bembo's treatise *De Aetna* in 1495, Dante is a thoroughly modern interpretation of that venerable face.